I0819309

GROUP C
RACING

WORLD ENDURANCE CHAMPIONSHIP

1982–1992

BP
BP
VIDEO
CAR
HI-FI
VIDEO
KENWOOD
RICHARD MILLE
FRANÇAIS D'ASSURANCES
GOODYEAR

GROUP C RACING

WORLD ENDURANCE CHAMPIONSHIP 1982–1992

Johnny Tipler

THE CROWOOD PRESS

First published in 2025 by
The Crowood Press Ltd
Ramsbury, Marlborough
Wiltshire SN8 2HR

enquiries@crowood.com
www.crowood.com

British Library Cataloguing-in-Publication Data
A catalogue record for this book is available from the British Library.

For product safety-related questions, contact:
productsafety@crowood.com

ISBN 978 0 7198 4542 0

Front cover: Derek Bell drives the 2649cc twin KKK turbo Porsche 956 #002 in which he and Jacky Ickx won the 1982 Le Mans 24-Hours.

Back cover: The Sauber Mercedes C9/88 placed 2nd at Le Mans, 1989 with drivers Gianfranco Brancatelli/Mauro Baldi/Kenny Acheson, here leading the 7th place Mazda 767B of David Kennedy, Pierre Dieudonné and Chris Hodgetts.

Page 2: Mike Wilds enters Druids Hairpin at Brands Hatch in the Kenwood Porsche 956-101 that finished 3rd at Le Mans in 1983: 'Undoubtedly one of my all-time favourite race cars,' he says.

Page 3: presented in Shell livery, the works 3.0-litre Porsche 962C #137>009 driven by Hans Stuck won the ADAC Supercup round at Hockenheim in July 1987 as well as several other podiums in '87 and '88, including 2nd at Le Mans.

Typeset by Chennai Publishing Services

Cover design by Keith Wootton

Printed and bound in India by Parksons Graphics

CONTENTS

FOREWORD

Mike Wilds participated in Group C from 1982 to 1989, pictured here giving the author tuition on the RML track at Silverstone in a 997 GT3 RS.

First of all, I would like to thank Johnny for asking me to write the Foreword for his brilliant book on the history of the FIA Group C International Sportscar Championship, which must be one of the FIA's most successful-ever series. I feel very honoured to have been asked.

In 1982, the FIA introduced a category of sports car racing called Group C, run in two classes – Group C1 and Group C2 – and these two categories were to feature in the World Sportscar Championship.

At the end of 1983, my good friend, racing driver Ray Mallock, of RML (and Clubmans Formula U2 fame), called to inform me that the famous Scottish Le Mans-winning team, Ecurie Ecosse, was being reborn with the intention of competing in the new Group C2 World Championship. Would I be interested in joining the team? It took me nearly a whole millisecond to say 'Yes, please'!

Ray soon told me that Dorset Racing was selling its De Cadenet DFV-powered chassis (No. ADC78/1) and that Ecurie Ecosse was interested in buying the car, which RML would then convert to the new Group C2 regulations.

The car was completed at the beginning of 1984, and after a couple of test sessions in the UK, the team set off for our first event, the Monza 1,000km. It was held on 27 April on the iconic Italian GP circuit near Milan, with eager drivers David Duffield, Ray Mallock himself, and yours truly. We had a wonderful start to our campaign, finishing 2nd in Group C2 and 8th overall, which was not bad at all for our embryonic little team.

Following retirement in the Silverstone 1,000km on 12 May, the team set off for the Le Mans 24-Hour race to be held on the weekend of 14/15 June. When our Ecurie Ecosse team arrived at the Circuit de la Sarthe, the region of France where the race is held, it was agreed that I would drive the first practice laps. I was asked to take the car out for an initial installation lap to warm the DFV up and check all the systems, followed by some fast, slippery laps.

Having made a pit stop for engineering checks at the end of that initial lap, I set off for some more slippery. The car felt amazing. OK, on that second lap, I wasn't going flat out in top gear down the 3.7-mile (6km) long Mulsanne Straight, but the car felt so stable and driveable.

So, starting the third lap, I accelerated the car past the start/finish line with the Ford Cosworth V8 DFV behind me, singing up to our fairly low rev limit of 8,000rpm, chosen for longevity in endurance racing. And then I changed up, turning right and slightly uphill to fly under the famous Dunlop Bridge and then down towards the Esses. I was so enjoying this little car as we accelerated out of the Esses towards Tertre Rouge, the right-hander that leads onto the Mulsanne Straight.

Exiting Tertre Rouge, I let the car have its head in all the gears and finally settled down for the long trip towards the daunting Mulsanne 'kink' (pre-chicanes), which was about three-quarters of the way along the straight. The Ecosse was flying, and if my memory serves me well, Ray Mallock had worked out the gearing, taking the tyre growth – that's caused by centrifugal force – into consideration. This increases as the car goes faster, altering the gearing of the car – albeit slightly – while giving more top speed. I was watching the temperature and pressure gauges occasionally – but most of all, I was watching the rev-counter, which was rising... and rising... and rising as I sped along, straight as an arrow.

The Mulsanne Straight is normally a main road – the RN138, or *Ligne Droite des Hunaudières* as it's called in French when it is not being used as part of a racetrack – and it has the normal broken white line lane markers down the centre. It is usual for the slower cars to keep to the right-hand side of the road with the faster cars running on the left, and the broken white line travels past so quickly that it almost appears as one continuous line.

The rev-counter was now reaching towards its maximum of 8,000rpm in top gear, and the Ecosse was still totally stable. And quite why I thought it necessary I will never know – but I took my hands off the steering wheel and the car continued to head straight and true towards the Mulsanne kink at around 217mph.

I was in my element when suddenly there was a huge bang, and my forward vision almost totally disappeared. As you might imagine, this quickly caught my attention, and if I'm totally honest, it scared me witless! For a moment I froze, not knowing what had gone wrong. The cockpit filled with dust, accompanied by an immense noise like a tornado. It was like sitting in a large, over-inflated balloon that had just burst with an immense change in air pressure.

Not wanting to do anything too dramatic, my foot came off the throttle and was hovering over the brake pedal which I started to press gently. The car began to slow and as the dust settled, I checked on the steering – but all seemed to be OK. As the car slowed further, I began to look around to see where all the noise was coming from and as soon as I glanced to my right, I quickly saw that the driver's door had completely disappeared!

As the car was now down to below 100mph, I guess, the noise was slightly less dramatic. So, having checked all the controls, I drove back to the pits at a much-reduced speed for a debrief and post-mortem with the team.

We eventually worked out the root of the problem. It had been caused by aerodynamic pressure inside the cockpit, which resulted in it bursting outwards. We eventually managed to retrieve the door from the excellent marshals on the Mulsanne Straight, and it was then refitted – virtually undamaged. However, both doors now had holes drilled in them to relieve the pressure build-up in the cockpit, and we had no further issues.

During practice, we were one of the fastest, if not the fastest, C2 cars in the field – and we were also very fuel-efficient, which gave us all a lot of hope for a good result come race weekend.

Sadly, the race brought us a mechanical failure, and we retired. However, during that first season, we learned so much, and in 1986, we won the Group C2 Team World Championship, a fine result for a great little team.

I drove four seasons with Ecurie Ecosse and finished my Group C career driving a works Nissan R88C in Group C1 at Le Mans in 1988 with my friend Win Percy and veteran Australian driver Alan Grice, placing 15th overall.

Five fantastic seasons in what I consider to be one of the best formulae the FIA has ever devised – super-fast, super-competitive, and certainly the best category I have ever raced in!

Mike Wilds
August 2024

PREFACE

From the start of the Group C era, Jürgen Barth was President of the Endurance Commission of the BPICA (Bureau Permanent International des Constructeurs d'Automobiles) and created OSCAR (The Organisation for Sportscar Racing) with Chris Parsons and was responsible for organising all races from the outset until 1988. He also drove in a fair number. Here is his mission statement and summary of the decade.

Group C was introduced by the FIA to replace Group 5 (open to special production cars) and Group 6 (two-seater racing cars). Although the new category was introduced in 1982, we must dive back into the mid-1970s for its roots. During those days the French ACO introduced the GTP-category for the Le Mans 24-Hours. Limited to a weight of 800kg and a maximum fuel capacity of 100 litres, GTP cars were roofed prototypes using 3.0-litre engines such as those employed in Formula 1. It was a great loss that legendary cars such as the Porsche 917 and the Ferrari 512 became obsolete, as the big 5.0-litre engines were no longer allowed. When Ferrari decided to concentrate on Formula 1, Matra dominated Le Mans. Then, when Matra decided to follow Ferrari into Formula 1, it was Mirage from the UK with Derek Bell and Jacky Ickx who claimed victory at Circuit de la Sarthe with their GR8. A few years later, in 1980, Jean Rondeau won the Le Mans 24-Hours in his own Rondeau M379B, together with his fellow countryman Jean-Pierre Jaussaud.

In 1982, the BPICA and FIA created Group C for cars weighing a minimum of 800kg with a maximum fuel capacity of 100 litres. The racing distance was limited to 1,000 kilometres with a restriction of five refuelling stops during a single race. With these rules, the FIA hoped that manufacturers would shift their concentration away from the worrying climb in engine output. Ford and Porsche were the first manufacturers to enter the championship with the Ford C100 and Porsche 956.

They were followed by Aston Martin, Jaguar, Lancia, Mazda, Mercedes, Nissan and Toyota. Ever-rising costs remained a significant issue, so an additional category was developed in 1983 for privateers and smaller teams, initially known as Group C Junior. Instead of five refuelling stops within a 1,000-kilometre race distance, Group C Junior cars were allowed 330 litres per 1,000 kilometres. The minimum weight for these cars was 700kg. Different engine types were used, such as the 3.5-litre BMW M1 or the 3.3-litre Cosworth DFL. Lightweight turbo engines were used, as

Jürgen Lässig drove the Obermaier 956 to 4th place in the DRM round at Berlin's AVUS circuit on 1 February 1983.

well as engines from Austin-Rover. In 1984, the FIA renamed Group C Junior as Group C2. The engine must be out of an FIA Homologated Car so as not to allow special racing engines to be used.

Group C quickly grew in popularity, and Bernie Ecclestone also remarked that we had over eight manufacturers competing in Group C, and no one was building special F1 engines any more. So, at a meeting at London Airport, Max Mosley (FIA President) and Bernie came up with the new engine rules, ending the homologated engine with the fuel consumption limitations, and opening it up for racing engines of up to 3.5 litres. Under protest from most manufacturers, the new technical rules were adopted, and when Peugeot recorded the highest top speed during qualifying for the 1988 Le Mans 24-Hours, reaching 407km/h, the FIA adopted a new rule book that became effective in 1991. Category C1 was introduced to mandate normally aspirated 3.5 litre engines, similar to what were used in contemporary Formula 1, and generating less power than was found in Group C cars then. As these engines were not affordable to privateer and smaller teams, Group C started to die. At the start of the 1991 season, only a handful of C1 cars formed the grid. As a result, the FIA allowed cars complying with the pre-1991 Group C rules to participate. However, interest was lacking by now, and after a poorly supported World Sportscar race at Magny-Cours in 1992, the championship came to a premature end.

The diversity of cars that competed under Group C regulations, combined with their sheer speed, attracted vast crowds around the world. It was a shame to see the second most popular category in motorsports, just behind Formula 1, disappear so suddenly.

Nowadays, the Group C Racing Series hosted under the Peter Auto flag recreates the great days of endurance racing with cars that actually raced in the World Sportscar Championship. Across Europe, with races in Spain, Belgium, France and Italy, fans can still enjoy the sounds and shapes of these great cars. The highlight of the Peter Auto calendar is the biennial Le Mans Classic, which features a race for Group C cars from that particular era.

Jürgen Barth
August 2024

TIMELINE

1981
Group C is mooted as a replacement for Group 5 special production cars (e.g. Porsche 935) and Group 6 open-top sports prototypes (e.g. Lancia LC1, Porsche 936).

1982
Group C represents the FIA World Endurance Championship. Ford, Lancia and Porsche lead the way; Rothmans Porsche wins the Manufacturers' title with four out of eight race victories; Jacky Ickx is Champion Driver.

1983
Group C2 'Junior' class introduced, won by Gianni Alba. Group C also represents the European Endurance Championship for one season. Jacky Ickx wins the Drivers' title again, while Rothmans Porsche is also Manufacturers' Champion, winning six out of seven rounds.

1984
Rothmans Porsche takes the Manufacturers' title with seven out of eleven wins; Stefan Bellof is Champion Driver.

1985
Rothmans Porsche is Group C World Champion team, and Hans-Joachim Stuck and Derek Bell are joint Drivers' Champions. Teams' titles are introduced for Group C2 and GT cars, replacing the traditional Manufacturers' awards. Group C2 Drivers' and Teams' titles are won by Gordon Spice and Ray Bellm of Spice Engineering.

1986
Group C represents the FIA World Sports Prototype Championship. Brun Motorsport (Porsche 956/962C) wins Teams' title; Derek Bell is Drivers' Champion.

1987
Silk Cut Jaguar wins the Teams' prize, with eight out of ten race victories. Raul Boesel is Champion C1 Driver. Fermin Vélez wins C2 Drivers' title, Spice is C2 Teams' winner.

1988
Silk Cut Jaguar win the Teams' World Sports Prototype Championship with six out of eleven race wins (to Sauber-Mercedes' five wins); Martin Brundle won the Drivers' title. Gordon Spice and Ray Bellm were joint winners of Group C2 Drivers, and Spice Engineering won Group C2 Teams.

1989
Sauber-Mercedes wins World Sports Prototype Championship for Teams, winning seven out of eight rounds, Jean-Louis Schlesser is Drivers' Champion; Chamberlain Engineering wins C2 Teams' prize, Fermin Vélez is top C2 driver. Last year of C2.

1990
Sauber-Mercedes wins the C1 Teams' prize and overall Championship with a magnificent eight out of nine race victories; Jean-Louis Schlesser takes the Drivers' title.

1991
Group C now represents the FIA World Sportscar Championship, with Group C divided into Categories 1 and 2, dependent on compliance with new regulations. Silk Cut Jaguar wins the Teams' title from Peugeot Talbot Sport; Teo Fabi is the Drivers' Champion.

1992
Peugeot Talbot Sport wins the Teams' title with five out of six race victories in a shortened Championship schedule.

Derek Warwick and Yannik Dalmas are joint Drivers' Champions. The Championship fizzles out in the final round at Magny-Cours, and in October 1992, after four decades, the FIA officially cancelled what became known as the Sportscar World Championship.

1993

Le Mans composes a special prototype category for Group C cars. Peugeot Talbot Sport takes the first three places, with Toyota taking 4 to 6.

1994

Last appearance of Group C cars at Le Mans: Dauer-Porsche 962 take 1st and 3rd places, with Toyota 2nd.

2002

Start of the Group C Revival. The category flourishes over the two following decades, from 2016 under the dedicated classic racing Peter Auto administration, with rounds held at Spa Classic, Paul Ricard, Le Mans Classic, Dijon, Estoril and Mugello, plus Silverstone Classic, Goodwood Members and Donington Historic.

2025

Group C relaunched as a standalone series in the Masters' Historic Championship.

Group C represented other international sports-prototype race series, including the All-Japan Sports Prototype Championship (1983–92), the DRM and ADAC Supercup in Germany, the UK's Thundersports, and Europe's Interserie Championships. Broadly similar rules were used in the North American IMSA Grand Touring Prototype (GTP) series (1981–93), with plenty of top-line crossover IMSA entries participating in certain Group C events, especially the Le Mans 24-Hours.

Mario and Michael Andretti debuted their 962 #001 on pole position for the 1984 Daytona 24 Hours but retired after 127 laps with engine cooling issues.

INTRODUCTION

The Mercedes-Benz C11 of reigning champions Jean-Louis Schlesser and Jochen Mass heads the C291 of Karl Wendlinger, Michael Schumacher and Fritz Kreutzpointner at Le Mans 1991, the lead car retiring at 22 hours when a broken alternator bracket compromised the water pump, destroying the engine.

In its 1980s heyday, Group C was the zenith of long-distance sports-prototype competition and, viewed retrospectively, one of the most exciting and intense periods of motor racing in history. The Group C category was synonymous with the FIA's World Endurance Championship from 1982 to 1985, the retitled World Sports Prototype Championship from 1986 to 1990, and the World Sportscar Championship from 1991 to 1992.

Whilst plenty of Group C entrants also ran in IMSA's GTP category in North America, I do not cover them here as, realistically, that constitutes a book in its own right. Nor do I venture into the All-Japan Sports Prototype Championship, where, again, the rules and duration were broadly similar, for the same reason.

The first manufacturers to join the series were Lancia, Ford and Porsche, quickly followed by other automotive titans, including Jaguar, Mercedes-Benz, Nissan, Toyota, Mazda and Aston Martin. Many of these teams also took part in the North American IMSA Championship, since its GTP class had similar regulations. A year after Group C was introduced, a junior category called Group C2 was introduced, attracting a swathe of smaller privateer teams such as Spice Engineering, Ecurie Ecosse, Argo, Alba, Lola and Tiga, employing engines such as Ford-Cosworth, Chevrolet V8 and BMW sixes. Thereafter, grids comprised both Group C1 and C2 cars, till C2 was dropped at the end of the 1989 season as new rules were announced.

Support for Group C from the main motor manufacturers grew steadily, with each make adding to the diversity of the series, and whilst turbocharged engines were commonplace, it was theoretically possible for large-capacity, naturally-aspirated engines to compete with smaller forced-induction engines, which amounted to C1 versus C2, though in practice C2 cars never quite matched the C1s for outright wins. Race distances were over at least 1,000 kilometres and usually lasted more than six hours, emphasising the

The 3.9-litre Ford-Cosworth DFL V8 Lola T610 of Guy Edwards, Rupert Keegan and Nick Faure is fettled in the Le Mans pitlane ahead of the 1982 race, as the Andretti's Mirage M12 passes by.

endurance aspect of the events. Again, the rules changed for 1990 to more than halve race distances. The ongoing fuel consumption regulations placed the onus on race teams to conserve fuel over the course of a race, and only throw caution to the wind when the result depended on deploying the throttle pedal.

FASTER THAN F1

In 1988, a French WM-Peugeot recorded the highest-ever speed achieved along Le Mans' Mulsanne Straight, doing 405km/h (252mph), way faster than Formula 1 cars – though the gearing for such a long 6km (3.7 miles) straight is a key factor in attaining such a speed. However, the authorities then decided not merely to construct enormous chicanes at two locations along the straight to reduce speeds (acting like half-roundabouts) but also to restrict the performance of cars built to the original rules, such as the Porsche 962C that was used by many privateers.

This directive eventually benefited the larger and wealthier manufacturer teams, such as latecomers Peugeot, who were using F1-derived 3.5-litre engines. Whether intentional or not, the move brought about the rapid downfall of Group C because the smaller private teams, such as Spice and ADA, lacked the budgets for brand-new F1 engines. The 1993 Group C Championship was cancelled before the first race due to a lack of entries. The ACO, organisers of the standout race, the Le Mans 24-Hours, still permitted Group C cars to run, though the 1994 race was the last one in which any Group C cars participated. A new category introduced by race organisers drew in modified Group C cars. One such, the Dauer-Porsche 962 – a former C1 car disguised as a road-legal GT car – won the 1994 race, and the open-top TWR-Porsche WSC-95 won Le Mans in 1996 and 1997. By this time, the real Group C cars had been pensioned off – not for good, though – as they would have another more secure bite of the cherry, running as historic racing cars from 2007 going forward.

REVIVAL

Today, there is a dedicated Group C Championship featuring many of the original protagonists, running in conjunction with the French Peter Auto race promoter under the auspices of Group C Racing –– with rounds at Classic Le Mans, Spa and Silverstone Classics, amongst others. From 2025, a new championship for Group C cars was scheduled to launch in the Masters' Historic Racing series, organised by Masters boss Frederick Fatien. The aptly named Historic Group C Collection is located at specialist and driver Henry Pearman's barns in rural Kent, containing at least 30 cars – Porsches, Jaguars and Toyota.

GROUP C TEAMS

The C1 series' main contenders were the factory-enabled teams of Jaguar, Sauber-Mercedes (Mercedes-Benz), Lancia, Porsche, Peugeot, Mazda, Nissan and Toyota, with top-line privateer teams such as Kremer Racing, Brun Motorsport and Joest (Jöst) Racing, and a surprisingly large number of independent constructors including Spice, Tiga, Ecosse, Gebhardt and Alba, to name but a few, running in the C2 Junior category. There was never any sign of a Ferrari works team – although the Lancias used Ferrari engines – and Ford was an early drop-out.

Jaguar's XJR series of racing prototypes were campaigned from 1983–91 in both Group C and IMSA GTP, with the early cars developed by Group 44 in the USA, followed by a switch to Tom Walkinshaw Racing (TWR). Jaguar scored three World Championship titles – in 1987,

The 7.0-litre V12 TWR Jaguar XJR-8 that won the Spa-Francorchamps 1,000km in 1987 is fettled in the modern Spa pitlane during the 2022 Spa Classic meeting.

Designed by Lee Dykstra with aerodynamicists Max Schenkel and Randy Wittine, the 600bhp Jaguar XJR-5 V12 was built by Bob Tullius' Group 44 Team in August 1982, pictured here in Henry Pearman's Historic Group C collection. At Le Mans 1985, one of the two Group 44 XJR-5s, driven by Tullius, Chip Robinson and Claude Ballot-Léna, placed 13th, the first time a Jaguar had finished Le Mans since 1963.

The third round of the 1989 WSPC at Jarama was the 480km Repsol Trophy, won by the Sauber-Mercedes C9 of Jean-Louis Schlesser and Jochen Mass, seen here passing the TWR-Jaguar XJR-9 of John Nielson and Andy Wallace, which came 6th.

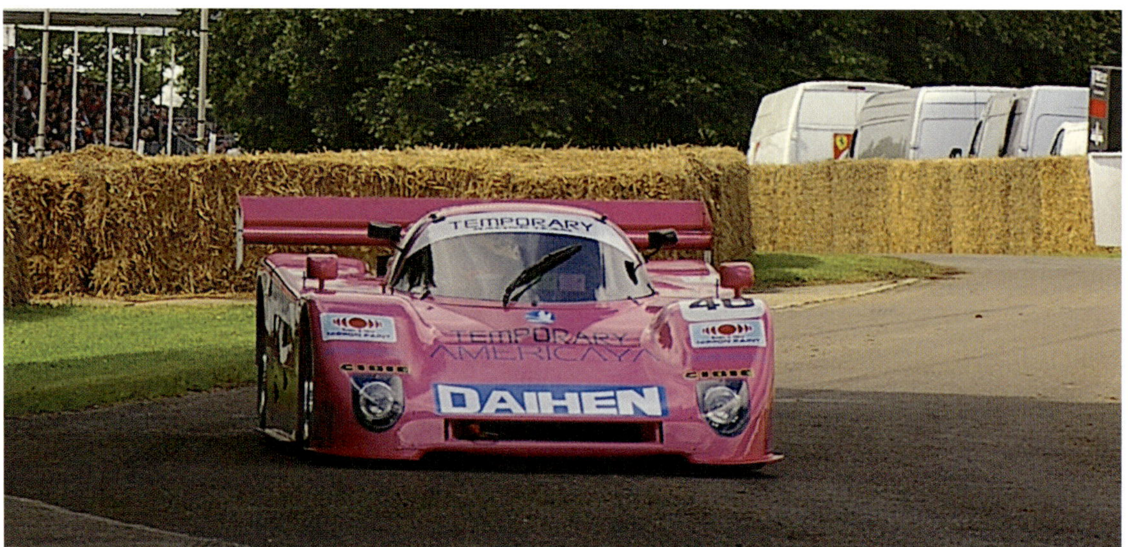

The 1990 Spice SE90C driven by Desiré Wilson/Lyn St James/Cathy Muller in the1991 Le Mans 24hrs (DNF), getting a run up Goodwood Hill. 'The Pink Spice', chassis SE90-C-017 was one of the last C1 Spices built.

1988 and 1991 – including two overall Le Mans wins in 1988 and 1990. The powertrain evolved from the V12 through Turbo V6 and, latterly, the Cosworth-built 3.5-litre V10 XJR 14, which also provided the basis post-Group C for the double Le Mans winning TWR-Porsche of 1996 and 1997.

Lancia's LC2 was the successor to its open-topped Group 6 LC1 and was campaigned from 1983 to 1986, with privately operated LC2s continuing as late as 1991, though with no outstanding success. The works Lancias won a World Championship race in 1983, 1984 and 1985, often dominating qualifying but fading with reliability issues against the more reliable Porsches and Jaguars. From the outset, Mazda entered the C2 category, then embraced C1. Johnny Herbert, Bertrand Gachot and Volker Weidler drove a 787B in IMSA GTP trim to a surprise victory at Le Mans in 1991. Mazda's rotary 'Wankel' engine was also notoriously deafening.

Peter Sauber's Sauber squad embraced the series from the outset, truly coming into its own as a Mercedes-Benz satellite in 1985. In 1990, Sauber-Mercedes morphed into a full-on Mercedes-Benz team, with the 5.0-litre twin-turbo V8-powered C11 replacing the Sauber C9. With several top-line drivers, including Jochen Mass, Jean-Louis Schlesser and Michael Schumacher on the driver roster, the C11s won all but one of the races entered, easily winning the 1990 World Sports Prototype Championship. Reliability issues with the replacement car meant the C11 continued to be used until mid-season when the C291 was introduced. In 1993, Sauber embraced F1 and, one way or another, has never left.

Perhaps surprisingly for a major player, Nissan's Group C entries were based on the customer March chassis with Lola underpinnings, which were theoretically available to any private team. Although Nissan's R90C drivers took Japanese domestic Championship honours every year from 1990 to 1992, on the international stage there were just seven podium finishes across the 1989 and 1990 seasons, but no wins, with 5th overall at Le Mans in 1990.

Aston Martin supplied engines to the Nimrod and EMKA (see Pink Floyd) teams in the early years of Group C.

In 1989, the works' spin-off Proteus Technology team built five Group C chassis, designated AMR/1–5, running Callaway-tuned 5.3-litre V8 engines, but despite high-calibre drivers like Brian Redman, they were also-rans in a competitive field. The team closed in 1990.

Toyota's early Group C cars were built by Dome and then by TOM'S, which moved in-house in 1987. There was little success until 1992 when the first race for the 3.5-litre V10-powered TS010 yielded a win at Monza and an All-Japan title in 1993.

Peugeot's 905, powered by the 3.5-litre V10, debuted in late 1990, notching up nine race wins, including overall victory at Le Mans in 1992 and the diminished Sportscar World Championship in 1992, plus the post-SWC event in 1993.

Stalwarts of the WSPC and WSC, Porsche embraced Group C from the get-go with its 956, which, together with its successor, the 962 (essentially the same car but with its chassis tub extended so the driver's feet were behind the front axle rather than ahead of it) is the most successful racing car of all time. It won the World Sports Prototype and Sports Car Championship five times in succession, also an unparalleled achievement in the sport. Stateside, it won the IMSA Championship three times, despite not being allowed

Standing on its airjacks in the Silverstone pitlane, the Brun Motorsport 956 #106 came 9th in the 1986 1,000km, driven by Walter Brun and Frank Jelinski.

to enter for the first two years of its life, and in 1991, in its tenth season of racing, it was still good enough to win the Daytona 24-Hours outright – and for the fifth time.

Between 1982 and 1991, 27 examples of the 956 (including four 956B evolutions) and 120 units of the 962 (including ten works cars) were built. After Porsche withdrew at the end of 1988, customer teams such as Kremer Racing, Richard Lloyd's GTi Engineering, Brun Motorsport and Joest Racing continued to operate the cars and develop them to some extent, such as substituting aluminium tubs with honeycomb cells.

DRIVERS

Across the board, Group C was peppered with well-known drivers, many from F1 and others being recent Le Mans winners.

In the Porsche camp alone, we find Derek Bell, Jacky Ickx, Jochen Mass, Mario Andretti, John Watson, John Fitzpatrick, Hans-Joachim Stuck, Klaus Ludwig, Stefan Bellof, Mike Wilds and Vern Schuppan.

Private teams abounded, including Brun, Fitzpatrick and Jöst in C1, and Spice, Tiga and Ecurie Ecosse in C2. At Sauber Mercedes-Benz, future F1 stars Michael Schumacher, Karl Wendlinger and Heinz-Harald Frentzen were groomed under the tutelage of 1990s' champion drivers Jean-Louis Schlesser and Mauro Baldi. Inevitably, some drivers flitted between teams, slipping backwards and forwards from one to another in a high-octane game of musical chairs, with some, such as Jochen Mass, Jean-Louis Schlesser, Mauro Baldi, John Watson and Johnny Dumfries sampling multiple marques in the course of the era. At TWR Jaguar, Andy Wallace, Jan Lammers, Johnny Dumfries, Stefan Johansson, Michele Alboreto, Tom Kristensen, Johnny Herbert and Martin Brundle played the starring roles; Mazda hired Yojiro Terada, Johnny Herbert, Bertrand Gachot and Volker Weidler, while Mark Blundell, Julian Bailey, Kenny Acheson, Geoff Lees and a host of others drove the Nissans, and Derek Warwick, Phillipe Alliot and Geoff Brabham were colleagues at Peugeot. As the chapters unfold, we will get the names of numerous drivers who starred in Group C2 as well, including Ray Mallock, David Leslie, Gordon Spice, Ray Bellm, Tim Lee-Davey, and our Foreword writer Mike Wilds – to name but a few.

STREET CARS NAMED DESIRE

Two Porsche-driving race- and title-winners, Derek Bell and Vern Schuppan, had road-going versions of the 962 made in their own names, though proving somewhat disastrous for Vern in commercial terms. I had a go in the one-and-only Derek Bell car when Antony Fraser and I journeyed to the Forest of Dean to review it, courtesy of Porsche racer and collector Paul Howells, who owned it at the time. The Derek Bell Signature Edition 962 was built by the former head of Sauber's F1 team at the cost of around £1.3m, based on a Fabcar monocoque and an integral multi-tubular roll-cage. It was equipped with a twin-turbo 3.6-litre 993 GT2 engine, producing 580bhp and 546lb/ft of torque, with an all-up weight of just 830kg. The suspension was by coil-over Koni adjustable dampers, with adjustable ride height, and stopped by 350mm floating Brembo discs with adjustable bias. It poured with rain on our visit, but Paul magnanimously let us loose on the local country roads despite the weather. Notwithstanding its road-going set-up, I can only reflect on how amazing this car would be on a racetrack.

As for the Schuppan version, Vern sought to emulate teams such as Kremer Racing, Team Jöst and designer John

Derek Bell and Jacky Ickx enjoy a moment with Ferry Porsche.

Works Porsche drivers take a break at Spa-Francorchamps during the 1,000km, 1984: from left, Stefan Bellof, Derek Bell, Jochen Mass, Jacky Ickx, Vern Schuppan and John Watson. Winners were Bell/Bellof, with Ickx/Mass 2nd, and Watson/Schuppan 6th.

Thompson, who were developing bespoke components and even entire chassis for the 962C. With design input from ex-Lotus F1 stylist Ralph Bellamy, the road-legal 962 was based on a Team Schuppan Le Mans 962, which enabled it to pass the type-approval process. The Schuppan 962 LM was created on the Advanced Composite Technology (ACT) carbon-fibre chassis and powered by the 962's 2.65-litre turbocharged quad-cam 24-valve flat-six engine. Just three cars were built in the Tiga Cars factory. With a planned production run of 50 units, the project foundered in 1991 when Schuppan's Japanese client and sponsors bailed on him.

Having competed in F3000 and F1, firm friends Mark Blundell and Julian Bailey were teammates at Nissan Motorsports in 1989 and 1990, and, subsequently, the BTCC. Blundell also shared the winning Peugeot 905 at Le Mans in 1992, while Bailey returned briefly to F1 and then Touring Cars.

There was – and still is – another way for humbler mortals to emulate the Group C gods on the open road, and it is called the Ultima. From 1982, Group C imagery and performance were available to regular sportscar drivers in the shape of the road-going Ultima. Hinckley-based automotive engineer and designer Lee Noble launched Noble Motorsport with the Ultima Mk1. With looks that would not disgrace a C2 car, the Ultima was built on a square-tube spaceframe chassis, and its V6 engine and transmission were taken from a Renault R30 with other components from the Ford, Lancia and Austin-Rover parts bins. Cars were assembled at the factory or sold as kits for self-build. Campaigned in domestic club events, by 1991 it was proving too successful on track and was banned from racing. It was re-engineered by Ultima's first customer, Ted Marlow, to run with a small block Formula 5000 Chevrolet V8, increasing potency somewhat. The Marlow family, under Richard Marlow, acquired the Ultima marque in 1992, and it has gone from strength to strength, with the Ultima GTR appearing in

Weighing just over 1,800lb, the Fabcar chassis Derek Bell Signature Edition 962C was surely one of the most beautiful racing cars to hit the road.

THE GENESIS OF GROUP C REGULATIONS

One of the key instigators of the rules and regulations for Group C was Jürgen Barth, son of the illustrious Porsche pilot of the 1950s and early '60s, and winner of the Le Mans 24-Hours in 1977 in a Porsche 936. It is not widely known that the dimensions of a Group C race car correspond with those of the 917, and it is thanks to Jürgen's background as a Porsche factory technician, works driver and emissary that he was able to convince the FIA to accept them. Nevertheless, it was Group C's stringent fuel restrictions that gave the constructors pause for thought prior to the series getting under way.

Here is Jürgen's assessment of how the scene was set for the implementation of the new category:

The World Sportscar Championship regulations in play between 1976 and 1980 were aimed at attracting the top manufacturer teams, but the Group 5 silhouette racing cars – like the Porsche 935 – that emerged were innovative in the quest for brute power but lacked the elegance and pioneering quest for technical evolution that sports-prototypes represented. Furthermore, the FIA allowed Group 6 prototypes – like the Porsche 936 – to race in parallel with the silhouette cars, and it wasn't only Porsche who felt it was time for a change under the circumstances.

Jürgen Barth remembers well the initial discussions back in 1979 at the International Permanent Office for Vehicle Construction (BPICA) in Paris:

As no manufacturer's board existed at the FIA at that time, all topics related to the car manufacturers were sorted out first at the BPICA, and afterwards presented to the respective FIA boards. At the time, I was chairman of the BPICA's sportscar board, and our basic aim was to attract more manufacturers into long-distance endurance world championships as well as national championships. First of all, we needed to implement free regulations for racing cars without specific reference to existing production vehicles. During the course of this procedure, I vividly remember dropping by the Porsche Museum at Zuffenhausen on my way to a board meeting in Paris, in order to calculate the interior width and the windscreen proportions of a Type 917, and thus glean a set of measurements that would serve as the basic interior dimensions for the new Group C chassis. What I had in mind then was a vehicle corresponding to the Ferrari 512 prototype, or, in this case, the Porsche 917.

It was an ambitious proposition, but all the manufacturers interested in establishing and participating in the new Group C formula did indeed accept those actual dimensions. Participating manufacturers included Ford, Mercedes-Benz, Lancia, Jaguar, Peugeot, Porsche, Nissan, Mazda, Toyota, and Aston Martin.

Jürgen explained:

From the start the board agreed that fresh ground needed to be broken in terms of propulsion and power delivery. Two options were considered: restrict the intake airflow rate or standardise the fuel consumption. Eventually, the decision was taken in favour of restricting fuel consumption. This effectively meant that the engine had either to originate from a homologated Group A or Group B series-production vehicle

The privately entered 2.7-litre twin-turbo Porsche 936C of Ernst Schuster, Siegfried Brunn and Rudi Seher came 6th overall in the 1986 Le Mans 24-Hours.

Thanks to Jürgen Barth, the inner dimensions of a Group C race car, like the 956, correspond with those of the Porsche 917, such as Claudio Roddaro's 1969 ex-works car, driven here by the author at Donington Park circuit fifty years later.

or from a manufacturer of vehicles already homologated by the FIA. Needless to say, the whole engine did not necessarily have to be used as an off-the-shelf unit, though its most fundamental parts, the engine block and the cylinders and cylinderheads, certainly did. All other parts could be subject to any modification whatsoever.

There was some fine detail as well.

The total amount of fuel that could be carried on board was limited to a maximum of 100 litres. Nevertheless, given that the fuel lingering within the pipes still had to be taken into account, the actual amount that could be stored in the fuel tank ended up being approximately 98 litres.

That rule provided a basis for regulating the number of pit stops permitted for refuelling during the race, as follows:

Races of less than 165 km: No refuelling permitted.
Races of 165 to 330 km: 1 pit stop permitted.
Races of 330 to 500 km: 2 pit stops permitted.
Races of 500 to 665 km: 3 pit stops permitted.
Races of 665 to 830 km: 4 pit stops permitted.
Races of 830 to 1,000 km: 5 pit stops permitted.
12-Hour Races: 12 pit stops permitted.
24-Hour Races: 25 pit stops permitted.

This resulted in an average fuel consumption of 60 litres per 100km, which still seems quite generous today. However, when Group C racing regulations came into effect in 1982, a further reduction to approximately 50 litres per 100km was stipulated for the 1984 season. As Jürgen admits:

That still seems a lot of fuel today, but remember that we are talking about engines with an output of 600bhp, which did not benefit from today's state-of-the-art electronics, so this really was a milestone – not least because of the incentives and hurdles that faced the technicians and race engineers involved, who applied their skills to make the engines and fuel systems attain and operate at that limit.

Moreover, evolving developments like injection electronics, along with newly introduced materials for the coating of cylinders and so on, contributed further to the reduction of fuel consumption. This was technology that also benefited the general public, as such revelations from the race track soon filtered down into series production vehicles.

So, in 1984, the practical consequences were as follows:

Races of 800 km (or 500 miles): Up to a maximum of 425 litres permitted.
Races of 1,000 km: Up to a maximum of 510 litres permitted.
9-Hour Races: Up to a maximum of 830 litres permitted.
12-Hour Races: Up to a maximum of 1,105 litres permitted.
24-Hour Races: Up to a maximum of 2,210 litres permitted.

As with many innovative regulations, scepticism was rife, as Jürgen concedes:

The atmosphere and tension at the first races of the season was wound up to a fever pitch, and malicious gossip amongst the pessimists and pundits suggested that none of the racing cars would cross the finish line as they would inevitably run out of fuel out on the circuit during the race. But it didn't turn out like that at all. During the Group C era, Porsche won the World Sportscar Championship in 1982, 1983 and 1984, with Jacky Ickx crowned World Endurance Drivers' Champion in '82 and '83; Stefan Bellof was the Drivers' title winner in '84. The Norbert Singer-designed Type 956 was superseded in '84 by the Type 962 evolution, which won the World Sportscar Championship in 1985 and 1986 and helped Derek Bell to win the Drivers' title. Many of the 91 cars built raced successfully as works and private team entries in the concurrent IMSA, Interserie and Japanese endurance series, and the 962 was still a race winner in 1992.

Nocturnal pit stop for the winning 962C #003 of Hans Stuck, Derek Bell and Al Holbert, Le Mans 1986.

The Derek Bell Signature Edition 962C used push-rod suspension and was powered by a 580bhp 3.6-litre twin-turbo 993 GT2 flat-six, producing 546lb ft of torque.

1997, the updated Evolution model arriving in 2015 and the RS available in 2021.

While the Ultima was originally conceived as a ringer for a Group C car, other road-going brands might legitimately propose their own products as deserving of the C2 mantle. For example, Lotus's Esprit S300 – which ran at Le Mans in 1993 and '94 – and BMW's M1 Procar, examples of which were seen in the early WEC rounds, were worthy candidates.

Austerely minimalist like its racing counterparts, exemplified by the flat-bottomed steering-wheel rim, built-in roll-cage, carbon-fibre seats, bare dashboard and race-car-style instrumentation, and of course the recumbent driving position as demonstrated by the author, the cockpit of the Derek Bell 962C had no creature comforts, not even in the upholstery.

One way for the Group C fan to experience the thrills of racing was in an Ultima Evo.

CHAPTER 1

DESIGN AND SPECIFICATION

The Group C racing category's history harks back to the mid-1970s, when motor sport's ruling body – the Federation International Automobile (FIA) – adopted the Le Mans 24-Hour race organisers' then-current GTP (Grand Touring Prototype) category. This was a class for closed-roof prototypes with certain dimensional restrictions, but instead of imposing limits on engine capacity (which had caused the demise of the highly successful Porsche 917 and Ferrari 512 after 1971), it placed limits on fuel consumption. There was a minimum weight limit of 800kg and a maximum fuel capacity of 100 litres; with cars restricted to five refuelling stops within a 1,000-kilometre distance – a typical distance for an endurance race, for example the Monza 1,000km – the cars were effectively allowed to consume 600 litres of fuel per 1,000 kilometres. The FIA's objective was to dissuade manufacturers from focusing on producing ever more powerful engines, which could be achieved by simply increasing turbocharger boost pressure. At the time, the 3.2-litre twin-turbo Porsche 935 (1977–81) developed more than 800bhp.

ANTECEDENTS

Group C cars' bodywork had come a long way since the days of Porsche's all-conquering 917 (1969–71); in the late 1970s, Formula 1 car design espoused ground-effect bodywork (*see* the groundbreaking Lotus 78 and 79 F1 cars), an aerodynamic phenomenon responsible for huge decreases in lap times, mostly due to the vastly quicker cornering speeds that were enabled by the downforce generated by the skirts, spoilers and diffusers surrounding the extremities of the car's bodywork. By trapping the air beneath the car, it was effectively and literally sucked down onto the track surface. Following in the wake of F1, Group C racing cars had ground-effect aerodynamics designed into their configurations from the word go. They were, therefore, much faster than the preceding generation of sports-prototype racing cars.

Equally fundamental to the construction of Group C racing cars was their chassis material and configuration. Again, whilst Formula 1 (and the majority of single-seater racing cars) had employed monocoque aluminium tub chassis since the early

The 5.3-litre Nimrod Aston Martin NRAC2 of Viscount Downe, driven by Ray Mallock, Mike Salmon and Simon Phillips, came 7th overall at Le Mans in 1982.

1960s, Porsche, for example, built its sports racing prototypes on complex aluminium multi-tubular spaceframe chassis, up to and including the open-top 936 that won Le Mans in 1977 and 1981. So, like their F1 counterparts, Group C cars utilised angular aluminium central monocoque hulls or tubs that supported subframes which provided locations for the sophisticated suspension pick-up points and engine mounts – plus the cockpit (more a survival cell with integral steel roll-bars) – all clad in suitably streamlined aerodynamic bodywork. And, just as the F1 chassis morphed at the same time from aluminium into lighter, stronger carbon-fibre honeycomb and Kevlar, the same happened to Group C cars. Metal tubular subframes supported the various ancillaries front and rear, such as oil coolers, fluid reservoirs and wing mounts.

MANUFACTURERS' ATTRACTION

From the outset, Group C was essentially a series based on fuel consumption. Anything was possible in terms of engines, provided they could do a whole race on a limited amount of fuel, and this allowed production engines like Aston Martin and Mercedes-Benz V8s and Jaguar V12s to compete head to head with Mazda's Wankel rotary engines and Ford's Cosworth V8s. Some criticised the formula, saying that cars had to hold back early on or back off late in the race in order to go the distance, but it produced a great variety of solutions, attracted many manufacturers and provided some great racing. The sights and sounds of Jaguars racing against Sauber-Mercedes and Porsche, along with the Japanese manufacturers Mazda, Nissan and Toyota, as well as Aston Martin, Spice, Tiga, Ecurie Ecosse and Gebhardt competing in the Group C2 category, were truly epic.

LE MANS SPRINGBOARD

Just as many sportscar racing series do, Group C started off at Le Mans. In 1978, Renault had won with a Group 6 open two-seater sportscar, but in the cause of better aerodynamics, they had fitted a bubble top with a small slit in front for driver visibility and a hole in the roof so that the car remained open to the elements and complied with the rules as they then were. This was the catalyst for the sports-GT-prototype class that started at Le Mans, bearing similarities to the sports-racing cars of the late 1960s and early 1970s, like the Ferrari 512S and Porsche 917, which were closed-cockpit Group 6 cars.

The new Group C regulations for 1982 endurance racing called for recognised engines homologated for Group

Alain de Cadenet, whom the author interviewed in 2007 in Snowmass, Colorado, created two eponymous cars in 1975, #HU1 placing 3rd at Le Mans in 1976 and 3rd again in 1980. Based on Lola T380-Cosworth V8s with Thompson-built chassis, one morphed into an Ecosse C2, another into an ADA-Ford C2. De Cadenet also managed the Rondeau Team, and he drove the GRID Plaza C2 in 1982, Charles Ivey's 956 in 1984, and then for Courage Compétition, placing 15th in 1985's Le Mans and 11th in 1986.

A or Group B production cars, but of unlimited capacity. By restricting fuel tank size and specifying a minimum of 102.5 miles (165 kilometres) between refuelling pit stops, fuel consumption needed to be at least 4.6 miles per gallon. Wheels were not permitted to have a rim width exceeding 16in, minimum weight with a two-seater body of specified windscreen area must not be less than 800 kilogrammes without fuel, and to some extent, ground-effect downforces were reduced by under-shield requirements.

Le Mans regular Jean Rondeau was one of the first constructors to embrace the rules, building his cars specially for Le Mans and achieving a remarkable victory in 1980 as an owner-driver. The WM-Peugeots were early exponents of the class, recording the fastest-ever speed on the 3.7-mile-long Mulsanne Straight, pre-1990 chicanes, at 252mph. The fastest speed recorded with the chicanes in place is 227mph, set by Mark Blundell in a Nissan R90CK.

The very early days of Group C at an international level saw some weird and wonderful oddities. The Lola T600 was the first shot at a production Group C car, but had to run with a hole in its roof before the FIA ratified the Group

The WM-Peugeot P83 PRV was driven at Le Mans in 1983 by Jean-Daniel Raulet/Michel Pignard/Didier Theys, with Roger Dorchy in reserve.

C rules. The Kremer brothers Erwin and Manfred turned the clock back and built a Porsche 917 out of spare parts and raced it at Le Mans in 1981, without achieving anything approaching a revival. Then, in 1982, the Porsche 956 arrived on the scene. The 956 and subsequent 962 offspring became the core Group C cars for at least three-quarters of the series' duration, and, whilst the factory fielded a Rothmans-sponsored works team for the first half of the series, several private teams enjoyed great success with the 956 and 962, notably Reinhold Jöst's Joest Racing Team, Walter Brün's Brün Motorsport Team and Richard Lloyd Racing.

Over the years, Lancia won fifteen World Rally Championships, as well as the World Championship for Makes between 1979 and 1981 with a Group 5 Beta Montecarlo 1.4 turbo, but this was not eligible for the WEC so they created LC2 and recruited F1 drivers Riccardo Patrese and Andrea De Cesaris who could put an LC2 on pole, although they lacked reliability, and the Porsches were always there to pick up the pieces. Porsche's early stranglehold on Group C was defused by Jaguar's US entrant Bob Tullius running Group 44 Jaguars at Le Mans in 1984, scoring respectable finishes in 1984 and 1985.

ETCC winner Tom Walkinshaw was retained by Jaguar and created a run of carbon-fibre monocoque TWR Jaguar XJR-6s that ran well at Le Mans, Brands Hatch and Spa-Francorchamps in 1985. In 1986, the XJR-6s raced in Silk Cut livery, winning the 1,000km at Silverstone. Also in 1986, the Kouros-backed Sauber-Mercedes V8 arrived and was straight away on the pace of the Porsches and Jaguars, though in 1987, Jaguars won eight out of ten races in the series. At Le Mans, the battle between the formerly dominant Porsches and the Jaguars raged on until dawn, but the Jaguars finally fell by the wayside, and Porsche took the victory once more.

The Sauber-Mercedes only ran in European rounds for the moment and the works Porsches withdrew mid-season as the firm's IndyCar project started to consume corporate resources. In 1988, Mercedes-Benz stepped out of the Sauber shadow and, clad in AEG (part of Daimler-Benz) livery, they took on Jaguar head to head. The first race fell to them, but the series and, at last, Le Mans went to Jaguar. Le Mans saw the works factory Porsches back in business, but despite a titanic battle, Jaguar took the victory. TWR's US team were victorious at the Daytona 24-Hours and the Sebring 12-Hours, giving Jaguar a clean sweep of the top-line endurance races that year.

GROUP C2: JUNIOR SCHOOL

From the earliest days of Group C, one of its strengths was the C Junior, later C2 class. Cars tended to be slightly smaller, less powerful, weirder-looking in some cases, and crewed by drivers lower down the pecking order. This enabled privateers to enter on a small budget and swell the fields to sensible numbers. The downside was that C1 drivers might complain of slow and erratic C2 drivers, but it was a two-way street, and it was not unknown for C1 drivers to push C2 cars off the track if they felt that they needed the bit of road the C2 was on.

C2 was discontinued in 1990 when the FIA decided that privateers would be much happier running cars with F1 engines. Even top C2 teams like Spice, Gebhardt and Ecosse could not hope to compete with factory-backed operations such as Mercedes and Jaguar for outright honours, so they quietly moved on to other racing projects or went into liquidation.

The Mako Team's C2 3.3-litre Cosworth DFL V8-powered Spice-Fiero SE88C of Don Shead, Robbie Stirling and Ross Hyett came 16th at Le Mans in 1989.

CHAPTER 2

MAKES AND MANUFACTURERS

The Sauber-Mercedes C9 driven by Kenny Acheson and Mauro Baldi won the Brands Hatch 480km, the fourth round of the 1989 WEC.

The decade encompassing Group C – effectively from 1982 to 1992 – attracted several top-line manufacturers, including Ford, Porsche, Lancia, Mercedes-Benz, Jaguar, Nissan, Mazda, Toyota and Peugeot, all of whom hosted competitions departments or racing teams, along with a host of smaller commercially run and privateer squads that made up the bulk of Group C2, of which Spice Engineering, Ecurie Ecosse and Tiga were the most prominent. The works teams hired the best drivers available, and, in respect of long-distance racing, Porsche already had the best of them on its roster. So, it is not surprising that Porsche was, overall, the most committed and consistently successful team, certainly in the first half of the 1980s. The following alphabetical cross-section of participating makes is packed with smaller ventures bent on resounding success, most of whom occupied the Group C2 category that came into being in 1983 and lasted until 1990. The appendix contains a complete list of participating teams.

ADA ENGINEERING

Chris Crawford and Ian Harrower created ADA Engineering in 1977. Getting their start as an engineering design and consultancy firm, they ran a Gebhardt C2 in the World Endurance Championship in 1985, having some success the following year with a class win in the Le Mans 24-Hours. ADA chassis 88-02 was built in 1987 and debuted at the Brands Hatch 1,000km. In a practice session for the Kyalami 1,000km in South Africa the car driven by Michael Briggs and Mario Hytten was quickest C2, but was destroyed in a huge startline accident. It was rebuilt in 1988 with some modifications, resulting in ADA C2-02B, with chassis 03 entered in the World Sportscar Championship in 1988. Harrower entered the 1988 24 Hours of Le Mans with co-drivers Jiro Yoneyama and Hideo Fukuyama finishing 18th overall and claiming 2nd place in C2.

ALBA

Alba was a small Italian company based in Moncalieri near Turin, founded in 1982 by Giorgio Stirano, a former Osella engineer. The carbon-fibre composite AR2 was built to compete in Group C Junior powered by a four-cylinder 1.8 turbocharged engine. Martino Finotto and Carlo Facetti debuted it at the 1983 WSC event at Silverstone, winning Group C Junior. Another class win at the Nürburgring was followed by podium finishes in the UK and South Africa, earning Alba the Group C Junior title. In 1984, in quick succession, the Alba-Ford AR3, AR4, AR5 and AR6 were launched, but they could not match the previous year's successes, with 8th in the 1985 Mugello 1,000km as their best result.

In play between 1990 and 1992 – though often a non-starter – the Alba AR20 resembled its predecessors with its lobster-claw front end, although it was powered by a heavy 560bhp Motori Moderni 3.5-litre V12, designed by Carlo Chiti. The AR20 was driven by Marco Brand and Gianfranco Brancatelli with no notable success.

ALD AUTOMOBILES

ALD was the creation of Louis Descartes, a keen motor racing enthusiast who had begun his career in the French Hill Climb Championship driving such diverse cars as a Renault 8 Gordini and a Lola T298. The director of a public relations company from Levallois-Perret in Northwest Paris, Descartes formed his own racing team, 'Automobile Louis Descartes' (ALD) in 1984. Jean-Paul Sauvée was recruited to design and build a new Group C2 car for the team. Based around a conventional sheet-aluminium monocoque, the first ALD was powered by an ex-Schnitzer BMW M1-style, M80 3.5-litre 440bhp six-cylinder engine. The ALD '01' made its debut at Le Mans in 1985, driven by Louis Descartes himself, Jacques Heuclin (the mayor of Seine-et-Marne) and Daniel Hubert, who had designed the car's bodywork. As a small private constructor, the team did well to make the finish line of the 24-hour race.

Between 1986 and 1988, ALD continued to develop the original car and produced chassis '02', '03' and '04'. All were BMW-powered, and most of the C2 WEC/WSC rounds were entered. In 1989, chassis numbers #05 and #06 were built as customer cars for Didier Bonnet, while a new works car was constructed using a carbon-fibre/honeycomb chassis powered by a 3.3-litre Ford-Cosworth DFL V8. Designated 'C289', the car represented a quantum leap forward technologically and was campaigned in all the WSC rounds of 1989, including the Le Mans 24-Hours.

In 1990, with the demise of the C2 class, a 3.5-litre Cosworth DFZ was installed, and once again, the team entered all rounds of the championship. With four full-time employees, a plastics moulder and a dozen volunteers, Descartes and his team's return on their huge investment of effort and cost was always likely to be small against the works teams of Mercedes-Benz, Porsche, Jaguar, Nissan and Toyota. Although adept at attracting a myriad small sponsors, Descartes was never able to secure a wealthy enough long-term sponsor. Drivers such as François Migault were ALD regulars, but often less-experienced drivers had to be taken on board in order to fund the team, and leader-board results were always going to be a challenge.

Team founder Descartes was killed at Christmas 1991 when his road car hit a tree near Paris, and after his death, Team MP Racing entered the ALD C289 at the 1992 Le Mans with a V6 PRV Peugeot engine, but the car failed to qualify when the car was found to be underweight in post-qualifying scrutineering.

ARGO RACING CARS

Swiss designer Jo Marquart and British mechanic Nick Jordan came together with a vast amount of experience in designing single-seater racing cars, including Lotus, McLaren, GRD and Modus, and founded Argo Racing Cars in 1977. In addition to constructing cars for Formula 3, Formula Atlantic and Formula Super Vee, morphing from JM1 to JM18, Argo also built sports prototypes for the World Sportscar Championship under Group C rules and the US IMSA GT Championship. Argo's JM19 appeared in 1987 and was a development of the earlier JM16 that raced in the IMSA GT Championship. The 1983 IMSA Camel Lights class was won by Argo, with Jim Downing and co-driver John Maffucci winning almost everything between 1985 and 1987.

Three versions of the JM19 were developed, taking the constructor into the early '90s. Marquart next partnered with Austrian designer Achim Storz, who used carbon-fibre composites to reduce weight. The Argo JM19B C and D models were mainly used under Group C rules and equipped with different engines from Zakspeed, Cosworth and even a Minardi Motori Moderni fitted by Jean-Pierre Frey. Former European rally cross champion Martin Schanche from Norway and Briton Will Hoy were often the fastest pair in the C2 class between 1986 and 1988. Sponsored by Lucky Strike, they had a string of pole positions and the fastest laps with a Zakspeed 1.8 turbo-powered engine. JM19Cs were driven by various drivers, including Schanche/Hoy in the '87 and '88 Le Mans 24-hours 1987/88, who scored several pole positions in an Argo JM19C in the World Sportscar Championship between 1986 and 1988. This was Argo's first car to be powered by a Cosworth DFV, and the JM19D was followed by the JM20, designed for privateers in Group C1, but apart from one for a customer in Switzerland and one for German pairing Fredy Lienhard and Eugen Strähl to run in Interserie, no further chassis were constructed.

ASTON MARTIN

A partnership between Peter Livanos, Victor Gauntlett, Richard Williams and Ray Mallock was formed in late 1987 to create Proteus Technology, which developed and raced the AMR1. Max Bostrom and Ray Mallock designed the car, which would appear in the 1989 World Sports Prototype Championship. Five cars were built and powered by a 740bhp Aston Martin 6.3-litre V8. Weighing in at just 904 kilogrammes, it was the lightest and most powerful of the cars. During its period career, chassis AMR1/05 was driven by Brian Redman, David Leslie, David Sears and Stanley Dickens. The car competed in three world championship events in 1989 at Donington Park, Spa-Francorchamps and Mexico, with best finishes 6th and 7th at Donington and 7th at Spa.

CHEETAH AUTOMOBILES

Cheetah Automobiles was founded in 1971 in Lausanne, Switzerland, by Swiss-American engineer and racing driver Chuck Graemiger. In 1974, he built his first car, the 01G. He then built two Group C cars – the G603 in 1983 and the G604 in 1984. The G603 was powered by a 4.0-litre Cosworth DFV, and the G604 used an Aston Martin V8. Graemiger then built a third car, designated the G606, which ran in his own works team. With Loris Kessel, Laurent Ferrier and Florian Vetsch driving, the G603 debuted at Spa-Francorchamps in 1983. The G604 ran in 1984 and 1985 but without success. Graemiger's next car was the G606, renamed SGR001, reflecting that Graemiger had a new partner, Fred Statler and his team, Racing Organisation Corse. The ROC 002 entered the 1991 Le Mans, driven by Pascal Fabre and Bernard Thuner, but retiring with transmission problems.

COURAGE COMPÉTITION

Yves Courage started racing and hill climbing in 1972 and founded Courage Compétition in 1981. At that year's Le Mans 24-hours, he finished 18th, co-driven by Jean-Philippe Grand, winning their class. Courage built his own car, the Cougar C01, to Group C regulations, and after 78 laps of Le Mans in '82, it was forced to retire. The Courage C01 was followed by the C02 in 1984, though compromised by vibrations from the Ford-Cosworth V8 engines. From 1985, the chassis was adapted to accommodate Porsche turbocharged flat-6 engines, and the new car was designated the Cougar

Michel Trollé and Claude Bourbonnais brought the Courage Compétition 3.2-litre Porsche 935 turbo-powered Cougar C26S home in 9th place at the 1991 Silverstone 430kms.

C12, with Primagaz sponsorship, finishing the 1986 Le Mans 24-Hours in 18th place. The Porsche-engined Cougar C30 LM Group C contested Le Mans four times, twice with Mario Andretti at the wheel.

DOME

Minoru Hayashi built his first racing car in 1965, going on to found Dome in 1975. His road cars, such as the Dome Zero and Dome P2, were not a success, so Dome continued building sportscars for Toyota's motorsport department. Initially, these cars competed in the All-Japan Super Silhouette Championship, with Group C following in the All-Japan Sports Prototype Championship. For the 1982 Le Mans, Dome built the RC82, which utilised a chassis constructed by March Engineering. The car was intended to compete in the C1 category and was eventually fitted with an 8.8-litre Chevrolet V8 engine. The Dome RC82 never finished a race, though, and was followed by the RC83. Dome constructed the chassis this time and fitted a 4.0-litre Cosworth DFL V8 engine. The car debuted at the 1983 Fuji 1,000km but retired after 31 laps because of transmission failure. Although the car finished other events, it basically was not a success. *See also* Toyota.

ECURIE ECOSSE

David Murray, a Scottish businessman and racing driver, founded Ecurie Ecosse in 1951. The team's Aston Martins scored two legendary Le Mans 24-Hours victories back to back in 1956 and 1957. Encountering financial problems during the mid-1960s, the team shut down, returning to the sport between 1969 and 1971, competing sporadically in F2. During the early '80s, Scottish businessman Hugh McCaigh resurrected Ecurie Ecosse's immortal name, and there were plans to enter the Le Mans 24-Hours in 1983 with a Chevron B52/54 Sports 2000, although the Ecosse C284 was already under construction to participate in the 1984 race. This Group C2 race car was powered by a 3.3-litre Ford Cosworth DFL mounted in a De Cadenet-Lola

Parked outside its pits garage at the 1989 Le Mans 24-Hours is the Courage Compétition race team's Cougar R89V – aka March 88S – of Takao Wada, Akio Morimoto and Anders Olofsson. Its 3.0-litre Nissan VG30 twin turbo V6 expired in the 16th hour.

The Ecosse C286 #003 of Mike Wilds and Marc Duez finished 10th at Brands Hatch's Shell/Gemini 1,000km in 1987.

chassis, and debuted at the Monza 1,000km in 1984, and also participated at Silverstone and Le Mans. A 2nd place in the C2 class at Monza was the best result that year. In 1985, former Clubmans U2 constructor Ray Mallock designed the Ecosse C285, which proved very competitive. The C285 was powered by a 3.3-litre Ford Cosworth DFV, and was derived from the earlier C284, although it had a new chassis and improved aerodynamics. The C285 won the C2 class at Silverstone, Brands Hatch and Hockenheim, taking Ecurie Ecosse to 2nd overall in the 1985 C2 championship. The third and final car was the Ecosse C286, powered by the Rover V6 engine that was also employed in the MG Metro 6R4 Group B rally car. At the 1986 Le Mans, the C286 led the C2 class for much of the 24 hours. Although the Rover engine proved reliable, a blown rear tyre led to disaster. The car managed to get back to the pits, but the driver refilled the C286 with boiled water by accident, which led to its disqualification due to strict fluid rules.

EMKA

EMKA Racing was founded by Pink Floyd's manager, Steve O'Rourke, engaging Maurice Gomm and Protoco to build the chassis for the Len Bailey-designed EMKA Aston Martin for Group C. It was powered by an Aston Martin 5,340cc V8 that was redesigned by Bailey. EMKA C83/1 debuted at the 1983 Silverstone 1,000km race, and C83/1 ran at Le Mans, finishing 17th overall. EMKA C84/1 was developed for the 1985 season and featured new bodywork, although lacking the ground-effect system of the previous cars. C84/1 proved much quicker, and its best result was 11th overall at Le Mans.

FORD

Ford entered Group C with the C100, designed by Len Bailey and active from 1981. Initially intended to be a Group 6 contender, it ran in Group C in 1982, though it was dogged

Pit stop during the 1983 Silverstone 1,000km for the EMKA Aston Martin C83-1 of Tiff Needell, Jeff Allam and Steve O'Rourke.

with reliability problems. Bailey then left the project and was replaced by FI designer Tony Southgate. Although several parts of the car were redeveloped, Ford decided to hand the project to Zakspeed. The German team modified a chassis into C1/4, powered by a 1.8-litre Zakspeed turbo engine from their Group 5 Capri. A stiffer chassis and improved aerodynamics led to the C1/8, which was powered by a 4.0-litre Cosworth DFL V8.

It was a missed opportunity: given proper manufacturer support, so much more could have been achieved. As it was, the C100 was never going to reprise the mid-1960s when the GT40 was dominant.

Entered by Ford-Werke AG Zakspeed, the 4.0-litre Cosworth DFL-powered Ford C100 of Klaus Ludwig and Mark Surer, pictured in the Le Mans pitlane ahead of the 1982 24-Hours, retired in the seventh hour due to electrical problems. The same malady afflicted its sister car of Manfred Winkelhock and Klaus Niedzwiedz, which also retired in the seventh hour.

GEBHARDT

Günther and Fritz Gebhardt produced the Gebhardt JC842 and JC843 for the 1983 and 1984 editions of the Le Mans 24-Hours, managing top ten finishes, bowing out in 1987, and re-emerging in 1991 when the Gebhardt C91 flirted with both the North American IMSA Championship and the FIA Sportscar World Championship.

The C91 ran in the IMSA Championship powered by a 2.1-litre turbocharged Audi engine, where it was allowed to enter the GTP category, making three appearances at Topeka, Watkins Glen and Road America. Its best result was 17th place at Topeka, driven by Giampiero Moretti. In 1992, Gebhardt Motorsport ran in the FIA World Sportscar Championship, switching to a 3.5-litre Ford Cosworth V8 DFR. The car was driven by Almo Coppelli and Frank Kraemer, scoring 4th in the Monza 500km race but retiring from the Silverstone 500km when the engine broke.

GRID

Grid Racing was founded by Giuseppe Risi and Ian Dawson, who ran a Lola T600 in the FIA World Championship for Emilio de Villota and Guy Edwards. Former Lotus FI designer Geoff Aldridge designed the Grid Plaza S1, which was powered by a 3.3-litre Cosworth DFL V8 and featured advanced aerodynamics – Aldridge had been involved with the Lotus Type 78 and 79 FI cars that pioneered ground-effect aero. Plagued by a troublesome DFL engine, the S1 was followed by the S2 at the beginning of 1984. Remarkably, this car was powered by a twin-turbo Porsche 935 engine. After debuting at an IMSA race in Florida, it appeared at WEC races at Monza and Le Mans. In March 1985, the S2 made its final appearance, where it also featured a Porsche 956-style nosecone.

The 3.3-litre GRID Racing Grid-Plaza S1-Cosworth DFV of Emilio de Villota, Desiré Wilson and Alain de Cadenet was an early retiree at Le Mans in 1982.

HARRIER

The Mazda-powered Harrier RX83C was the first Group C Junior car. It was developed by Lester Ray, based on an aluminium sheet monocoque chassis and powered by a Mazda rotary engine. It debuted in 1983 at the Monza 1,000km and was soon entrusted to JQF Engineering. Equipped with reworked suspension and revised fuel and cooling systems, it finished 14th at Spa-Francorchamps. Two weeks later, the Harrier made its final appearance at Brands Hatch.

JAGUAR

A major presence in endurance racing during the 1950s and early '60s, Jaguar's renaissance in top-line motorsport began with the support for Bob Tullius' Group 44 and, subsequently, Tom Walkinshaw's TWR Racing activities, resulting in an outstanding series of Jaguar XJR sports cars. Group 44 participated in the North American-based IMSA GTP Championship with the XJR-5, while TWR Racing won the FIA European Touring Car Championship with the XJS, moving on to contest Group C and the World Sportscar Championship with the British Racing Green-hued XJR-6.

Jaguar's XJR-6 was designed by Tony Southgate and built on a carbon-composite monocoque. Two XJR-6s debuted at the 1985 World Endurance Championship race at Mosport Park, where Martin Brundle, Mike Thackwell and Jean-Louis Schlesser finished 3rd behind two works Rothmans Porsche 962s. Six XJR-6s were produced. The Jaguar XJR-6 was followed by the maroon-and-white Silk Cut cigarette-sponsored XJR-8, which appeared in 1987; the XJR-7 was an IMSA car, as were the XJR-10 and XJR-16/17.

TWR Jaguar XJRs in the paddock garages at Goodwood during the 2020 Speedweek meeting, including the XJR-6 of Brundle/Thackwell, the XJR-8s of Watson/Lammers and Cheever/Boesel, and the XJR-9 of Dumfries/Wallace/Lammers.

Ahead of the 1987 Spa-Francorchamps 1,000km, Johnny Dumfries and Martin Brundle contemplate the controls of their ultimately victorious Jaguar XJR-8 #TWR-J12C-387.

Although the XJR-8 was similar to the XJR-6, retaining the Silk Cut livery, it used a 7.0-litre V12 engine developing 720bhp, scoring victories at Silverstone, the Nürburgring and Spa-Francorchamps on the way to winning the '87 World Championship. Jaguar had entered three cars for the Le Mans 24-Hours, and while two did not finish, the third car finished 5th after being delayed by transmission problems.

Jaguar debuted the XJR-9 at the 1988 Daytona 24-Hours. It was an evolution of the XJR-8, again designed by Tony Southgate, and five cars were entered for Le Mans. The first car retired from the race early due to transmission problems, and a second car was eliminated by an engine problem. With Jan Lammers leading the race in chassis J-12-C-488, he drove much of it in fourth gear, realising that making a single gearshift could have ended the car's run. Thus, Lammers, Andy Wallace and Johnny Dumfries claimed Jaguar's first Le Mans victory since 1957, ending Porsche's seven-year winning streak in the process.

As the TWR-built V12 engine struggled against the might of the contemporary Mercedes-Benz engines, Jaguar decided to use the Rover 3.5-litre V6, initially designed for the MG

A pensive Martin Brundle on the grid with his Jaguar XJR-8 for the 1987 Spa-Francorchamps 1,000km, which he and Johnny Dumfries would go on to win.

Metro 6R4 Group B rally car, in the XJR-11. Two versions were developed: a 3.0-litre for use in the IMSA Championship and a 3.5-litre variant for the World Sportscar Championship. Both capacities were fitted with a pair of Garrett turbochargers, generating 659bhp and 750bhp respectively. Jan Lammers and Patrick Tambay debuted the car in the 1989

WSC round at Brands Hatch, finishing 6th, and the team managed just a single victory during the 1990 season due to reliability issues. Now in Silk Cut's all-mauve livery, presenting a less cluttered and more mature image, the Tony Southgate-designed 7.0-litre V12 XJR-12 was developed for the 1990 season and won both the Le Mans 24-Hours and the Daytona 24-Hours enduros.

The Jaguar XJR-14 was TWR's offering for the new 3.5-litre formula, which replaced the Group C regulations. After nine years, the FIA banned turbocharged engines in favour of normally aspirated 3.5-litre engines. Since only a handful of cars were entered in the 3.5-litre formula, Group C cars with restricted performance were allowed to participate in the new C2 category.

Accordingly, Jaguar produced the brand-new XJR-14, designed by Ross Brawn and John Piper and built by Tom Walkinshaw Racing. Sporting radically different aerodynamics and a lower kerb weight of just 750kg, the XJR-14 had a much higher cornering speed than rival front-runners from the Group C era. As the earlier twin-turbo engine from the XJR-11 was no longer permitted, Jaguar adopted the 3.5-litre Ford HB V8 engine, sourced from the Benetton Formula 1 team, downgraded from 13,000rpm to 11,500rpm, and reducing available power from 700bhp to 650bhp. TWR built three chassis, #591, #691 and #791 for the 1991 World Sportscar Championship, though they decided not to enter the XJR-14 at Le Mans as they were unsure that the Cosworth HB engine would last 24 hours. However, the XJR-14 outclassed competitors, namely the

The 3.5-litre JV6 turbo engine of this TWR Jaguar XJR-11 is fine-tuned in the Silverstone pitlane during the Silverstone 480km meeting, 1990. Andy Wallace and Jan Lammers drove this car to 2nd place behind its winning sister car of Martin Brundle and Alain Ferté.

The 3.5-litre Cosworth HB V8-engined TWR Jaguar XJR-14 of Martin Brundle finished 3rd in the 1991 Silverstone 430km, a race won by its sister car driven by Teo Fabi/Derek Warwick.

Peugeot 905 and the Mercedes-Benz C291, and although Peugeot entered the upgraded 905B, TWR-Jaguar managed to secure the manufacturers' title with three wins. At this point, Jaguar decided to bow out of the World Sportscar Championship in favour of the IMSA championship.

KONRAD

The Konrad KM-011 was the result of a partnership between Konrad Motorsport and Italian tractor and supercar manufacturer Lamborghini. Franz Konrad was an established racing driver who had founded Konrad Motorsport in 1976. He entered the World Sportscar Championship with a Porsche 962 in 1990 and 1991. As his Porsche 962 was not allowed to run under the rules for the 1992 season, his choice was to use a customer chassis or to build his own car that was compliant with the new 3.5-litre regulations. As both the World Sportscar Championship and Formula 1 applied similar engine rules, Konrad decided to use an engine available from Lamborghini. The Italian manufacturer was owned by Chrysler at that time, while Team Lotus, Ligier, Minardi and (in-house) Modena used Lamborghini V12 engines in their F1 cars between 1990 and 1992.

KM-011 was designed by Geoff Kingston and made its debut in the 5th round of the 1991 World Sportscar Championship at the Nürburgring, driven by Franz Konrad and Stefan Johansson, though despite having two talented drivers, it failed to qualify. Konrad entered the next round at Magny-Cours but lasted only eighteen laps. After a single round of the Interserie championship at the Nürburgring, the car never raced again.

KREMER-PORSCHE CK5 AND CK6

For over 50 years, the name Kremer was synonymous with Porsche racing cars – not least the extraordinary 911-based 935K3 – but it was the servicing of road cars that set the two brothers, Erwin and Manfred, on the road to success.

The highlight of the team's 32 appearances at Le Mans was its tenth showing, in 1979 when the slant-nose 935 K3 – a Kevlar-panelled Group 5 car built and modified at Kremer's Cologne base, driven by Klaus Ludwig and Americans Bill and Don Whittington – took the lead at midnight. At the 4.00pm finish the following day it was several laps ahead of the Dick Barbour 935 driven by actor Paul Newman and Rolf Stommelen, and the other Kremer 935 that had been delayed by a drive-shaft failure. Just as remarkably, it was the first time for many years that a production-based car (however remotely connected) had won the event.

Four years later, in 1983, Kremer almost took the win again. By now, the mighty Group C ground-effect turbo era was in full swing, and the Kenwood-liveried 959/101 crewed by father and son Mario and Michael Andretti, plus Philippe Alliot, was running 2nd in the early hours. The problem was, it was gulping too much fuel. Erwin Kremer had to ration the allocated 2,500 litres to make it to the finish, and that ruled out an attack on the two leading works cars. Third place was a consolation of sorts.

There is a strong attraction about the longevity of the Kremer enterprise. For 32 years in a row, Kremer Racing

The Porsche-Kremer CK5 of Richard Cleare, John Cooper and David Leslie pictured at Brands Hatch during the 1984 1,000km.

had an entry at Le Mans, all but one of them with Porsches, winning the race in 1979 with the slant-nose 935 K3. No other team or driver could match that, and more recently, Erwin Kremer's fabulous 962 CK6s were among the leading lights in the Group C revival.

Jacky Ickx once asked Erwin Kremer how many years he had raced at Le Mans – 32 consecutively, Erwin replied. 'You're more crazy than me!' said the Belgian ace. 'I've only been there 30 times.' But Ickx was too expensive for Kremer. Mario Andretti would normally have been too dear, as well, but his personal Budweiser sponsorship appeared on the car and race overalls; likewise, Keke Rosberg with *Playboy* magazine when he drove for Kremer at the Norisring.

We find the late Frenchman Bob Wollek becoming a regular, along with Englishmen John Fitzpatrick, Guy Edwards and Nick Faure, who shared a Kremer 935 K2 in 1977. In more than 1,000 races, Kremer has engaged 350 drivers of international repute, from GP stars like Alliot, Lehto, Stuck and Boutsen to sports- and touring-car specialists like Bellof, Weaver, Surer, Schickentanz, Jelinski, Ongais and Barth. In 1984, a Kremer Le Mans 962 was handled by Alan Jones, Vern Schuppan and Jean-Pierre Jarier: big names. But the story was not without tragedy. Rising talents Jo Gartner and Manfred Winkelhock were both killed in Kremer cars. Erwin was understandably devastated. 'It's very hard to take, and very difficult to come to terms with,' he said. 'Actually, you never stop thinking about it.'

From 1976, Kremer ran two cars every year at Le Mans, apart from 1982, including an evolution of the Group 5 slant-nose 935, designated K3 because it was the team's third project. It was this model that won in 1979. They also constructed a 917 for the 1981 event, a decade after its glory days, and it was an anachronism even then, but it remains the only 917 built outside the Porsche factory. Unfortunately, the engine failed after seven hours.

Now, though, Kremer Racing had entered a new phase. Not content with running factory race cars, it reconstructed them, making sweeping changes to the bodywork, as in the CK5, and rebuilding most of the mechanicals to its own specifications and tolerances.

Charming and quietly spoken, Erwin discussed the team's strategies:

> *After every race, the drivers would discuss the shortcomings and how we could improve the cars, and so we would make minor adjustments and bring them to the next race. The factory did not do that. They remained with the same specification all season. Because we are a private team, we can be more adaptable, more flexible.*

The CK5 was Kremer's singleton entry at La Sarthe in 1982, a project based on successful 908 and 936 forerunners but updated and running with a 'bread van'-style engine cover. On both occasions when it ran – 1982 and 1983 – the car retired with mechanical problems.

The following eleven seasons, Kremer ran the Group C 956 and its 962C and CK6 evolutions. By any standards, they were immensely successful: John Fitzpatrick won the IMSA title in the USA, Klaus Ludwig won the German championship, and Alan Jones won the Australian series. Kremer Racing delivered consistent results for a private team. Best placings at Le Mans during the Group C era with the 956 and 962 were 3rd in 1983, 6th in 1984, 5th in 1985, 4th in 1987, 8th in 1988, and finally 7th in 1992.

As the Group C era ended completely in 1993, Honda Germany engaged Kremer to build a pair of carbon-fibre NSX coupés to run in the national Meisterschaft (championship) and three cars for Le Mans. With a cast of personnel that would not disgrace a modern F1 team, Kremer-Honda brought all three cars home; it was the first time a three-car team finished on its debut at Le Mans.

Team principals pow-wow: CEO of TWR/Silk Cut Jaguar Tom Walkinshaw confers with veteran Porsche privateer and Cologne-based team owner Erwin Kremer during the 1991 Silverstone enduro.

The Porsche-Kremer CK5 of Richard Cleare, John Cooper and David Leslie on the run-up to Druids at Brands Hatch during the 1984 1,000km.

On a visit to Kremer Racing in 2016, the author was let loose in the latest incarnation of the KR 935 K3, based on a 997 GT3 Cup – on a wet road in the countryside near Cologne.

Erwin pointed out that his cars participating in the Group C revival were all running short tails, which provide better turn-in stability through corners than the long-tail bodywork featured on the works Rothmans 962s, which was really only appropriate on long straights at Le Mans or maybe Monza. Additionally, he believed that the gearbox-mounted rear wings gave far superior downforce than the bodywork extensions seen back in the mid-1980s. Indeed, one of the Leyton House 962 CK6s has a wing on the leading edge of the nose, a feature not in the car's original specification. The two Leyton House 962 CK6s had quite different engines; one was even powered by the original Porsche GT1 motor and had air and water intercooling with intakes at the sides. 'The lower the temperature, the higher the horsepower,' said Erwin simply.

In its heyday, a Group C 962 – or its Kremer-built CK6 derivative – cost in the region of $700,000 (nearly £400,000) to build, with assembly of the 1000bhp flat-six engine taking 250 hours. Sophisticated electronic cameras were used in the suspension set-up for optimum tracking and camber alignment. It cost up to $2m (£1.1m) to run two cars at international level (not counting the build costs) and, unsurprisingly, sponsorship was a crucial adjunct. Kremer's main backers over the years, Kenwood, Jägermeister, Leyton House and Repsol, remained loyal for long periods. Erwin claimed:

> *There is a book in the Kenwood 962. It was the blue Andretti car, then that changed to red, then red and black. The complete deal lasted over ten years. With Jägermeister, it was seven years, and Leyton House was five. Nobody gives that degree of commitment anymore. It's a two-way thing – the team must give equal commitment to the sponsor. But you can't do that in the short term – you must build up to it.*

LANCIA

In 1982, the Group 6 Lancia LC1 appeared in the World Sportscar Championship powered by a small-capacity 1425cc straight-4 single turbo engine. At 1.5/1.65 bar boost, the engine produced an impressive 460bhp. Lancia used a Dallara spyder chassis fitted with a Hewland TG500 gearbox.

The incoming Group C regulations meant the LC1 saw limited action, though the LC1 was permitted to race in the new category even though it was built under Group 6 regulations. The LC1 was light and agile and did not have to comply to Group C fuel consumption regulations, and it scored three victories in 1982 at the Silverstone 1,000km, the Nürburgring 1,000km and the 6 hours of Mugello. Although Lancia entered two cars for the 1982 Le Mans 24-Hours, both retired with electrical problems.

The Giampiero Dallara and Gianni Tonti-designed Lancia LC2 got the go-ahead from the Fiat board in July 1982, and the aluminium monocoque chassis with its pontoon sides was constructed at Dallara's Varano workshops and the carbon-Kevlar body fashioned in the Fiat wind tunnel at Orbassano. The 268C twin-KKK turbo engine was developed by Ferrari's Nicola Materazzi. It was unveiled in February 1983 and endured till 1991.

Pictured at the 2021 Goodwood Festival of Speed, helmed by Jochen Mass, the 1982 Lancia LC1 was a Group 6 car eligible for WEC Group C Driver points but not the Constructors' championship. By dint of eight wins, Riccardo Patrese finished the season as runner-up in the Drivers' charts.

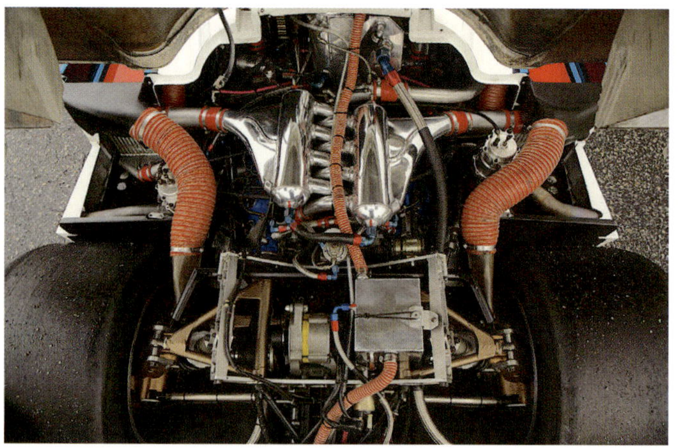

The driveline of the Lancia LC2 featured the twin-turbo Ferrari 308C V8, configured as 2,599 cc or 3,014 cc V8, originally mated to a Hewland 5-speed manual transmission and Abarth-cased from 1984.

The aluminium monocoque cockpit hull of the Lancia LC2, with cooling tube and turbo boost control prominent.

Lancia introduced the LC2 for the 1983 World Sportscar Championship, designed by Giampaolo Dallara and Abarth, under the race direction of Cesare Fiorio. Power came from a 3.0-litre Ferrari V8 downsized to 2.6-litre and fitted with twin KKK turbochargers to produce around 850bhp.

The Lancia LC2 debuted at the 1983 Monza 1,000km and claimed pole position, beating the already dominant Porsche 956 by nearly a second. However, the Pirelli tyres were problematic, and the leading car retired. Engine reliability issues also hampered the LC2 throughout 1983. Fitted with redesigned suspension and Dunlop tyres, the LC2 scored a podium finish during the opening round of 1984 at Monza. Lancia occupied the entire front row for the 1984 Le Mans

24-Hours, though the Rothmans Porsche factory team was not present. Although Bob Wollek and Sandro Nannini led the race, at half distance gearbox problems on both Lancias dropped them back. Ricardo Patrese and Sandro Nannini finally scored a 1–2 at Kyalami.

The LC2 switched to Michelin tyres for the 1985 season, but despite often outclassing the dominant Porsche 956 in qualifying, the Lancias lacked reliability. Only at the shortened round at Spa, curtailed due to Stefan Bellof's death, did Lancia manage to win its first championship over the Porsche factory team. After experiencing ongoing reliability problems in 1986, Lancia pulled out of the championship.

This Lola T600-Cosworth won the 1981 Brands Hatch 1,000km driven by Guy Edwards and Emilio de Villota, pictured here at Le Mans Classic in 2018 by Sarah Hall.

LOLA

On the back of over two decades of producing top-line sports-racing prototypes – viz Mk 6, T70, T212, etc. – Lola introduced the T610 in 1982. It was based on the previous year's T600, an aluminium monocoque designed by Max Sardou that incorporated ground-effect generating venturi, the first prototype GT car to do so. The T610 was powered by a 600bhp 6.0-litre Chevrolet V8. Cooke-Woods Racing acquired the first one, and Guy Edwards and Rupert Keegan debuted it at the Monza 1,000km.

The T610 was different in several ways from the T600. Lola employed an aluminium monocoque with aluminium skins, although the floor was made of carbon fibre. Instead of the Chevrolet V8 of the T600, a Ford-Cosworth 3.9 V8 DFL was used for the T610, with two cars built. The T616 of 1984 was also based on the T600, though this time, Lola adopted a Mazda (2616cc) rotary engine and debuted the car at the season-opening Daytona 24 Hours. A single T616 ran at the Monza 1,000km, and the Mazda engine turned out to be reliable enough for John Morton, Yoshimi Katayama and John O'Steen to win the C2 class at Le Mans. The BF Goodrich Lola team finished 2nd in the 1984 World Championship.

Lola's final contribution to Group C was the T92/10 that appeared in 1992, designed by Wiet Huidekoper for private customers. The T92/10 was focused on downforce and powered by a 650bhp Judd GV10 V10 with an overall weight of 770kg. Euro Racing was managed and owned by Dutchman Charles Zwolsman, who bought two cars, debuting at the Interserie round at Mugello in 1991. At Monza, Euro Racing entered both cars for Charles Zwolsman/Cor Euser and Stefan Johansson/Jesús Pareja. Just three cars were built, and T92/10-HU1 is still active in historic motorsports.

Entered by BF Goodrich Tyres, the distinctly wedge-shaped Lola T616 #HU3 powered by the Mazda 13B 1308cc twin-rotary engine, was driven to 12th place at Le Mans 1984 by Jim Busby, Boy Hayje and Rick Knoop.

MARCH ENGINEERING

March Engineering was founded in 1969 by Max Mosley, Alan Rees, Robin Herd and Graham Coaker – hence MARCH. From its inception, March Engineering had a go at anything, creating chassis across the board, from its own works F1, F2, F3 and Formula Atlantic chassis to F5000, Can-Am and virtually everything in between. Although therefore ubiquitous, customer teams could rely on a degree of state-of-the-art competitiveness and potential success at all levels. The March 82G was the company's first GTP-eligible sports car for IMSA regulations and arrived

Bob Garretson ran the 5.8-litre March 82G-Chevrolet at Le Mans 1982, with drivers Bobby Rahal, Skeeter McKitterick and Jim Trueman. The fuel cell gave up in the seventh hour.

in 1982. Designed by Adrian Newey, the 82G was based on the monocoque chassis March had developed for the BMW M1C in 1981 and fitted with a Chevrolet V8. Bobby Rahal, Bruce Canepa and Jim Trueman put the debutant March 82G on pole for the 1982 Daytona 24-Hours, but they were sidelined by a broken gearbox. However, they came 2nd overall in the Sebring 12 hours. The 82G was followed by the 83G, and five cars were produced for the 1983 season – four for participation in the IMSA championship and a single car for Nissan to run under Group C regulations.

One of the four chassis built for the IMSA championship 83G/04 won every race of the 1983 championship, taking Al Holbert to the title. Adrian Newey also designed the March 85G that appeared in 1985 as the final evolution of the March 82G. Of the eleven chassis built, four were equipped with Porsche 956 engines. Both BMW and Nissan ordered cars from March, and a March-Nissan won the Fuji round of the World Sportscar Championship.

March developed the 86G for Group C and IMSA in 1986, where it was known as the BMW GTP Buick Hawk or Nissan R86V, depending on which engine was used. March built eleven cars, of which four were sold to BMW and five to Nissan. The remaining cars were sold to privately run teams. BMW used the M12/14 2.0-litre inline-four, and Nissan used the VG30ET V6, while Buick adapted the 3.0-litre turbo V6 as well as a 4.5-litre naturally aspirated V6. Finally, March built three cars for Nissan based on the March 87G, equipped with the new 3.0-litre VEJ30 V-8 engine.

Randy Lanier and Bill Wittington won the IMSA GTP 1984 Riverside Six Hours in the 5.8-litre Chevrolet V8-powered Blue Thunder Racing March 84G #4, demonstrated here at the 2021 Goodwood Festival of Speed.

The 2.9-litre turbo March 85G-Porsche of Richard Cleare, Lionel Robert and Jack Newsum came 14th overall and 1st in the IMSA/GTP category at Le Mans, 1986.

MAZDA

Mazda began their GT campaign in 1979 with the rotary-engined RX7, entering Group C in 1983 with their new 717C, designed by Takura Yura of Mooncraft. He selected a rotary engine, notionally 1.3-litre, that had been used in the RX7, fitted with a Bosch electronic fuel injection system, generating 310bhp at 9,000rpm. The sleek all-enveloping bodywork featured enclosed rear wheels, and the 717C was 4m in length, weighing 760kg. The 717C debuted at the 1983 Silverstone 1,000km, driven by Pete Lovett and Youjiro Terada, who qualified 21st overall, but a loose wheel ended its run. At Le Mans, a second car was driven by Jeff Allam, Steve Soper and James Weaver. The two Mazda 717Cs were the only finishers in Group C Junior, finishing 12th and 18th overall, respectively. Mazda had proved that 'Wankel' rotary power was a viable player on the international stage. How is the rotary engine categorised in terms of displacement compared with a conventional piston engine? The cubic capacity of a 'Wankel' rotary engine such as Mazda's is calculated by multiplying the displacement volume of one chamber by the total number of chambers in the engine: cubic capacity

The 1983 Mazda 717C was designed by Takuya Yura at Mazda's in-house Mooncraft division, with aluminium chassis and Kevlar bodyshell. The new 13B twin-rotor rotary engine displacement was 1308cc, rated as 2.6-litre under the equivalence formula, developing 320bhp and maximum speed of 305km/h (190mph). Two cars ran at Le Mans in 1983, with Alan Docking as team manager with Jeff Allam, Steve Soper and James Weaver placing 18th in one car and Yojiro Terada, Yoshimi Katayama and Takashi Yorino coming 12th in the second one (pictured).

Fabulous shot of two of the Mazda 787Bs approaching the end of the Mulsanne Straight during their successful run at Le Mans 1991: the winning car of Johnny Herbert, Volker Weidler and Bertrand Gachot leads the sister car of Stefan Johansson, David Kennedy and Maurizio Sandro Sala, which finished 6th.

equals the displacement volume of one chamber times the number of chambers.

The 717C was followed by the 727C in 1984. The 727C was fitted with the same engine as the 717: a 310-bhp Mazda 13B rotary engine. Two cars ran at Le Mans, and although #86 had transmission issues and was involved in a collision, and #87 had suspension problems, they finished 4th and 6th in Group C2, respectively.

The 737C of 1985 was the final evolution of the 717C and used the same Mazda 13B rotary engine. The factory entered two 737Cs for the '85 Le Mans 24-Hours, and despite problems, both cars completed the race, finishing 3rd and 6th in Group C2. Mazda had by now created a new rotary engine capable of generating 450bhp and commissioned British designer Nigel Stroud to design a new Group C/GTP race car – the Mazda 757. The 757 was built on an aluminium monocoque chassis clad in a carbon-fibre body. One car debuted at the Suzuka 500km in April 1986, followed by two entries at Silverstone's 1,000km. Although they were the fastest cars in the GTP class at Le Mans, both cars retired with gearbox problems. Mazda went on to refine the 757 for the 1987 season, fitting a three-rotor engine calculated to displace 1962cc, generating 450bhp. The pair of 757s entered for Le Mans were lighter, with several technical improvements over the previous model. However, two hours into the race, one car stopped with engine failure, and the second car had wiper problems as well as a broken left rear suspension, fixed in a pit stop. With the top teams retired due to multiple crashes, the Mazda 757 went on to score the best finish ever for a Japanese car: 7th overall and 1st in IMSA GTP/GTX.

The 767 of 1988 was developed with Mazda's new four-rotor motor, although the chassis was shorter and still based on the 757. Mazda entered Le Mans with two new 767s and an earlier 757. Although the two 767s fought their way into the top three, a cracked exhaust manifold and damaged water pump hampered progress. Yoshimi Katayama, David Leslie and Marc Duez finished 17th in the Mazdaspeed 767, with Takashi Yorino, Hervé Regout and Will Hoy 19th. Mazda fared better in the IMSA GTP class, ending the season 1st, 2nd and 3rd.

In 1989, Mazda scored class victories at Le Mans, winning the IMSA GTP Class for the third time in a row with the improved 767B. David Kennedy, Pierre Dieudonné and Chris Hodgetts won the IMSA GTP Class and finished 7th overall, while Takashi Yorino, Hervé Regout and Elliot Forbes-Robinson placed 2nd in IMSA/GTP and 9th overall, with Yojiro Terada, Marc Duez and Volker Weidler coming 12th overall. In 1990, Mazda entered two 787s and a single 767B for Le Mans, but all three cars encountered technical problems, and only the 767B lasted the full distance, claiming top spot in the IMSA GTP class despite finishing 20th overall – though finishing Le Mans is an achievement in itself. However, the manufacturer teams had not been able to comply with the AC de L'Ouest's impending regulation changes, which were accordingly delayed a year, giving Mazda one more shot. The 787 chassis composition and bodywork aerodynamics were radically improved; the radiator was moved from the side of the body to the front, so the body was 50mm narrower than that of its predecessor and drag was reduced by 30 per cent. Instead of outright speed, Mazda shifted the focus onto vehicle dynamics, including a

The Mazdaspeed-entered Mazda 767B powered by the Mazda 13J (2.6-litre) 4-Rotor engine, and driven by Pierre Dieudonné and David Kennedy, came 13th overall at the 1989 Brands Hatch 480km.

While Mazda claimed the honours at Le Mans in 1991, the next three places were taken by TWR Jaguar XJR-12LMs, one of which pursues the victorious Mazda here.

carbon composite braking system, steel struts and bigger wheels and tyres. Two 787Bs and a 787 were entered and lined up in 19th, 23rd and 30th places on the grid. With 22 hours gone, # 55 inherited the lead as the leading Mercedes C11 dropped back with mechanical problems. Thus, Johnny Herbert, Volker Weidler and Bertrand Gachot gave Mazda the victory, making it the first Japanese manufacturer in history to win the Le Mans 24-Hours.

NISSAN

Nissan's Group C contender, the R85V, was created on an aluminium monocoque March 85G chassis, of which three out of eleven made were delivered to Nissan. Nissan equipped the 85V with several different engines. Two of the three cars used a V6 engine, while the third used a turbocharged LZ20B four-cylinder unit that proved unsuccessful. The VG30T/C V6 was derived from the VG30 engine known to car buffs as the power unit of the 300ZX road car, but was equipped with twin turbochargers and an aluminium block. This engine was used in the Nissan GTP ZX-Turbo, which took part in the IMSA GT championship. Nissan's R85V V6 racing engine produced 690bhp, although in qualifying trim it could reach over 1,000bhp. For the 1986 racing season, Nissan bought three 86G chassis in March and identified them as Nissan R86V, with side radiators to improve the aerodynamics. The R86V debuted at Le Mans in 1986.

Johnny Herbert raced extensively in F1, coming 4th in the 1994 World Drivers' Championship. He also frequented the All-Japan Sports Prototype series over three years, and in the Group C WEC category he won Le Mans in 1991 for Mazda.

The works Lola-based Nissan R89C #02 of Geoff Brabham, Chip Robinson and Arie Luyendyk started the 1989 Le Mans race from 15th but dropped out due to an oil leak.

Kazuyoshi Hoshino, Kejii Matsumoto and Aguri Suzuki qualified the car 24th but retired during the race. The following year, Nissan received three March 87G chassis featuring some minor improvements and equipped with the VEJ30 engine, which was designated the R87E. However, none of the cars entered for Le Mans in 1987 made the finish due to engine failures. Next up, Nissan's R88C was powered by a newly developed engine, the 750bhp 3.0-litre twin IHI turbo VHR30 and it had a longer wheelbase to improve driver comfort, while a higher boost level made 1000bhp possible. The car finished 15th overall in the 1988 Le Mans 24-Hours.

Nissan Motorsports International's Nissan R90CK was powered by the turbocharged 3.5-litre Nissan VRH35Z V8 engine. The team struggled at the 1990 Silverstone 480km, with the Blundell/Brancatelli car failing to complete 75 per cent of the winner's 101 laps, and the Bailey/Acheson car retiring at 92 laps.

For the 1989 season, Nissan switched from the March chassis to a Lola chassis with sleeker bodywork and badged the R89C, powered by the 800bhp VRH35 engine. Three cars ran at Le Mans in 1989, though none finished.

The following year, the Nissan R90C ran in both the World Sportscar Championship and the All-Japan Sports Prototype Championship. Nissan also continued to use the R89C chassis since much of the construction componentry was the same for the R90C. Although Nissan employed a Lola chassis – T90/10 – two-thirds of the parts were made by Nissan and NISMO, its in-house tuning, motorsports and performance subsidiary. Nissan continued to employ the twin-turbo 800bhp 3,496cc VRH35Z engine, as used in the R89C. Nissan Performance Technology Incorporated – NPTI – developed the Nissan NPT-90, and instead of using the Lola chassis, Nissan's North American motorsports division developed a brand-new car fitted with the 3.0 litre turbocharged VG30 V6 engine. It was an immediate success, placing 1st and 2nd in the Sebring 12-Hours.

Nissan elected to compete in both the World Sportscar Championship and the All-Japan Sports Prototype Championship, so two different cars were developed – the R90CK and R90CP.

The R90CK was constructed by NISMO Europe and had a different engine cover and rear spoiler, and was entered for the 1990 World Sportscar Championship and the North American IMSA GT Championship. Of Aston Martin and Ecosse fame, Ray Mallock Limited carried out the design and development of the R90CK, which ran at Le Mans in 1990 and 1991. The R90CP was built in Japan and differed from the R90CK in having more of a low downforce design, featuring redesigned front wings (fenders) as the headlights were placed vertically instead of horizontally. The low downforce design also used a much lower-set rear wing, and the rear bodywork was extended to connect with the rear wing endplates. Although Nissan withdrew as a factory team from the World Sportscar Championship in 1991, NISMO evolved the R90CP into the R91 and R92.

PEUGEOT

Peugeot Talbot Sport was set up in November 1988 under the control of Jean Todt in the Parisian suburb of Vélizy-Villacoublay. Aimed to comply with the impending WSC rules for 1991, the Peugeot 905 was built on a carbon-fibre chassis, engineered by Dassault and powered by the SA35-A1 3,499cc normally aspirated V10 engine, similar to contemporary F1 engines. Designed by Andre de Cortanze, the 905 was officially unveiled on 4 July 1990 at the Circuit de Nevers Magny-Cours, with Jean-Pierre Jabouille driving. The 905 sports prototype entered the fray in the last two rounds of the WSC at Montreal and Mexico City, driven by Jabouille and Keke Rosberg.

The earlier races of the 1991 season did not work out, with Peugeot suffering reliability and performance issues – especially at Le Mans, where neither of the two cars made it beyond the four-hour mark. Peugeot's response was the heavily revised 905B, with aerodynamics including a two-tier rear wing, an optional full-width front wing, and the more powerful SA35-A2 engine. The upshot was that Peugeot came 1st and 2nd in the WSC rounds at Magny-Cours and Mexico.

Albeit latecomers to the by now rapidly disintegrating Group C world, Peugeot was on something of a roll, though lacking many challengers. In 1992, the 905B finished 1st and 3rd at Le Mans, and although the World Sportscar Championship drew to an ignominious close at the end of 1992, Peugeot entered the 1993 Le Mans with the 905 Evo 1B. Christophe Bouchut, Eric Helary and Geoff Brabham scored a third consecutive victory, with Thierry Boutsen, Yannick Dalmas and Teo Fabi in 2nd and Philippe Alliot, Mauro Baldi and Jean-Pierre Jabouille 3rd.

In 1992, the Peugeot 905B, with its F1-derived 3.5-litre V10 engine, won five out of six races in the FIA World Sportscar Championship, including the marque's first win at Le Mans in the hands of Derek Warwick, Yannick Dalmas and Mark Blundell, taking both the Drivers' and Teams' titles in 1992.

PORSCHE

There is a certain inevitability that Porsche gets the largest slice of the action here, not because of any personal predilection on my part, but simply because the marque was in contention for pretty much the entire WEC Group C series – IMSA and the All-Japan series included – and it made many more cars than any other manufacturer, in the shape of the 956 and 962, which, after the inaugural year, were bought and run by several private teams.

In 1981, the challenge at Weissach was to build a new and powerful yet low fuel consumption vehicle in record time. A separate main department for motorsport was set up at Porsche for the first time to meet the challenge, and the competition department's Chief Designer and Engineer, Norbert Singer, first had a 1:5-scale wooden model built. He recounted the story:

> *Ferry Porsche took a look at the model and said: 'I wish you good luck,' and that was it. To him, it was just another racing car. He had presented so many over the years, and of course, no one knew at the time what would happen with the car. Could it be successful?*

The team then went into the wind tunnel to create an aerodynamics concept – one that would employ massive downforce to stick the car to the track surface, known as ground-effect, a phenomenon applied to F1 cars in the five seasons ahead of Group C, which are described in a bit more detail later on. Another novelty for the engineers was the pure aluminium monocoque. Norbert Singer said:

> *It was mainly a case of learning by doing. We had no idea how to build monocoques, and we sought help from the aircraft manufacturer Dornier. We built various boxes, joined them together and, in the end, we actually had a monocoque. We had started thinking about a carbon monocoque in 1982, when synthetic materials were just emerging in Formula 1. But our team was just too small to develop an aluminium monocoque and a carbon monocoque at the same time.*

Derek Bell recalled the sense of promise at the time:

> *I had previously driven a Porsche 936 with Jacky Ickx, and we had won Le Mans in 1981, and afterwards, I was invited to the factory by the Head of*

> *Development, Dr Helmuth Bott, to talk about the future. Dr Bott told me, 'Next year, we're starting in Group C,' but I had no idea what that was. He said: 'The car will have a monocoque chassis. We've never done anything like this before. We're also going to use ground-effect, and we've never done that before either.' But he also said: 'We've never been wrong.'*

For the powertrain, Singer opted for the twin-turbo six-cylinder boxer unit from the Porsche 935/76, an enhanced version of the 911 engine optimised for racing. All other components were newly developed. The racing team was obliged to work under extreme time pressure: the final version of the Group C regulations was not released until October 1981, but the upcoming season was set to start at the beginning of 1982. Two of the three works cars were only really ready to go a couple of weeks before Le Mans, and the third was completed just a few days before the event.

Le Mans 1985, and Peter Falk, Dr Helmuth Bott and Norbert Singer discuss an ACO lap times bulletin. As head of the pre-series and racing department, Peter Falk enabled cars from Porsche's most successful racing era, ranging from 917 to 956, 962 and Paris–Dakar 959. Dr Bott was head of R&D during Porsche's rise to World Championship-winning status during the 1960s and '70s, as well as designing the Weissach test track, while Norbert Singer transformed the 911 into a successful racing car and designed the bodywork of the 956 and 962.

In January 1982, Derek Bell shook down the new 956 at the Paul Ricard circuit at Le Castellet. It was a hit straight out of the box. He recalled: 'It was fantastic, the car was perfect. It was incredibly fast in the corners and was also very stable.' Jochen Mass was among the first drivers, and he, too, remembered being blown away by the 956:

> *It was so different to all the other racing cars before it. It had so much more downforce and was efficient in every detail. With the 956 so many corners just weren't there any more. The car was so good that it was now possible to drive through them at full throttle. It was also very comfortable to drive, not least on longer runs, because the seats were cushioned, and you sat well in them.*

Board Member for Development, Dr Helmuth Bott, of all people, was among the few sceptics. He could not imagine that a 620bhp racing car would be faster than its predecessor, the 917, which, latterly, in Can-Am trim, had 1000bhp at its disposal. To ensure Singer could not put one past him, Dr Bott personally chose the driver for a comparison, entrusting the task to freelance driver Derek Bell. Singer was vindicated: 'Ultimately, the 956 was 2.0 seconds faster. Bott was satisfied, and even climbed into the racing car himself to get a feel for it.' At Le Mans, Derek Bell and Jacky Ickx won the 1982 race in the 956. Jochen Mass and Vern Schuppan took 2nd and Hurley Haywood, Al Holbert and Jürgen Barth came 3rd in their 956. In the end, the cars crossed the line in the order of their race numbers: 1, 2 and 3.

Saving fuel was a key concern from the outset, and the formula is so crucial to the story that it bears repeating. Singer explained:

> *For the first time, there was a very clear fuel consumption rule for endurance races. You could have a maximum of 100 litres on board, and you had to do five pit stops. A maximum of 600 litres were allowed for the entire race distance. But you could never drive the cars down to empty – the danger of getting stuck out there somewhere was too great. It did nevertheless happen on occasion that someone would run out of fuel with two laps to go and would have to wait on the side of the track until they could get filled up there.*

Saving fuel was also a precarious undertaking, however, as Derek Bell recalled:

> *We had to tape a piece of paper about five by seven centimetres to the centre of the steering wheel. Across the top, it said: 11, 12, 13. Down the side it had the numbers 1 to 13. On the instrument panel, there was an indicator of how much fuel we had used at a certain point. So, we went out for 11, 12 or 13 laps. If we did 11 laps with the fuel, we were really fast. But that also meant more fuel stops. Every pit stop meant three to four minutes of lost time. We could do 13 laps – very economically, but also very boringly for everyone involved.*

The calculating was one thing, but the reading was another thing altogether.

> *We were doing 360km/h on the Mulsanne Straight, and at the same time, we had to look at this little piece of paper and figure out how many laps we'd set out to do. Believe me, we had a tough job in those cars.*

Hans-Joachim Stuck joined the Porsche team in 1985:

> *I drove in a team with Derek. I could rely on him one hundred per cent. We never had any internal rivalry. Sometimes he was faster, sometimes I was. Peter Falk had taught us how we could save extra fuel at Le Mans, for example, while braking after the very long Mulsanne Straight. Normally we braked 200 metres before the corner, but were now supposed to ease off the accelerator 400 metres before it and just let the car roll. There were about ten more corners, so we did it the same way there. This made the distance travelled with the accelerator pedal floored considerably less. What a brilliant idea – that's how we beat them all.*

The factory team also had some unusual ideas that helped solve the fuel problem: because the quality of the fuel at the respective racetracks was completely inconsistent at the time, the teams never knew how they should tune their engines. Helmut Schmid, an engine man, recalled:

> *We got the notion of using Norbert Singer's company car, the 944 Turbo. We installed a measuring device and then compared conventional petrol with that at the track. Maximum rpm, full-on brakes till everything was glowing. That's how we got to the knock limit of the engine. And that gave us an advantage because then we knew how to tune the engines in terms of ignition injection parameters and so on. Later we piggy-backed the knock control from the 944 on the steering apparatus in the 962.*

Singer summed up:

> *A comparison at Spa in 1982 and 1985 showed that the average lap time over the entire race in that period got seven per cent faster, while fuel consumption dropped by 23 per cent.*

Singer and his development team completed the first prototype on 27 March 1982. Singer had just a single goal, which was to enter that year's Le Mans 24-Hours. Only a few weeks after the cars were completed the Rothmans-Porsche team took three 956s – chassis 2, 3 and 4 – to Le Mans. On their debut, they scored an emphatic 1–2–3 victory, Jacky Ickx and Derek Bell winning, followed by Jochen Mass and Vern Schuppan, with Hurley Haywood, Al Holbert and Jürgen Barth crewing the third 956. Porsche and Ickx also claimed the 1982 World Championship, then lifting the crown in 1983, 1984 and 1985. In 1983, in a works 956, Stefan Bellof set an astonishing lap record on the Nordschleife at 6 minutes 11.13sec, a record that stood for 35 years. Private teams such as Joest Racing, Obermaier Racing, John Fitzpatrick Racing, Richard Lloyd Racing, Kremer Racing and Brun Motorsport used the 956 as a customer car from 1983. Kremer Racing and Joest Racing had to wait until 1983 for their 956s, and meanwhile, they created new bodywork, including fairing in a roof on their existing open-top 936s. Kremer Racing designated their car CK5 01, and Joest Racing's car was designated a 936C JR005.

Twenty-eight 956s were built between 1982 and 1984, while Richard Lloyd Racing created an unofficial 29th chassis out of spare parts. As top speed on the 6km (3.7-mile) Mulsanne Straight during the 1980s was crucial, Porsche used two different rear wing designs on the 956. For Le Mans, the 956 was fitted with a noticeably lower and smaller rear wing. Some privateer teams experimented with a front wing to increase downforce on tighter tracks.

THE PORSCHE 956

The 956 was a milestone model for Porsche, just as the 917 had been in 1969. It was radically different to any previous Porsche racing cars, mainly in having a monocoque chassis as its basis, rather than the triangulated tubular spaceframes that went before. The 956 is described here in some depth because it set certain standards and reveals similar construction methods to those employed by its competitors.

In contrast to the open-top Type 936 (in action 1976–82), the 956 monocoque had relatively narrow side members. This distinction was possible because the fuel tanks were no longer housed inside the car. Instead, the fuel tank of the 956 was located behind the cockpit, theoretically the safest location within the chassis, holding 99.5 litres or 26.3 gallons of fuel. The passenger cell was encompassed by a roll-cage, which served to stiffen the chassis. The flat-six engine was bolted to the rear wall of the fuel tank. In between the engine and transmission, there was a 40cm spacer (15.75in) with a cast integral cross member. Bracing tubes connected the cross member to the roll-cage. The cross member also served as the pickup point for the rear suspension's upper A-arms. The engine crankcase and upper tubular structure were designed to act as a single stressed load-carrying member. The front and rear suspension design deliberately went down an established path because the obligatory flat plate underneath the car – 100 centimetres wide by at least 80 centimetres long – introduced completely different airflow relationships and behaviours to any precedents, familiar, for example, from newly established F1 ground-effect practice. Because on the 956, incoming air had to be directed very low under the flat plate and, therefore, below the lower A-arm to the rear, the front suspension components were not directly exposed to the airstream, so their shapes did not have to be especially aerodynamically configured. The rear suspension appeared unconventional because the pair of Bilstein gas dampers were not mounted outboard, as on the front suspension, but inboard in a broad V configuration. Here too, the reason was revealing. Behind the flat plate required by the rules, two air tunnels, one on either side, lead under the engine, rising and widening slightly towards the back, allowing an escape for the tightly bound airflow from the nose. Outboard spring-damper units would have disturbed the airflow in this complex path. Because the lower rear A-arms still protruded into these air channels, these lower arms, like the transmission housing, were enclosed. After the flat plate, the Porsche engineers' greatest obstacle in designing a race car with high downforce was initially the flat-six engine.

Norbert Singer (second left) supervises the construction of the 956 monocoque tub.

In Weissach, engineers were convinced that they could achieve better downforce using a narrow-angle V6 engine, but at the time the 956 was being designed, there was no other engine available in-house other than the classic flat-six. Its initial disadvantages compared to competing designs were more than compensated for by years of painstaking, detailed engineering.

The outboard brakes were attached to magnesium spindles and were a new Porsche development. The single-piece aluminium alloy fixed calipers each contained four pistons. The brake discs measured 330 millimetres in diameter and about 30 millimetres thick and were internally vented and perforated, except for 12- and 24-hour races. The wheels were designed by Horst Reitter and produced by Speedline in the UK as single-piece magnesium castings as opposed to split-rims. Contrarily, customer 956s were fitted with standard three-piece BBS wheels. The works wheels were lighter and had the added advantage of allowing the inclusion of a tyre pressure warning system. In the cockpit, four red dashboard lights signalled a loss of air in one or more tyres, and the driver could then head for the pits at reduced speed to have the wheel replaced, precluding more serious damage.

The bodywork was fabricated by Porsche's in-house plastics and composites craftsmen and consisted primarily of fibreglass-reinforced plastic – GRP – with reinforcing ribs of carbon fibre. There were problems with the windshield shape because the top edge of the windshield was specified by the rules as a measurement point, a maximum of 1.10mm above ground level. The engineers chose a curved windshield to keep the car as low as possible, about 1.03 metres at that uppermost point. This meant that the laminated safety-glass windshield had to have a compound curve. This was a difficult assignment, which the glazing company Südglas in Bietigheim, Stuttgart, only achieved on their 31st attempt. The first 30 goes shattered because, up to this point, there was no mould or sufficient experience with manufacturing such compound curves.

The twin-turbocharged inter-cooled flat-six engine displaced 2.65 litres, and, in principle, was identical to that which had powered the 936 to victory at Le Mans in 1981. The six four-valve water-cooled cylinderheads were individually welded to the air-cooled aluminium alloy cylinder barrels. Two overhead camshafts per cylinder bank controlled the flow of combustion air into and exhaust gases out of the flat-six power plant. Despite the engine's proven abilities, Director of Racing Engine Development Valentin Schäffer subjected the design to a thorough revamping in order to reduce fuel consumption, since the Group C rules were a fuel consumption formula, and achieved the necessary fuel economy improvement from the outset by reducing peak engine revs and raising the compression ratio. There was also a compromise between boost pressure and compression ratio, so the air- and water-cooled flat-six with a 7.2:1 compression ratio immediately produced 620bhp.

By the end of 1985, the compression ratio had risen in stages to 9.01, while power output remained roughly constant. Fuel consumption continued to drop to the point where the car easily met the tighter fuel restrictions imposed for 1985. In real terms, the fuel consumption of the works Porsche 956 and 962 for the 1985 season was uniformly below 50 litres of premium petrol per 100 race kilometres, which translates as 4.7 miles per gallon. Although the comparison is not entirely appropriate from an engineering standpoint, this would be like a conventional 100bhp production car getting 29mpg running at full throttle.

A spare 2,659cc 935/76 flat-six engine for a 956 in the Porsche pits garage at Brands Hatch, 1984.

The 956 began its racing career using Bosch mechanical fuel injection, but as early as September 1982 at the Spa 1,000km, engine control functions were served by a fully electronic Bosch Motronic system. This also marked the beginning of the rapid rise of electronics in motorsport, and without the Motronics map ignition concept it would not have been possible at that time to achieve such fuel economy with this particular engine. In a departure from the earlier practice of locating the turbochargers behind the engine, the 956 had them mounted at the sides of the cylinderheads, taking advantage of the car's more spacious engine bay, with shorter air passages. This had several advantages, including better throttle response and a small increase in power. The correspondingly short exhaust pipes exited on both sides of the bodywork. Each side of the car had one radiator for the cylinderheads, an intercooler for that side's turbocharger and an oil cooler located on either side of the fuel tank. In the first version of the 956, cooling air still entered through NACA ducts in the horizontal surfaces and the doors and exited through horizontal openings in the rear bodywork. This version was never used in a race, as testing quickly proved the design to be impractical. The reworked engine with all its ancillary equipment weighed 192kg (423lb). The Porsche 5-speed synchromesh manual transmission used a magnesium case specially made for the 956, which provided all the pickup points for the rear suspension. The gear ratios and individual gears were largely taken over from the Type 935, while the final drive was by a spindle or limited slip diff.

RONDEAU

Jean Rondeau is the only driver to have won Le Mans in a car bearing his own name, and since we are using the 24-Hours as a performance yardstick, that achievement counts for something. Rondeau also built cars for Group C, but before developing his own cars, he appeared at Le Mans as a guest driver. In 1976, he entered Le Mans with an Inaltera GTP designed by Bureau Jean Rondeau, a Group 6 race car that was sponsored by wallpaper producer Inaltera and powered by a Ford Cosworth DFV engine. The naturally aspirated Cosworth V8 engine was no match for the turbo-engined cars, finishing some forty laps behind the winning Porsche 936, but Henri Pescarolo and Jean-Pierre Beltoise won the GTP class, beating Peugeot, Aston-Martin and Ferrari-powered cars. Four years later, Jean Rondeau and Jean-Pierre Jaussaud won the 1980 Le Mans in the Rondeau.

In 1980, Jean Rondeau won the Le Mans 24-Hours in his own Rondeau M379B, together with his fellow countryman Jean-Pierre Jaussaud. Jean Rondeau was one of the first constructors to embrace incoming Group C rules, building his cars specially to contest Le Mans.

Henri Pescarolo demonstrates a Rondeau-built Inaltera at the 2018 Le Mans Classic event. Pescarolo and Jean-Pierre Beltoise enjoyed class successes with the Inalrera – named after a wallpaper company – at Le Mans in 1976 and '77. Two Cosworth DFV-powered Inalteras ran in the Le Mans GTP class cars at the 1977 Daytona 24-Hours and provided the inspiration for the IMSA GTP class rules developed in 1980. Meanwhile, Jean Rondeau kept the blueprints, and these served to produce his own car with which he won Le Mans in 1980.

When Inaltera pulled out, a modified version of the Inaltera bore the Rondeau name, and Rondeau got sponsored by Otis Elevator. He had his ups and downs, though the M378 was introduced in 1978, followed a year later by the M379. In 1979, Rondeau took a surprise class win and 3rd at Le Mans. Fired up by his triumph in 1980, Rondeau entered the 24-hour race in 1981 with five cars, finishing 2nd and 3rd, overshadowed by the death of Rondeau's driver Jean-Louis Lafosse who was killed during the opening stages. In 1982, the M382 appeared, in fact, the first car that was designed and built by Automobiles Jean Rondeau to comply with the Group C technical regulations. The M382 was largely based on the earlier M379, although it had a larger wheelbase, new rear suspension, and improved aerodynamics and brakes. Rondeau used a 3.3-litre Cosworth DFL V8, although it was decided to use the more powerful 3.9-litre engine at Le Mans. Two cars debuted at the Daytona 24-Hours, but due to a lack of preparation and a number of unscheduled stops, neither made it to the finish. The team's primary sponsor, Otis, withdrew in 1983, after which Rondeau entered a partnership with Ford and appeared at the start of Le Mans with the M482. When it turned out that the 3.3 litre and 3.9 litre DFL were unreliable and Rondeau had problems with the development of ground-effect aerodynamics, it was concluded that the French manufacturer could no longer match the success of the past. At the end of that year the team was subsequently disbanded. Unfortunately, Jean Rondeau was killed two years later when his 911 got stuck on a railway level crossing.

SAUBER-MERCEDES & MERCEDES-BENZ

Peter Sauber's private team participated in the Group C World Sportscar Championship from 1982 to 1991, racing its own designs, which were initially powered by BMW or Ford Cosworth engines. Contacts were established with Daimler-Benz, which enabled Sauber to use the Untertürkheim wind tunnel for the development of its racing cars. Mercedes-Benz engineers Rüdiger Faul and Leo

Ress had also worked on a Group C car in 1980/81, powered by a Mercedes-Benz V8 engine used in the C 111-IV in 1979, and elements of the Group C design were incorporated into the development of the C6 Group C car for the 1982 season. This came to fruition as a collaboration project between Sauber and Seger & Hoffmann, another Swiss company, a manufacturer of composite components for racing and rally cars.

As a result of the disastrous 1982 season, which, after a hopeful start, saw numerous Cosworth engine failures, largely on account of vibration, the two Swiss collaborators parted ways, and the deck was reshuffled. Sauber produced the C7, which was again optimised in the Untertürkheim wind tunnel and, in 1983, equipped with a BMW engine. It competed in the Le Mans 24-Hours, the only race it did in Europe, where it finished 9th. In 1985, Leo Ress moved in as a chassis specialist from Daimler-Benz to the Sauber team via a brief stopover at BMW, and Rüdiger Faul continued to support Sauber on a part-time basis. The new C8, which had evolved from the C7, acted as a beacon of hope. Since the contacts between Sauber and Daimler-Benz had become much closer by then, the Stuttgart-based company had contributed its 5-litre V8, which had meanwhile been further developed into a racing engine – the C8. Two KKK turbochargers helped it to achieve a peak output of around 515 kW/700 hp. However, the power unit, which was based on the production engine of the M 117 series, was not only considerably more powerful but also more expansive and heavier than BMW's 3.5-litre inline six, which the original C7 was designed to accommodate. With its aluminium housing, the large-volume production V8 was ideally suited to its intended task. To be on par in terms of performance with the dominant Porsche 962 C and Jaguar XJR-6, despite the fuel consumption regulations, only relatively unintrusive tuning measures were required beyond turbocharging. The engine was turned into an absolutely competitive power unit, not only in terms of power, but also in terms of reliability and fuel consumption, by installing a two-valve cylinderhead with larger valves adopted (as in the 500 SLC rally car of 1980) from the 5.6-litre version of the M 117 then under development as well as racing pistons, titanium conrods, a lightened crankshaft, a dry sump lubrication system, and a much more powerful cooling system, working in concert with a modified injection system and a Bosch Motronic engine control unit. The power of the turbocharged eight-cylinder engine was transmitted directly to the rear axle via a 5-speed Hewland gearbox.

Peter Sauber, right, helps push the one-off Sauber C7 out of the Hockenheim pits garage ahead of a shakedown.

The privately entered Bellanger-Bassaler Sauber SHS C2, powered by the BMW M88 3.5-litre straight-six, was driven by Roland Bassaler, Dominique Lacaud and Yvon Tapy and finished 23rd in the 1985 Le Mans.

Leo Ress had the task of implanting this engine from his former employer into the C8. Since its aluminium monocoque, as well as the complete chassis with double wishbone axles, suspension struts and front and rear stabilisers, had essentially been adopted from the C7, Ress had to limit himself to the construction of a steel subframe to house the new engine instead of the inline 6-cylinder originally planned. Sauber set itself the ambitious goal of competing at Le Mans with the barely tested C8 as early as mid-June. However, initial test drives undertaken in May already showed that the new drive configuration entailed problems. On the one hand, the aluminium monocoque proved not to be torsionally stiff enough to cope with the immense performance potential of the Mercedes-Benz V8. On the other hand, the C8 produced too little downforce at high speed. The excursion to Le Mans began quite promisingly. Peter Sauber's one-car team with the renowned driver team John Nielsen/Dieter Quester/Max Welti still managed to take 18th place in the pre-qualification that traditionally takes place before the race. During the actual practice runs to determine the starting positions immediately before the race weekend, the Dane John Nielsen then met with a serious accident. About 500 metres before the end of the 6km-long Mulsanne Straight, the airflow under the car lifted the C8 up in the air after passing over a small crest at about 370 km/h. It flew about 200 metres through the air and fortunately landed on its rear end. The engine was still running, and the doors opened effortlessly. Miraculously, the driver was unhurt, but the car was so badly damaged that a start in the race was ruled out. After this incident, the team ended the season and turned to working on the remaining technical weaknesses and teething troubles of the C8. They wanted to compete with a mature car with new-found strength. Indeed, the Group C World Sportscar Championship, which comprised nine rounds in the new season, got off to an auspicious start. In addition to John Nielsen, Henri Pescarolo and Mike Thackwell were signed as regular drivers. In the first two events, a sprint race at Monza and a 1,000-kilometre race at Silverstone, the prototype – now called the Kouros-Mercedes C8, thanks to the new sponsor Yves Saint-Laurent and its perfume brand Kouros – finished in 8th and 9th places. This time, however, the two-vehicle entry in the Le Mans 24-Hour race ended in total failure.

In the pits during the 1986 Silverstone 1,000km, the Kouros Racing 5.0-litre V8 Sauber C8 #02 was driven to 8th place by Henri Pescarolo (on right), Mike Thackwell and John Nielsen.

After that, the team did not compete again until the end of August at the traditional Nürburgring 1,000km. In the terrible weather conditions that prevailed on race day in the Eifel, the aluminium monocoque's continued lack of torsional rigidity had a rather positive effect, and the duo Pescarolo/Thackwell achieved the first overall victory for the C8 in a world championship race. When the race was abandoned after about two-thirds distance due to the rain, car #61 was leading by two laps over three trailing Porsches. Three weeks later, at the 1,000-kilometre race at Spa-Francorchamps, the upward trend was confirmed. The pairing of Thackwell/Pescarolo crossed the finish line in sixth place after a race duration of around five and a half hours. This was the last appearance of the C8 in Group C racing under the Sauber team name. In the overall standings of the World Sportscar Championship, competing as the Kouros Racing Team, Sauber finished in a respectable sixth place. The French privateer Noël del Bello bought one of the three existing C8s after the season and competed with it in a total of eight further rounds of the World Sportscar Championship in 1987 and 1988 but was forced to retire early from each of the races.

In 1987, Sauber developed a car in which the conceptual weaknesses of the C8 were eliminated. Above all, it was important to make the Mercedes-Benz 5.0-litre V8 turbo engine an integral part of the chassis design right from the start. The design of the bodywork also had to be completely revised to achieve higher downforce. Leo Ress designed a much more torsionally stiff monocoque made of aluminium sheets of varying thicknesses. In this chassis the engine was embedded in two subframes and acted as a supporting element. The suspension consisted of double wishbones front and rear and, following a new design trend, the positioning of the spring/damper units on the rear axle, with the wheel movements transmitted via thrust arms to the suspension struts, which were now horizontal in the direction of travel. A new brake system with carbon discs, as well as new light-alloy wheels, completed the revision. The sandwich construction of the C9 model's outer skin reflected the search for more downforce: voluminous side pods with integrated air ducts, together with the overall design of the body and the rear wing extending across the entire width of the car produced twice as much downforce as the previous C8 model. The Mercedes-Benz engine, which was based on the production V8 of the M 117 engine series, was turbocharged by two KKK turbos with maximum power set to 500 kW/680 hp in race trim and even to 577 kW/785 hp in qualification mode; it had proved to be absolutely reliable as well as economical within the regulations. It was only modified in detail and was used in the 1987 season.

The Sauber squad, still registered as the Kouros Racing Team, faced the competition for the first time with the new C9 in May in the fourth round – the Silverstone 1,000km. However, the car driven by Thackwell and Pescarolo retired early with suspension failure, and the two-car line-up at Le Mans was equally disappointing. The driver trios Dumfries/Ganassi/Thackwell and Thackwell/Pescarolo/Okada were let down by gearbox and tyre failures, respectively. The only tangible result in the 1987 world championship season was a 7th in the Spa-Francorchamps 1,000km at the beginning of September. However, Jean-Louis Schlesser showed the true potential of the C9 in the Nürburgring Supersprint, a round of the international ADAC Würth Supercup, when he took victory against strong competition. The success was completed by third place for Mike Thackwell in the sister car.

Clearly, ways had to be found to further improve the race performance for a more convincing result in the following year's Group C World Championship. Even the previous 5.0-litre biturbo V8 with its two-valve cylinderhead no longer offered sufficient prospects in the medium term, so the ball was in Daimler-Benz's court. It transpired that the motorsport bug had infected even board members in the company, and the topic of an official re-entry into the national and international racing scene, which had been floating around for years, finally gelled around the turn of the year 1987/88: on 15 January 1988 Daimler-Benz AG finally announced that the factory would once again be involved in motorsport. The explicit focus was on the highly publicised DTM German Touring Car Championship, which the 190 E 2.3-16 targeted, and the World Sportscar Championship with Group C cars in close collaboration with the Swiss Sauber team. As the sponsorship programme with the French perfume label Kouros had expired at the end of 1987, the C9 models sported a new outfit with the main sponsor AEG Olympia at

The 5.0-litre M119 V8 engine of the Sauber-Mercedes C9 revealed during a pit stop at the Donington 480km race in 1989, where they finished 1st and 2nd.

Sauber's sponsorship deal with Kouros was not renewed for 1988, and the team was renamed Sauber-Mercedes, coinciding with a change of Mercedes-Benz senior management and the announcement in January '88 by new deputy chairman Prof. Dr Werner Niefer that the company would support Group C sportscars, with backing from AEG-Olympia, which was owned by Daimler-Benz at the time. Team management was bolstered by former BMW team manager and Porsche race-driver Jochen Neerpasch and Swiss driver Max Welti.

Jean-Louis Schlesser in the Sauber-Mercedes C9 leads Jochen Dauer's 962C and Franz Konrad in the Jöst 962C during the Diepholz Supercup (a round of the ADAC Würth Supercup) at Flugplatz Diepholz in August 1988.

The C9 was a development of Sauber's previous C8, an aluminium monocoque with redesigned rear suspension, which changed from vertically positioned spring/damper units arranged over the top of the gearbox to a horizontal layout aligned with the longitudinal axis of the car.

their first action – the first round of the world championship in Jerez de la Frontera, Spain. The base coat looked almost black but was the Daimler-Benz dark blue hue (code DB 904). No significant technical changes had been made to the cars, while the increased input from Mercedes-Benz initially manifested itself in the establishment of increased overall reliability. However, they already had a new engine lined up, which was to be used at the beginning of the 1989 season.

From the first race of the 1988 season, it became apparent that the C9 Sauber-Mercedes had been developed over the winter into a serious title contender. In the four races preceding the Le Mans 24-Hours, the Sauber-Mercedes team took one victory, three 2nd places and one 3rd place. The driver line-up was augmented by Mauro Baldi and Jochen Mass, two more experienced drivers who made the Sauber-Mercedes line-up even more potent. However, the performance at the season's highlight at Le Mans was not a success. Tyre problems in practice resulted in Klaus Niedzwiedz blowing a tyre at high speed, and the team management decided not to allow the two entered C9s to start for safety reasons. Despite this, the team proved that, with four wins in the remaining six rounds of the season, they had left Porsche behind them after the latter's years of domination.

In the final WRC standings, they were bested only by the TWR factory Jaguars. To carry the momentum of success forward into the following season and, more specifically, to aim for the title, Mercedes-Benz prepared a new power unit for 1989. The new power unit was also a production-based V8 – the 5.0-litre M 119 engine with four-valve cylinderheads and two overhead camshafts, a further development of the previous V8, including a lightened crankshaft, titanium con-rods and racing pistons, making it 30 per cent lighter than its production counterpart.

A dry sump lubrication system was installed, while the two KKK turbochargers were the latest design with boost pressure of 0.9 bar. In this configuration, the new power unit produced a maximum output of 720bhp. In qualifying trim, the boost pressure was increased to 925bhp. Transmission

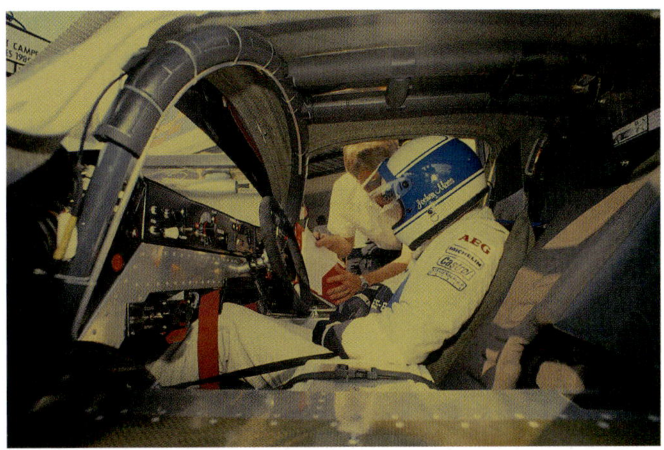

The cockpit of the Sauber-Mercedes C9 is a neat yet purposeful environment, with comprehensive crash safety structures and coordinated switchgear. Jochen Mass takes stock during his 3rd place outing with Jean-Louis Schlesser at Brands Hatch, 1989.

The Sauber-Mercedes C9 of Mauro Baldi, Gianfranco Brancatelli and Kenny Acheson heads three of the TWR Jaguar XJR-9s and the 962C of Franz Konrad, Rudi Seher and Andres Vilariño at the start of the 1989 Le Mans 24-Hours. The Sauber Mercedes C9s finished 1st and 2nd, with Mass/Reuter/Dickens taking the win.

was by a Hewland five-speed gearbox optimised by the Mercedes-Benz technicians. Apart from minor modifications to the bodywork and further technical fine-tuning the C9 remained otherwise unchanged for the 1989 season. Highly symbolically, the cars were now presented in silver, evoking the brand's racing tradition. Of the eight races scheduled, the Sauber-Mercedes two-car team won seven events, three of them 1–2 finishes. In the only race not won by the C9, the Coupe de Dijon at the Dijon-Prénois circuit, C9s numbers 62 and 61 finished second and third. The undisputed highlight of the season was the 1–2 double victory at Le Mans. Even though it was not a world championship race in 1989, it was still one of the most demanding, and it was the first victory for the brand at La Sarthe since 1952. After a distance of 5,265 kilometres, the Jochen Mass/Manuel Reuter/Stanley Dickens crew took the chequered flag with a five-lap lead over their 2nd-placed teammates Mauro Baldi/Kenny Acheson/Gianfranco Brancatelli, with the French trio Jean-Louis Schlesser/Jean-Pierre Jabouille/Alain Cudini placing 5th.

The cockpit of the 1990 Sauber-Mercedes C11 reveals the carbon-Kevlar panels used in its construction, plus the Momo wheel and five-speed shift lever.

Reigning 1989 WEC champions Sauber-Mercedes C11s were dominant in 1990, with Jochen Mass/Karl Wendlinger in #2 victorious at the Spa-Francorchamps 480km, with Mauro Baldi/Jean-Louis Schlesser 8th in #1, having set fastest lap.

The C9's dominance throughout the season won the World Championship title for Sauber-Mercedes, and in the Drivers' Championship, the first four places went to drivers Jean-Louis Schlesser, Jochen Mass, Mauro Baldi and Kenny Acheson.

After the title win with the C9 in both the teams' and drivers' championships, Sauber-Mercedes set about developing a new car for the 1990 Group C World Championship season. It was given the designation C11 because C10 was perceived as a tongue-twister in German and therefore not used. The development focus was primarily on a new chassis; while the four-valve V8 engine introduced the previous year was optimised in the areas of valve control, injection and electronics, gaining a slight increase in maximum output by 11bhp to 730bhp, the new carbon/Kevlar monocoque marked the beginning of a new era.

Although the completely redesigned chassis was somewhat heavier than the previous glued and riveted aluminium monocoque, it provided twice the torsional stiffness which benefited the handling. The chassis structure also had significantly higher safety reserves for the driver in the event of an accident. The new car's wheelbase was longer by 70mm, with a correspondingly modified rear subframe to accommodate the power unit and modifications to the rear axle, chiefly in that the longitudinal suspension struts actuated by pushrods in the C9 were now designed to lie transversely to the direction of travel in the C11.

Another significant changeover that led to faster lap times was the change of tyre supplier, switching from Michelin to Goodyear. The silver bodyshell of the C11 appeared almost unchanged externally, since despite the longer wheelbase, the total vehicle length of 4,800mm was the same as the C9. However, the underbody of the new carbon-fibre chassis was optimised for improved downforce, and in fact the C11 in the configuration specified by the regulations weighed less than the prescribed 900kg. So, in order to comply, lead ballast weights were placed in the tub's passenger side.

Gaining the 1989 World title was the incentive the parent company needed to pitch into the limelight: for the 1990 World Sportscar Championship, the car was entered as the Mercedes-Benz C11, the first racing car to carry the legendary brand name after Daimler-Benz withdrew from factory racing at the end of the 1955 season. However, at Suzuka in the first of the nine world championship rounds, Sauber-Mercedes still ran the C9s, the pairings of Schlesser/Baldi and Mass/Wendlinger duly placing 1st and 2nd. Then, at Monza three weeks later, the Sauber-built C11s proved their worth, and the same two driver duos finished in the same order as in Japan. As the season progressed, the C11s won six of the remaining seven rounds to secure the team title ahead of Jaguar and Nissan, and in the drivers' standings, Jean-Louis Schlesser, Mauro Baldi and Jochen Mass took the top three places. For the whole season, Mass took the up-and-coming 21-year-olds Karl Wendlinger, Michael Schumacher and Heinz-Harald Frentzen under his wing to teach them about life in a top-line works race team.

Pit stop drama at Suzuka 1989 in round 1 of the World Sports Prototype championship, with tyre change, refuel and driver swap-over for the winning Mauro Baldi/Jean-Louis Schlesser Sauber-Mercedes C9.

The Sauber-Mercedes C11 driven by Jochen Mass and Karl Wendlinger rounds La Source hairpin on its way to winning the Spa-Francorchamps 1,000km in 1990.

THE C291

Group C racing as a whole faced major changes in 1991. Three years earlier, the FIA had already decided to reform the World Sportscar Championship, the core of which was a new engine formula. From the 1991 season onwards, only 3.5-litre naturally aspirated engines were permitted in the top category C1 – as in Formula 1 at the time – while the minimum vehicle weight without operating fluids was set at 750 kilogrammes. Those who still wanted to start with the previous turbo engines were relegated to the C2 category. In the face of shrinking starting fields in prototype racing, the new regulations were an attempt to cut costs by relying on existing engines such as the Ford-Cosworth DFR V8, and thus attract new private teams. For a works-supported team like Sauber-Mercedes, this implied dramatically increased costs, as a power unit complying with the regulations was not available and would have to be developed from scratch. The rival Jaguar team was able to operate differently, simply by using the Cosworth V8 operating as it did within the expansive Ford cosmos – sourcing engines from the Benetton team. Only one newcomer rose to the FIA challenge. As part of its medium-term motorsport strategy, Peugeot saw participation in the World Sportscar Championship as an opportunity to gain experience with a newly designed 3.5-litre V10 engine, mounted amidships in its 905 sports prototype. Sauber-Mercedes had made the decision well in advance to contest the 1991 season with a completely redesigned car. The C291 differed significantly from the previous year's C11, and followed the Mercedes-Benz model series nomenclature in which the letter C designated a coupé and also referred to the 1991 racing season.

The C291 embraced a radical aerodynamic concept to which the redesigned drivetrain was to be subordinate as well. To achieve the lowest possible centre of gravity and an optimally designed underbody in terms of downforce, an unusual technical configuration was chosen, consisting of a 3.5-litre V12 engine installed at a slight angle to the direction of travel, in combination with a sequential 6-speed gearbox mounted transversely ahead of the rear axle. The 12-cylinder engine, with its 180-degree bank-angle, resembled the layout of a boxer engine more readily associated with its Zuffenhausen rivals, and contained a number of technical characteristics that went beyond the design mainstream. Some of these, such as the flat design of the V-engine and the central output by means of a shaft rotating at crankshaft speed that acted directly on the main shaft of the gearbox located transversely behind it, harmonised perfectly with the uncompromising aerodynamic concept. Here, the large-volume venturi duct in the underbody dictated the installation space available for the powertrain. What was equally surprising was the decision to dispense with a cylinderhead gasket and instead use a design in which the cylinder and cylinderhead were a one-piece integrated cast element. Although this design feature had historically been a characteristic feature of Mercedes-Benz racing engines for decades until the W196R Formula 1 racing car and the closely related 300 SLR racing sportscar of 1954 and 1955, it seemed decidedly exotic as an isolated technical solution at the start of the 1990s.

The cylinderhead itself was state of the art, with four-valve technology, two electronically controlled injection valves and dual ignition. The engine electronics relied on an MB-TAGtronic system specially developed by Mercedes-Benz and TAG-Heuer, which controlled both intake manifold injection and ignition pulses. During the first tests at the end of 1990, the flat twelve

The 5.0-litre V8 turbo-powered Mercedes-Benz C11 of Jochen Mass and Jean Louis Schlesser finished 4th overall at the 1991 Silverstone 430km.

In line with new FIA rules for 1991, the Mercedes-Benz C291 power unit was the normally aspirated M291 3.5-litre flat-12, developing 600bhp, rather less than the 750bhp produced by the previous twin-turbo 5.0-litre engine of the Sauber-Mercedes C11.

engine with its magnesium case produced a peak output of 550bhp at 13,000rpm. By the season première at Suzuka in mid-April, this had risen to 598bhp, achieved by tuning and performance-enhancing fuel mixtures. For the last race of the season at the end of October in Autopolis – also in Japan – a further evolutionary stage of the engine was used, which delivered 642bhp, placing it on a par with Peugeot and Jaguar in terms of performance.

Not only was the engine of the C291 completely redesigned in accordance with the revised Group C regulations, but the carbon-fibre chassis was also adapted for the new rules. A crash test was now mandatory to certify the strength of the monocoque structure, so there were also a number of revisions on the chassis side. Although the wheelbase of 2,700mm was carried over unchanged from the C11, the time-served double-wishbone front axle was switched to tension struts for the actuation of the coil spring/damper units, and the previous rear-axle design gave way to unusually high-positioned wishbones that left room for the venturi duct. The C291 bodyshell featured new air intakes at the front of the vehicle below the cockpit and on the flanks and, with a length of 4,650mm, was 150mm shorter than its predecessor.

The driver line-up remained essentially the same, with Michael Schumacher and Karl Wendlinger in the C291, and Jochen Mass and Jean-Louis Schlesser initially continuing to compete in the C11, relegated to the C2 category. In the first two rounds, the C291 still suffered from teething problems and retired prematurely, while the C11 managed 2nd and 3rd places overall. But in the third race in mid-May at Silverstone the C291 finished second in the hands of Schumacher/Wendlinger, with the C11 of Schlesser/Mass in fourth place.

The C291 was entered for Le Mans but was ultimately withdrawn, and the surviving C11 of Schumacher, Wendlinger and Kreutzpointner finished 5th in a race won by Mazda, with Jaguar filling the next three places. The hordes of Peugeot 905s fared no better.

Designed by Leo Ress, the 1991 Sauber Mercedes C11 tub was created entirely in carbon-fibre rather than the aluminium monocoque of its predecessors, and was built by Dave Price's Surrey-based DPS Composites.

Round 2 of the 1991 WSC was held at Monza, with the latest C1-spec cars versus previous C1 entries given a stay of execution to run in C2 that season. Thus, the 5.0-litre flat-12 Mercedes-Benz C11 ran in C2, whilst its replacement, the latest 3.5-litre C291, ran in C1. Mass/Schlesser's C11 came 3rd, but Schumacher/Wendlinger's C291, pictured, did not finish.

The C291s had no joy in the second half of the season; neither in their home race on the Nürburgring nor in the subsequent races at Magny-Cours and Mexico City did either of the two cars finish.

But in the final race at Autopolis, Michael Schumacher and Karl Wendlinger gave the C291 its first victory, beating both the factory Jaguar XJR-14 and Peugeot 905 models, and the second C291 of Schlesser/Mass crossed the finish line in fifth place. Although a successor to the C291, designated the C292, had been created to contest the 1992 season, Mercedes-Benz elected to end its involvement in Group C a few weeks after the season finale. The framework created by the FIA resulted in further reduced starting grids, and prototype racing in that format came to an end one year later. Accordingly, Mercedes-Benz concentrated its resources on the German Touring Car Championship (DTM), with the 190 E 2.5-16 Evolution II playing a prominent role.

The Mercedes-Benz C291 was built on a carbon-fibre-reinforced plastic monocoque incorporating the roof and roll-over bar, and powered by the M291 flat-12, canted upwards at the rear to make more space for underfloor venturi, and allied to a transverse 6-speed gearbox.

The 1991 Mexico City 430km was staged on 6 October at the Autodromo Hermanos Rodriguez, the penultimate race of the season. Michael Schumacher started the second Mercedes-Benz C291 from the front row of the grid alongside Alliot's Peugeot and set a new sportscar lap record. At 60 laps out of 98, the C291s were 3rd and 5th overall, but Schumacher/Wendlinger's retired with failed oil pressure and Mass/Schlesser's with rainwater flooding the electrical system.

Brembo carbon brake discs glow red-hot on the 5th placed Mercedes-Benz C291 of Karl Wendlinger/Michael Schumacher/Fritz Kreutzpointner at Le Mans 1991.

SPICE ENGINEERING

Spice Engineering was founded by racing drivers Gordon Spice and Ray Bellm in 1986. The former rejoiced in a long and successful career as a saloon car racer in the 1960s and '70s, while the latter raced Chevron B36 sports-prototypes in the '70s. They ran Group C2 Tiga sports cars in their early days, with Neil Crang as co-driver, and in 1985, they began to develop the Tiga GC85 chassis. They took five class wins in 1985, including the Le Mans 24-Hours and the Teams' championship.

The Spice SE86C was the team's first car, designed in conjunction with Pontiac, and resembling the Pontiac Fiero in silhouette to justify Pontiac's financial backing for the project. Spice and Bellm drove chassis 001 to C2 class victory and a 2nd place in its first two races in 1986. After another win, followed by multiple podium finishes, Spice and Bellm took the Group C2 Drivers' World Championship. At Le Mans in 1987, Spice, Fermin Vélez and Philippe de Henning came 5th overall, with Spice winning the Drivers World Championship again in 1987.

Spice Engineering designed and developed the Spice SE87C for the Group C2 World Sportscar Championship in 1987, but unlike the very successful SE86, the SE87C suffered from numerous reliability problems. However, when the format of the World Sportscar Championship was changed to 480km races instead of the longer 1,000km races, the SE87C managed to finish several times. Besides participating in the WSC, the SE87C was entered in the German Interserie Championship.

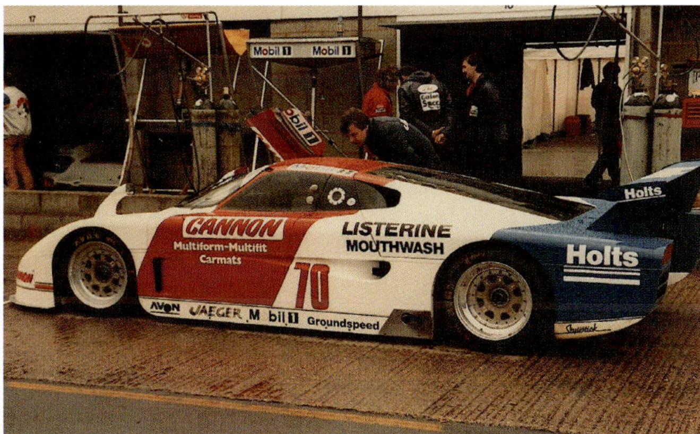

The Spice SE86C presents a sleek profile in the pitlane for the 1986 Silverstone 1,000km, in which Gordon Spice and Ray Bellm came 14th.

For the 1988 racing season, Spice Engineering introduced the SE88C, a second-generation sports prototype which was available to customer teams. There was a range of engines to choose from, allowing the car to be used in Group C, Group C2 GTP, and GTP Lights. The Spice SE88C succeeded the SE86C and SE87C in the WSC, and Spice and Bellm dominated the Group C2 class with their factory entries. In 1988, Spice Engineering won the C2 class in ten out of eleven rounds, including Le Mans, with Gordon Spice, Ray Bellm and Pierre de Thoisy driving. De Thoisy drove for several teams in Group C, including the Rondeau M482, Gebhardt JC853, Brun Motorsport 962C, the works Spice SE88C and SE90C, the Team Davey 962 'Schuppan', and Les Alméras Frères' 962C 'Thompson'.

In 1989, Group C regulations changed once more, and Spice Engineering entered the C1 category in the World Sportscar Championship, but, as it turned out, the SE89C failed to deliver in either the C1 or C2 classes. New cars were built for the 1990 season, which were basically identical to the previous cars. Designed by Graham Humphrey, the Spice SE90 was offered to customer teams in two versions: the SE90C to comply with the C1 and C2 categories of the WSC, or the SE90P version designed for the IMSA Championship and the GTP and GTP Light categories. The SE90 was one of the most successful Spice models, with different versions having won several championships. Spice Engineering built the SE91C and SE92C for 1991 and 1992, and Spice Engineering's story came to an end after winning the constructors' title for Oldsmobile in 1994.

TIGA

Two former F1 drivers, Tim Schenken from Australia and New Zealander Howden Ganley, founded Tiga Race Cars in the UK. It's pronounced Tiger, not Tigger, although the word is made up of Tim and Ganley. The company was known for various types of racing cars ranging from Formula Ford to sports cars built for the World Sportscar Championship. Schenken raced at Le Mans in 1973 as a Ferrari prototype works driver, with a 16th place in 1976 as his best result. Ganley gained more success at La Sarthe, with a 2nd place during the 1972 edition, partnering François Cevert in a Matra MS 670. In 1984, the Tiga GC84, also known as GC284, appeared with a Ford Cosworth DFL V8 engine. The car was an evolution of a sportscar originally built for Australian racer Neil Crang back in 1983. For the

The Ford-Cosworth-powered Tiga GC84 was created by Tim Schenken and Howden Ganley and driven here at Brands Hatch in 1984 by Neil Crang, Gordon Spice and Ray Bellm.

Cosmik Racing's Dudley Wood and Costas Los finished 15th overall in their 3.3-litre Cosworth DFL-powered Tiga GC287 at Silverstone's Autoglass 1,000km in 1987.

The C2 Tiga GC289 #373 powered by a 3.3-litre Ford-Cosworth DFL V8 entered by Didier Bonnet and driven by Gérard Tremblay and Joel Aulen ran in the 1989 Wheatcroft Gold Cup at Donington Park but hit gearbox problems.

1984 24-Hours of Le Mans, Crang teamed up with Gordon Spice and Ray Bellm under the Tiga-Spice Engineering flag. Unfortunately, the team ran into engine problems, and their first participation in Le Mans was unsuccessful. However, once the engine problems were resolved, the GC84 proved to be a formidable car. At the end of the year, the GC84 won the World Championship in the C2 class. Building on the success of the GC84, the GC85 was introduced in 1985, also known as the GC285, in fact, an evolution of the earlier GC84. Gordon Spice, Ray Bellm and Mark Galvin took a class win at Le Mans, finishing fourteenth overall. Spice entered the GC85 as a Spice-Tiga for the World Championship, and alongside winning at the Le Mans, they were crowned World Champions in the C2 division. The Tiga GC86/GC286 for the 1986 season was a development of the GC284 and GC285 both designed by Howden Ganley. This car was, in fact, Tiga's first ground-effect C2 and IMSA Light sportscar. Several types of engines were used, such as the Mazda 13B rotary Cosworth DFZ Chevrolet V8 Ford BDT, and even one from a Porsche 962. For its first season in 1986, this car was powered by a Ford Cosworth BDT-E 1.7 litre turbo engine, but by the time they got to the 24-Hours of Daytona in 1987, the engine was replaced by a Ford Cosworth DFL 3.3-litre V8. The final outing for the GC86/286 was in the Interserie Championship. For the 1987 season, Ganley modified the GC86/286 resulting in the Tiga GC87/287. Tiga was unable to build on the successes of previous years with the GC87/287, though. Just a single victory in the World Championship was scored while the brand struggled on in the North American IMSA championship. Later that year, Ganley sold his company. The GC288 (1988) and GC289 (1989) appeared before Tiga Race Cars ceased operations in 1989.

TOYOTA

Toyota's main interest in Group C was solely aimed at capitalising on the publicity accruing from participation and potential success in the Le Mans 24-Hours, an ambition shared with fellow Japanese manufacturers. In 1985, ten years after their first entry there – when the Sigma MC75 ran a Toyota engine – two TOM'S Toyota 85Cs powered by the 2.1-litre, 4-cylinder turbocharged engine installed in a TOM'S-Dome aluminium monocoque contested the 24-Hours enduro, with one driven by Satoru Nakajima, Masanori Sekiya and Kaoru Hoshino finishing in 12th place. TOM'S (Tachi Oiwa Motor Sport) was the brand's aftersales and tuning marketplace as well as its racing team moniker,

A pair of TOM'S Toyota 86Cs ran in the 1986 Le Mans 24-Hours. Powered by the 2.1-litre 4-cylinder turbocharged Toyota 4T-GT mounted on a TOM'S Dome aluminium monocoque, the bodywork was redesigned to harness more downforce. One 86C retired with engine trouble before dawn, while the other hit a terminal turbocharger problem with just an hour to go.

with race shops at Hingham, Norfolk (TOM'S GB – not a million miles from Lotus HQ at Hethel), and Tama, Tokyo.

In 1986, two TOM'S Toyota Dome 86Cs were entered for Le Mans, their bodies completely redesigned to gain an increase in downforce. Drivers were Geoff Lees, Satoru Nakajima and Masanori Sekiya, and Eje Elgh, Beppe Gabbiani and Toshio Suzuki. One retired with engine trouble before dawn, while the other moved up to 7th before a turbo failed with just an hour remaining. In 1987, Toyota changed its name to Toyota Team TOM'S, and the car was redesignated the Toyota 87C and fitted with a 2.1-litre, 4-cylinder turbo engine. This Toyota 3S-GT unit manifested a power boost that enabled it to beat the dominant Porsche 962Cs to win the Fuji 1,000km, a round of the All-Japan Sports Prototype Car Endurance Championship. In the following month's Le Mans 24-Hours, two 87Cs ran strongly in 5th and 6th in the early stages, driven by Alan Jones/Eje Elgh/Geoff Lees, and Tiff Needell/Masanori Sekiya/Kaoru Hoshino, although both cars retired before the sixth hour – one out of fuel.

A further evolution logically dubbed the 88C was produced by TRD, while TOM'S took care of the racing operations. Its carbon monocoque chassis was fitted with a 3.2-litre twin-turbo V8 engine, and two cars competed in the 1988 Le Mans, managing 8th and 10th in qualifying with Geoff Lees/Masanori Sekiya/Kaoru Hoshino finishing 12th and Paolo Barilla/Hitoshi Ogawa/Tiff Needell coming 24th. The 88C underwent further refinement while competing in the JSPC series and, for 1989, Toyota was obliged to comply with a new rule requiring participants to enter all the races counting towards the World Sports Prototype Championship in order to race at Le Mans. Accordingly, TOM'S entered two further developments of the 88C-V in the WSPC series, an 89C taking pole position in the opening round at Suzuka. Two 89Cs driven by Hitoshi Ogawa, Paolo Barilla and Ross Cheever, and the Brit threesome Geoff Lees, Johnny Dumfries and John Watson, and an 88C crewed by Kaoru Hoshino, Didier Artzet and Keiichi Suzuki ran at Le Mans but all three retired due to accidents and mechanical problems. In 1990, the Toyota 90C-V competed in the JSPC series and ran at Le Mans, with one driven by Geoff Lees, Masanori Sekiya and Hitoshi Ogawa logging 6th place overall. When the FIA changed the technical regulations in 1991 to allow only cars with naturally aspirated 3.5-litre engines, Toyota withdrew from the series. Its best result at Le Mans came in 1992, with its Tony Southgate-designed TS010 running a V10 engine and driven by Masanori Sekiya, Pierre-Henri Raphanel and Kenny Acheson, in 2nd place, and in 1993, the one-on-one duel for victory with Peugeot ended with a 4th place finish for Eddie Irvine, Toshio Suzuki and Masanori Sekiya, with Geoff Lees, Jan Lammers and Juan-Manuel Fangio II coming 8th.

CHAPTER 3

PORSCHE PREVAILS 1982–96

The 962C #002 of Jacky Ickx and Jochen Mass won WEC rounds at Mugello, Silverstone and Shah Alam, winning the 1985 Team title along with Derek Bell and Hans Stuck.

There was certainly a note of optimism ahead of the 1982 race season, as World Championship Sports-Prototype Racing had been in decline for much of the previous decade, post 917 and 512, and the introduction of the Group C category looked capable of raising the stakes substantially. This first season, with its new regulations, was a new beginning, even though it was not yet possible to dispense with the last vestiges of the old order. Apart from the four new categories that were allowed to compete for the World Endurance Championship for Makes – Groups A, B, C and

N – for this first season, the old Groups 4, 5 and 6 cars were also permitted to take part, but only for the World Endurance Championship for Drivers, which was to be run concurrently, and, perversely, had more counting rounds than the Makes' Championship.

As Jürgen Barth explained, Group C was conceived by FISA's technical commission in 1981 in consultation with some of the world's automakers. Although it was obvious from the outset that the new regulations' general drift was in the right direction, several reservations from manufacturers were not settled until late 1981, resulting in the rules being amended as late as that December. Unsurprisingly, some Group C car build programmes were seriously delayed, leading to an early lack of competitive entries and the consequent postponement of the first two events on the calendar, Mugello and Brands Hatch, until later in the season. In the confusion, Lancia shrewdly decided to play a safe hand by concentrating on the Drivers' Championship, building a completely new car, but to the eight-year-old Group 6 regulations, thus avoiding the incoming fuel consumption rules. Not only was the 1.4-litre turbo Lancia LC1 virtually unbeatable in its own class, with Ricardo Patrese nearly winning the drivers' title, but it was also competitive in overall terms, winning the rounds at Silverstone, the Nürburgring and Mugello, and coming very close to success in the rain-shortened Brands Hatch race. This did not help consolidate or generate much enthusiasm for Group C, and FISA's embarrassment was compounded in late May when a 3.3-litre Porsche 930 Turbo driven by Fritz Müller and Georg Memminger finished 9th overall, 1st in Group B and 2nd in the combined Group C/B category at the Nürburgring 1,000km, claiming fifteen points towards the Manufacturers' Championship. This caused a furore that rumbled on right through the rest of the season, especially when it became obvious that the championship hung between Porsche and Rondeau, and was solely dependent on whether this one maverick Porsche's score stood, or not. This 930 #93A 007, entered by the Müllerbräu team, had nothing to do with the factory cars, so the argument went, so it was unfair to allow it to score points in the Makes series. Eventually, FISA decided in favour of Porsche, but the fact that the Müller/Memminger 930 was, in any case, the only Group B car to take part in the entire 1982 series, apart from an abortive attempt to qualify a Ferrari 308 GTB at Spa, heralded the early failure of the Group B category. Despite a Rondeau M382C winning the opening Monza round, after the Lancias had failed, it was also clear that the new Group C cars were having trouble with reliability. The attrition rate was abysmal; of the eight starters in Germany there was only one finisher, and even Porsche had trouble meeting the fuel consumption standards on the 956's debut at Silverstone in May. The quickest car on the track straight out of the box, the Jacky Ickx/Derek Bell 956, was obliged to slow down over the last half of the race to conserve fuel, handing a three-lap victory to the Patrese/Alboreto Lancia. Nevertheless, Weissach could only regard their new machine as being an outstanding success in its first year. It won the Manufacturers' title as well as the Drivers' title for Jacky Ickx, and four of the eight races in the full series, including 1st, 2nd and 3rd at Le Mans, with 935s in 5th and 6th, which saved FISA's embarrassment and was an omen for the subsequent five years.

The Group C category was intended to present a forward-looking approach during a time of increasing concerns over fuel crises and fuel consumption. Initially, the transition to Group C faced several challenges. For one, the overlap with the pre-existing Group 4, 5 and 6 classes meant that the racing field was somewhat fragmented, which complicated the evolution towards a more homogeneous and sustainable future. Teams were allowed to run cars from these older categories in the World Endurance Championship for Drivers, disrupting a full shift to the new regulations. Lancia's strategic decision to develop the LC1 under Group 6 regulations allowed them to sidestep the stringent fuel rules of Group C and achieve notable success with their 1.4-litre turbo engine. Their strategy paid off as they secured multiple wins and nearly clinched the drivers' title with Riccardo Patrese. This manoeuvre, while shrewd, underscored the turbulent nature of the season as new Group C cars contended with teething problems, consumption and reliability issues.

On the technical front, Porsche's 956 faced its own challenges in meeting fuel consumption requirements, especially evident in its debut at Silverstone. However, despite these early hurdles, the 956 demonstrated its potential by winning multiple races and securing the 1982 Manufacturers' and Drivers' titles. So, while the introduction of Group C was blemished by initial difficulties, transitional issues and calculated circumventions by certain teams, it laid the groundwork for a more competitive and technologically progressive era in sports-prototype racing. The successes and failures of 1982 set the stage for further refinements and the consolidation of Group C within another season or two as the premier category – alongside Stateside's IMSA GTP – in endurance racing that would last virtually a decade.

RACING IMPROVES THE BREED

There is no question that optimised engineering and mechanical innovations deployed in racing cars filter down to road cars. One such advancement was the much-vaunted Porsche double-clutch automatic transmission that is frequently used in the company's modern road cars, which goes back to Group C. PDK – *Doppelkupplung* – (Porsche double-clutch transmission) uses two clutches to provide quick gear changes, and was first used in racing in 1984 in the 956, and proved something of a relief for the drivers. Hans Stuck was one of its most eager testers, and when signed off, the finished PDK, which now no longer required too much power from the engine, with which lap times in testing were now faster than without it, and which finally demonstrated its reliability, was installed in the 962 in 1986/1987.

An IMSA rule change in 1984 turned the 956 into a 962. In North America, the only arena in which the 956 was not completely frowned upon was the Can-Am championship, into which John Fitzpatrick entered his JDavid-sponsored 956 for two rounds of the 1983 championship. He came third at Mosport, but at Road America – also known as Elkhart Lake – he won, the only time a 956 would win a major race in-period on American soil. But Can-Am was of no interest to IMSA, and when it became clear that IMSA was not prepared to compromise and let the 956 in, Porsche decided to turn the 956 into a car to which the IMSA authorities could not possibly object. Two areas in particular needed addressing: the engine and the location of the driver's feet. The former proved by far the easiest issue to sort, largely because Porsche had an entirely eligible single-cam, single-turbo, 12-valve air-cooled version of the flat-six engine already dominating IMSA in the 911-based 935. It had the requisite 2.8-litre capacity to allow it to run as a sub-4.0-litre car – there was a multiplication factor of 1.4-litres for turbocharged engines – and because it did not need to run to a fuel consumption formula, it could be boosted to give at least as much power as the far more technically sophisticated 956 motor, probably more.

The issue of how to bring the feet of the driver in line with the front axle was a problem of an altogether greater magnitude. What was certain was that either the driver would have to move back, or the wheels would have to move forward. In theory, reversing the driver within the cockpit was the preferable option from the point of view of mass management, but it simply was not possible without redesigning the entire car, because the driver sat against the rear bulkhead to which the engine and gearbox were bolted as stressed members so there was simply nowhere for him to go. Porsche would have to extend the wheelbase, which is how the 962 came to have a 109.1-inch wheelbase. This was a stretched limo in sports-racing terms; a 935 had a wheelbase almost 20 inches shorter. A corresponding amount was then chopped off the nose to keep the overall length of the car within permitted parameters. There are two easy ways of telling whether it is a 956 or a 962: if there is barely a hand's breadth between the front of the door and the back of the front wheelarch, it's a 956. Similarly, if the front overhang is small and seemingly abbreviated, it's a 962. Some say that the 956 is by some margin more aesthetically pleasing. This in no way affected the 962's competitiveness as a race car. In its debut year in 1984 and with little time to get cars to customers, it won five IMSA rounds, all thanks to the driving combo of Al Holbert and Derek Bell, and for the next three seasons it dominated the championship. Moreover, Porsche's efforts to comply with IMSA paid dividends in Group C, as an IMSA-inspired FIA mandate that feet could no longer protrude beyond the front axle line rendered the 956 obsolete. What was needed was a 962 with all the 956 mechanical trickery, and that was manifest as the 962C. So while Porsche would race 962s in America and 956s everywhere else throughout 1984, from 1985 onwards all its Group C cars would be 962Cs, even though privateer 956s continued to race up to the end of 1986.

At first at least, the 962C was little more than a 962 with 956B running gear mildly modified to improve fuel consumption. But it worked, probably beyond even Porsche's wildest imagination. By 1991 and the tenth consecutive season of competition for the 956 and 962, Porsche claimed 148 cars had been built, which, with 956 production totalling 27 units, puts total 962 production at over 120, of which just ten were works cars, but with the last five works cars using a production-numbered tub as the basis, unlike the 956. There was a total of 77 customer factory chassis numbers allocated, starting at '101', which splits down as five tubs used for works cars – 006 to 010, six tubs for Jöst/works cars 011 to 016, three tubs converted for the 1994 Dauer GT cars, eighteen IMSA spec cars, thirteen 962Cs up to 1988 for the World Championship teams, and five cars for Japan.

In 1987, Porsche stated they would end production at chassis 138, but post-1988 they were persuaded to produce a 1988 'works spec' car with fully water-cooled MP 1.7 engine starting at number 962-143 for Vern Schuppan, and went on to produce a further twelve examples for World

Run by Joest Racing, this 962C #015 Lang Heck (long-tail) placed 4th at Le Mans in 1990 in the hands of Hans Stuck, Derek Bell and Frank Jelinski.

Championship team use the following year, and eight examples for Japan, the remaining six numbers being made up of factory prototypes or spare tubs, which were also supplied to Japan.

Other new cars seen during 1982, designed or adapted to meet the new regulations, were the Group C version of Ford's C100, the Rondeau M382 and M482, the Robin Hamilton and Viscount Downe Nimrod Aston Martin, Peter Sauber's Sauber SHSC6, initially with Ford DFL power, later with BMW engines, Reinhold Jöst's Porsche 936C, the WM Peugeot, Grid S1, Kremer Porsche CK5, Lola T610, URDC81, Cougar C01, Dome 0RC82, ADA Lola, March 82G, and at Le Mans, the Tiga-built Mirage M12. This car passed scrutineering and qualified comfortably, only to be eliminated on the instructions of the ACO shortly before the start for having the oil cooler wrongly positioned. The car was never seen again in Europe but briefly appeared the following year in IMSA, driven by Tony Garcia and Albert Neon to seventh place in the Miami Grand Prix.

The Nimrod Aston Martin NRA C2 of Viscount Downe (John Dawnay), driven by Ray Mallock and Mike Salmon, came 7th in the 1983 Silverstone 1,000km.

Jacky Ickx describes a racing drama during our 2016 interview at the Goodwood Festival of Speed.

Distinctive black helmet with a white surround, endurance specialist and FI driver, off-road racer and motorcycling trials champion, Jacky Ickx is the consummate all-rounder. This is the man who, aged 24, rewrote the rules at Le Mans for good when, in 1969, he strolled insouciantly across the track in the traditional driver sprint start, eased – rather than jumped – into his GT40 and carefully buckled up. Ickx won the race, the first of his six Le Mans victories and one of just two not achieved in a Porsche; also, until the Le Mans Classic was introduced, there was never another traditional Le Mans sprint start. A potted history of his career includes winning the 50cc Zundapp trials championship as a teenager; three-wheeling the Lotus Cortina to win the Belgian touring car championship in 1965; his break into single-seaters with Ken Tyrrell when he was 3rd fastest around the Nordschleife in the F2 Matra in practice for the 1967 German GP; the five years with Ferrari that brought eight GP victories; how he licked Lauda in the wet Race of Champions in 1974 in a Lotus museum piece; the fiery Ensign crash at Watkins Glen in 1976; six Le Mans wins (1969 in a GT40 with Jackie Oliver, 1975 in a Mirage with Derek Bell, 1976 in a Porsche 936 with Gijs van Lennep, 1977 in a 936 with Hurley Heywood and Jürgen Barth, 1981 in a 936 with Derek Bell, and 1982 in a 956 with Derek Bell); in 1978 he was Can-Am champion in a Lola; and lastly came the Paris–Dakar win in a Mercedes in 1983.

Today, Jacky is a brand ambassador for Porsche-Audi, and a regular visitor to Goodwood and Rennsport Reunion.

Jacky is probably more readily associated with the Rothmans-liveried 956 and 962 which he won the WSC with in 1982 and 1983, but actually it was the 936 that he drove over the longest period – from 1976 to 1981 – and scored three Le Mans wins with, as opposed to one with the 956. Which one is his favourite? I ask. He reponds:

It was a privilege to do those ten years with Porsche, because I've been part of a number of interesting projects, and the 956 was probably the most incredible Group C car that's ever been built, because it also lasted roughly ten years with very little development. And there is the incredible four-wheel drive Paris–Dakar project where I was deeply involved, because the 953 and 959 were built to do 230km/h in the desert – I only did 210km/h because I wasn't brave enough but my teammate did 230km/h, and that's fast, but more incredible than this was the fact that this is a sophisticated 911 that was able to compete with the people who build four-wheel-drive off-road machines, and yes, we did it.

Jacky was known as the 'rain master' in the early 1970s – witness his amazing passing move in the JPS-Lotus 72 on Niki Lauda's Ferrari around the outside at Brands Hatch's Paddock Bend as rivers flowed across the track; he undoubtedly had very special skills in the wet, yet here is the modest response.

I had some abilities, and I think my style fits those conditions fairly well. I learned some of that in motorcycle trials where I was competing in a sport that most of the time you do in winter, in mud, ice and rivers, and also races like the Suzuki Grand Prix 50, and when you only have two wheels you cannot afford to be wrong: with a car you can put a wheel on the grass and hold it there, but it suits my style, probably, and I used that experience later on in the Paris–Dakar. I was doing some jumps with the car and I was still lifting the steering wheel, the same way as you do with a trials motorcycle – you lift the front wheel, and I was trying to do that in the car! It doesn't work in practice, but it does help psychologically!

His race career lasted three decades, from motorcycle trialling to the Paris–Dakar. That's impressive in itself.

Yes, I started in '61, and I finished in '92. My last real race as a professional was in '92 in the Paris–Dakar, and I'm probably the one who made the largest number of racing miles in their career because I did so many things at the same time. It adds up to a hell of a distance if you count touring cars, endurance racing, World Championship for Makes, GTs, Group C, Formula 1 and Formula 2, and Paris–Dakar. Usually, drivers are specialising in one thing, one category, and in the past there wasn't this exclusivity; we could race anything because there were not the compulsory sponsor activities. And that also meant I've been able to build up a number of good results, because I was very often with the right team, in the right place at the right time. You can't control that, it's just a fact, things are happening.

His Formula I career began to decline because of budget cuts at JPS Team Lotus in 1975. But he has those parallel ladders in his career, FI and the WSC, so, as he started to descend one, his ascent of the other took off in a big way with Porsche.

Yes, but that's with hindsight; you don't know at the time that it's going to last for ten years. Having no FI contract in '75 – and I had already been doing long-distance racing for a long time with Ford and Ferrari – and Porsche is offering me the most incredible cars (the 935 and 936), and it's a guarantee of winning, it's a no-brainer. The 935 was maybe the most powerful car in those days, 750bhp, let's call it a monster in a way, where we almost won every race in the '77 World Championship for Makes, the DRM and IMSA. And then came the Moby Dick (935/78), honestly, an incredible car, a spaceframe silhouette of a 911.

Jacky won the 1978 Silverstone 6-Hours with Jochen Mass in that car.

Yes, I think we were only four seconds slower than the FI lap record at the previous year's Grand Prix, and Moby Dick was also fastest car on the Mulsanne Straight that year with 228mph! It was a real surprise at first, but after 10–15 laps you got used to it. It's very powerful and very fast; nobody saw a car like that before. But I never drove it at Le Mans, I drove the 936. You know at Le Mans on the Mulsanne Straight, before the chicanes were installed, you could go 380km/h (236mph) and frankly, it's easy, you can smoke a cigarette at the same time in the '70s, and as you passed the restaurant in the middle of Hunaudiéres you could see the people eating at the table in front of the restaurant, and it was not easy to see if it was salmon or beef, but you could see more or less! You say 'How do you manage to stay six hours at the wheel?' or whatever, but it's very resting, the Mulsanne Straight, I don't say you can sleep, but almost.

An example of Jacky Ickx's versatility: he and Skeeter McKitterick came 2nd in the 1977 Mid-Ohio 3-Hours in the Vasek Polak 935, pictured here at Abbeville Circuit in France.

The Group C twin-turbo 956 from 1982 was Porsche's first aluminium monocoque and it had ground-effect bodywork. Jacky was involved in the testing of that:

We were all driving the prototypes. Weissach is the engineering centre of Porsche, and I'm sure you are aware that they do a lot of studies for other brands, even aeroplanes. I think the group of engineers today numbers maybe 3- or 4,000 people and you never know what they do, because it's all very secret. But in those days Weissach was the very first development centre, and there is a small racetrack surrounded by the office buildings, and we were testing all the cars there, so it was very special. The Rothmans 956 was made there, and starting the '82 season, we knew that it was the best possible toy on the Group C grid. We always did a lot of testing, mostly at Paul Ricard, before we went to Le Mans, and it's fast there, but we had no simulators in those days, few computers, and testing was fairly hands-on, trying out different spring settings on the cars, different aerodynamic styling, different camber, different torsion bars, different settings for the engine. It was all handmade, it was not computer designs, that's why it was fairly easy for the amateur, and it was an incredible result, and at the conclusion of that season I think we had four wins, and by the end of 1986, the Rothmans 956s and 962s had amassed 25 wins (not to mention numerous podiums).

What, I asked him, makes a successful endurance driver? A combination of driving talent, racecraft and mechanical sympathy?

What makes the success of a car, frankly, is not the driver, it's the group of people who stick together and design and build an incredible race car, and replace the parts at the right moment, and then you as the driver receive a winning car, and then you have to be lucky, and that's how it was for me. I was not too bad, okay, but without the right tool you're nobody. There are no possibilities of winning any kind of race if the background isn't perfect, and the team's not motivated and passionate about what they do. And as far as that's concerned it's clear that I had the perfect surroundings, including the perfect partners in long-distance racing. If you take for example drivers like Derek (Bell) or Hans (Stuck), or Mario Andretti, Brian Redman, Gijs van Lennep or Jackie Oliver, at the time they were the perfect teammates, and we shared that together. Maybe mathematically I am the one who won the largest number of long-distance races, but, if I reached that point, it is because I was surrounded by a lot of other talented drivers who share that equally.

And that's Jacky Ickx; perfect gentleman, worldly and astute, yet carrying that aura of greatness that only high achievers possess. As he says of himself, 'There are two drivers inside: there's the nice, polite one, and there's the wolf.' It's a privilege to have got to know one and seen the other in action.

GROUND-EFFECT

Extraordinary as it seems now, even though F1 was only just emerging from its full-on ground-effects era in 1982, and the FIA had written clauses allowing limited ground-effects in the new rules, a number of the cars only partially utilised the technology and some not at all. Notable among these were the Nimrod, which was a flat-bottom design, and the Ford C100, which ran without underbody ground-effects in some races.

I have presumptuously assumed that readers will comprehend the basics of ground-effect downforce aerodynamics, but if not, here is a bit of detail to bring everyone up to speed. In its original form, as seen on the trend-setting JPS-Lotus Types 78 and 79 Formula 1 cars of 1977 and 1978, by means of ducts in the side pods that funnelled the air through them, allied to flexible skirts running along the bottom edges of the side pods that closed the gap between car and track, the air that passed through and underneath the car was used, literally, to suck it onto the ground. The ground-effect system provided vastly more downforce than had hitherto been achieved by means of aerofoils, wings, splitters and spoilers. John Player Team Lotus stole a huge advantage over tardy practitioners of the phenomenon, with Mario Andretti winning the 1978 F1 title. Other F1 teams and formulae were not slow to catch on; ground-effect was now very much 'a thing'.

One of the clearest definitions of the nature of ground-effect I've ever heard was provided by Jochen Mass.

> *A designer like Norbert Singer and his engineers were totally into it. For example, at Hockenheim, my 956 was very good, and I was quickest, but it was mildly understeering in some places. So, I came in and said, 'Could we perhaps lower it a little bit at the front?' And Norbert Singer said, 'You know what, Jochen, just race it a bit and see how you get on. Just persevere with it.' So, I did, and of course it was fantastic. He spoke about it afterwards to make me understand what's happening with the car's aerodynamics, which is that a large amount of air compressing underneath the car gets accelerated earlier so the centre of pressure moves forward, sending the downforce further forward and glueing it to the track surface. We're only talking about a millimetre, and that's how efficient and how sensitive these cars were, though actually they looked big and bulky. But a millimetre made a major change. Most people hadn't understood that, and they were milling around putting on big spoilers, big splitters and wings and all that, so they had the downforce, but in a different way, and the balance was not the same. I've driven a few of those and I didn't like them compared to our cars. When I drove the 956 at Hockenheim in 1982, I said, 'Where's the corner? Oh, I just gone through it!'. It was that different. The car was so good it was a joke. It was fabulous. And there were no more corners. Most of them were flat anyway because of the efficiency of the ground-effect aerodynamics.*

By the early 1980s, though, there were concerns about increasing cornering speeds that saw cars bottoming out and losing all grip mid-corner, and in 1983, the FIA decided to ban full-on ground-effects altogether. Instead, teams were obliged to run flat-bottomed cars, a dictate that extended to the incoming Group C WEC cars as well. Nevertheless, ground-effect aero and the complex rear diffusers that followed still played a vital role in the devastatingly quick speeds achieved by all racing cars that employed it.

The Grid S1 #GA01 was powered by a 3.3-litre Ford-Cosworth DFL V8, driven by three big names – Steve Thompson, Tony Lanfranchi and Divina Galica – at the 1984 Brands Hatch 1,000km, but was disqualified for being pushed over the finish line.

EFFECTS OF IMSA RULING

Other complications had affected the sport's Paris-based FISA (*Fédération International Sport Automobile*) controlling body, even before the racing had started. The US-based IMSA (International Motor Sports Association) had decided that, for sound local reasons, it wanted nothing to do with the fuel consumption formula and went its own way for 1982 with its own GTP regulations, equating engine power to racing weight without citing any restriction on the amount of fuel used. Automatically, this removed effectively half the potential entrants from the FISA championship as well as most of the American circuits, including the classic Daytona 24-Hours, which until then had traditionally been the opening venue for the Sportscar Series. The only exception was Watkins Glen, which was in the original 1982 calendar, even after the IMSA/FISA split, due to the good offices of the ACCUS (Automobile Competition Committee for the United States).

GETTING THE SHOW OFF THE GROUND

It was not an auspicious beginning, though. Following the postponement of the opening races at Brands Hatch and Mugello, the World Endurance Championship finally took off at Monza on 18 April. Both those initial events were doomed from the outset, as they did not form qualifying rounds of the Manufacturers' Championship and did not attract major teams like Porsche or Ford. That, combined with conflicting events on the international calendar, ensured that any entries received were either of poor quality or were withdrawn because cars were not ready. The only manufacturer team that wanted to race at Brands Hatch was Lancia. As its car conformed to Group 6 rules and was therefore ineligible for manufacturer points, there was no reason to wait for the rescheduled opening manufacturers' round at Monza. Lancia had a car, though, and it needed to race so that it could grab the glory of winning the first contest in the new world championship. Lancia had to defend its hard-won endurance reputation, but it was obvious it could not construct a competitive Group C machine. The WEC Group C regulations saw to that. Without an engine of at least 3.0-litres capacity, a 2.0-litre turbocharged car weighing 800kg not hope to be competitive and conform to the restrictions placed on fuel consumption. So, Lancia plumped for Group 6, where the minimum weight limit was lower, and its 450bhp engine would be powerful enough to make the car competitive. Lancia retained its 1981 sponsors Martini and Rossi and assembled an impressive roster of drivers for the two cars. Grand Prix helmsmen Riccardo Patrese and Michele Alboreto, who were members of the Brabham and Tyrrell F1 teams respectively, were to crew the lead car, with former European F3 champion Piercarlo Ghinzani and F1 pilot Teo Fabi in the second car. As before, the Martini Lancia team would be managed by Cesare Fiorio and operate from Turin. The pressure was on Lancia right from the start, with the first race scheduled to take place on Italian soil. But after practice, choosing the winner looked to be a mere formality with both cars on the front row of the grid. However, there were furrowed brows in the Lancia pit on the morning of race day when the Ghinzani/Fabi car needed repairs to a collapsing nose cone. When the 1,000km race started, both Lancias assumed team formation comfortably clear of the rest of the 29-car field. But first, Ghinzani stopped with a puncture, and then a typically shambolic Lancia pit stop dropped Patrese from the lead. But worse was to come and, having staggered back to the pits after an electrical failure, Patrese then handed over to Alboreto, who finally stopped altogether with a broken distributor. They were joined minutes later by the sister car, whose nose cone troubles had spread to the radiator, but which also ground to a halt with the same distributor fault. Fiorio was mystified. The same Magneti Morelli parts had been used throughout the car's development and had not failed once. The Italians could only assume the distributors were from a bad batch.

LANCIA LUCKS IN

Lancia fared rather better at Silverstone on 16 May. Although they were out-qualified by the debutant Porsche 956, the Lancias were able to dictate the pace of the race thanks to the tight restraints on fuel consumption. Being a six-hour race, the Pace Petroleum-sponsored Silverstone event was around 1,150 kilometres in length, and with the number of stops for petrol restricted to five, the potentially faster Porsche risked running out of fuel by competing head to head with the more economical Lancias. However, Fiorio was rather lucky to come away from Silverstone with a win, because the victorious Patrese/Alboreto car collided with a backmarker in the chicane, then punctured a rear tyre and also suffered a flat battery. Ghinzani and Fabi, running in a secure 2nd place, inherited the lead, only to retire with engine failure.

To the uninitiated spectator, the performance of the new Group C Porsche 956 must have been puzzling; on pole position by 1.7 seconds, but then trundling around in the race nearly ten seconds slower than its practice time. The drivers, five times Le Mans winner Jacky Ickx and Derek Bell, had come to Silverstone, round two of the Manufacturers' Championship, to prepare for the Le Mans 24-hours in June. But they cannot have learned much about the 956's behaviour, being obliged to cruise around in 5th gear. In the first hour of the race, Ickx gradually speeded up until he was lapping around 1m 23sec, moving up from 7th to 4th and closing in on the Ford C100 of Manfred Winkelhock. But when the cars stopped to refuel after just 50 minutes, the Rothmans-Porsche team made sure that its drivers did not break into a fast canter again. Driving the car so far below its potential made it difficult to handle, according to Bell, because the ground-effect attributes only really came into play at high speed, and the fuel-eking drivers could use little of its 620bhp. Even so, the Rothmans-liveried 956 cruised into 2nd place, earning maximum Group C points, while the Lancia team got away with punctures, accidents and various other dramas, yet still claimed a resounding win. When the Lancias faltered in Monza, the French Rondeau team stepped into the breach with one of its 382 designs, powered by a 3.9-litre Cosworth DFL engine. This Group C update of the car, which had won Le Mans in 1980, was driven in Italy by the thrice Le Mans-winning Henry Pescarolo and the Alfa Romeo F1 team test driver, Giorgio Francia. The team was managed by Keith Greene, who had supervised Rondeau's Le Mans sorties, and before that, Alain de Cadenet.

Never renowned for its outright speed, the Rondeau was better known for its reliability, but it led the chase of the Lancias at Monza and was perfectly placed to pick up the pieces when the Italian cars broke down. Pescarolo also drove the same car at Silverstone, but this time he was joined by Group 1 tin-top racer Gordon Spice. At Monza, there were a few tense moments just short of the finish when the car refused to restart after a last-minute top-up with fuel. At Silverstone, it was more serious, and repairs to a broken suspension component cost the Rondeau 3rd place. Drivers of the new car were team patron and founder Jean Rondeau and former BRM F1 driver François Migault. The 482 was prone to all the usual new car problems and finally retired with an overheating engine.

Perhaps the most unfortunate Group C project was the Len Bailey-designed Ford C100. Promising in Group 6 guise, the Group C version debuted at Monza and retired early with an engine about to seize. An aluminium water pipe had fractured, and the consequent loss of coolant spelt disaster. One of the team drivers, Klaus Ludwig, raced a C100 in the German sports car championship, though poor performances led to its withdrawal. Then, the whole project was entrusted to Eric Zakowski's Zakspeed team, and when the car arrived at Silverstone, the only parts remaining from the original creation were the dampers, and immediately its fortunes took an upward turn. Fourth fastest in practice, Ludwig and Winkelhock held down 3rd place in the race, one lap behind the Lancias. Unfortunately, a stone holed the radiator, dropping it down the leaderboard, and then a fuel pump broke, which starved it of the last twenty litres of fuel. Finally, it lost its clutch and, running perilously low on petrol, the C100 crawled across the finish line in 8th place.

STANDOUT TEAMS

Two of the most distinctive entries in the World Endurance Championship were the Peter Sauber and Reinhold Jöst teams. The Sauber SHS C6 was sponsored by BASF Cassettes and was driven by Hans-Joachim Stuck and Hans Heyer. At Monza, it was the fastest Group C car in practice, but being brand new, it was not surprising when it retired from the race with a broken fuel pump. The Sauber's demise handed 4th place to the Joest – Joest Racing – Porsche 936C of Bob Wollek and the Martin brothers. More reliable, it finished 7th at Monza and 3rd at Silverstone on its last reserves of fuel. The Sauber was left on the grid at Silverstone when the starter motor jammed, and it eventually retired with the same problem, having first climbed from last to 6th place. The Nimrod Aston Martin also made its debut at Silverstone, driven by Bob Evans and Geoff Lees, with support from the private entry of Ray Mallock and Mike Salmon. In the race, Evans retired with distributor failure, while Mallock and Salmon soldiered on to finish 6th.

The first two rounds of the World Endurance Championship made it abundantly clear that the minimum weight limit for Group C cars made them uncompetitive with the lighter Lancias, which could run faster for longer. Restricting fuel capacity tied all cars down to the same number of fuel stops and, in terms of spectacle, deprived spectators of the dramas of refuelling scenarios and rendered the alacrity and skill of the mechanics somewhat superfluous. Limiting the capacity of fuel tanks on all cars would oblige entrants of more powerful cars to find ways of competing with smaller, less thirsty cars. Derisive pundits felt that, as the regulations stood, the WEC was more like an economy run.

At Le Mans 1982, the Belga Team's Joest Racing 2.5-litre twin-turbo Porsche 936, driven by Bob Wollek, Jean-Michel Martin and Philippe Martin, retired in the last hour with engine failure. Originally an open-cockpit car, the 936 was converted to Group C spec with a bonded-on roof.

SPA 1,000KM 1982

The extent of the book precludes the possibility of a race-by-race account of the series, year on year, but we shall review a few specific races as we go on to add a gloss to the general status quo. So, for example, the finale of the World Endurance Championship for manufacturers took place at Spa-Francorchamps on 5 September 1982. At this point, the crown was being contested by Ford, Rondeau and Porsche, with the French team leading the Rothmans-backed Porsche team into the final round by 60 points to 40. It was complicated because Porsche claimed fifteen points scored by a Group B 911 Turbo at the Nürburgring race, which the works Group C 956s did not attend. An anomaly in the regulations implied that Group B cars could score points towards the WEC. But FISA never intended this to be the case, as Group B cars are supposed to have their own GT championship. FISA issued a statement to this effect, but by the time Spa came around, Porsche still had not accepted the fact and continued to claim the championship points score of 55. This was the background against which the Spa race took place, with Rondeau needing to finish 4th or higher to secure the title if Porsche, as expected, won the race. If, however, FISA were to stand down on the issue, a win for Porsche would send the championship to Germany, wherever Rondeau finished. Spa was the first WEC race to be held since Porsche's steamroller victory at Le Mans, and Porsche brought two 956s to Spa for Jacky Ickx, Jochen Mass, Derek Bell and Vern Schuppan. After two wins as co-drivers, Ickx and Bell shared the same number of points in the WEC Drivers' Championship. A couple of weeks before Spa, Ickx decided it would be fairer for both he and Bell to drive different cars to give one or the other a better chance of winning the Drivers' title. That would be fine if both drivers were to receive equal status in terms of equipment. But with Ickx the undisputed Porsche number one, what his idea effectively meant was that Bell would be relegated to the second car and would finish behind him, unless he retired. So, Bell, the three times Le Mans winner, found himself in a car with Vern Schuppan, tasked with trying out some new modifications to the 2.65-litre turbocharged engine. In the event, Ickx very nearly had his nose put out of joint, for the new tweaks worked very well during the hot, dry practice sessions, and Bell was able to make a significant challenge to the Belgian's pole position. Unfortunately, the 144-lap race started on a wet track, and Bell's Porsche became something of a pig to drive. The engine was not responsive enough to allow the car to pass others, including backmarkers, without dropping down into a lower gear – and thereby consuming more fuel – so Derek was simply unable to run with Ickx, circulating in 3rd place between two Lancias. At the start, the Group 6 Martini-Lancia of Riccardo Patrese grabbed the lead from the Group C Ford C100 of Klaus Ludwig and Marc Surer.

Patrese and co-driver Teo Fabi qualified in third position behind the two works Porsches after a notably trouble-free practice. Lancia's only problem was a lack of horsepower, the 1.4-litre turbocharged engine only producing about 450bhp, making it difficult to push the cars up Spa's gradients. Passing slower cars was a particular problem, especially if the manoeuvre had to be carried out between Eau Rouge and Les Coombs. But the Lancias were by no means humbled by their more powerful opposition and made up for what they lacked in grunt with excellent handling. The second Lancia of Michele Alboreto and Piercarlo Ghinzani

The Ford C100 #005 of Klaus Ludwig and Marc Surer on the hill heading up to Raidillon during the 1982 Spa-Francorchamps 1,000km; they were sidelined by a fuel pump malady.

The Rondeau M382 #003 Cosworth of Christian Bussi/ Bernard de Dryver/ Pascal Witmeur leads the Lancia LC1 of Piercarlo Ghinzani/ Michele Alboreto through Eau Rouge during the 1982 Spa-Francorchamps 1,000km on its way to 13th overall. The Lancia retired with fuelling issues.

started from 4th on the grid. Behind this foursome came the unique Kremer Porsche CK5, which had made its debut at Le Mans. This bulbous yet effective design had featured at the front of German sports car championship races for some time and finally won its first DTM race at Hockenheim two weeks prior to Spa. At the Ardennes track, the car was driven by former Grand Prix driver and Porsche veteran Rolf Stommelen and F2 star Stefan Bellof. The CK5, powered by a turbocharged 2.6-litre Porsche engine, was the fastest in a straight line, with Stommelen describing its performance as fantastic. Starting the race from the inside of the third row, Stommelen quickly attached himself to Ickx's gearbox but was unable to make a significant challenge as Ickx carved confidently through the myriad tail-enders. After the first refuelling stop, Bellof took over the helm and maintained Kremer's position amongst the first five, but then struck problems as he prepared to hand over again to Stommelen. Descending the hill past the pits, the CK5 briefly misfired and then the engine died altogether as the driver turned into Eau Rouge. Bellof coasted to the top of Raidillon, where he attempted to coax the motor back to life. Although he managed to drive back to the pits, the engine's electrical and fuel systems were sufficiently compromised to cause its retirement.

Rondeau also hit trouble early on. For the start, the three M382Cs of Pescarolo and Boutsen, Jaussaud and Rondeau, Migault and Spice lined up directly behind one another on the grid. The cars ran reliably enough, but their Dunlop tyres did not offer enough grip. It transpired that Dunlop's race tyre was too soft and was going off very quickly, which also affected Stommelen's CK5 at the Hockenheimring. The promise shown by the Ford C100 soon evaporated as well. Fitted with new DFL Cosworth engines, which, like all the other 3.9-litre Fords, also featured revised crankshaft dampers after their Le Mans debacle, the C100s handled well but lacked straight-line speed. Klaus Ludwig, who had covered more miles in a C100 than anybody else, started from 6th place on the grid, while ATS F1 driver Manfred Winkelhock complained of suspension problems but nevertheless qualified 8th.

With the Ludwig Ford's demise, the BASF Sauber-Ford of Hans Stuck and Hans Heyer became the best-placed normally aspirated car in 5th. In practice, the GS tuning team's unloved 3.9-litre DFL engine had proved no quicker than the more reliable 3.3, so the team manager had it replaced with the latter for the race, only for the Sauber's engine to fall sick. Nimrod Aston Martin had come to Spa with the firm intention of securing third place in the Manufacturers' Championship, and Robin Hamilton's works team entered their latest chassis for Geoff Lees, who held the Spa lap record, and Tiff Needell. Ray Mallock in the Richard Williams-prepared car was partnered by veteran Mike Salmon. During practice, the 5.3-litre V8-engined cars struggled to find the right balance, suffering from understeer and oversteer, respectively. Mallock once again put one over on the factory when he set 13th fastest practice time. However, during the first refuelling stop, it fell off one of its air jacks, rupturing the oil cooler. A spare was fitted, but the car was down to 27th. From here, it gradually recovered to finish 7th in Group C and raise Nimrod Aston Martin to 3rd place in the Manufacturers' Championship. Mass and Ickx, meanwhile, took the lead after two hours and with their Porsche running faultlessly the chequered flag seemed assured. Alboreto and Ghinzani, however, kept inside 50 seconds in arrears. But as the Lancia, like the sister car of Patrese and Fabi, was consuming batteries at a heavy rate, they could not make any consistent impression on the leading Porsche. Bell and Schuppan, reluctant guinea pigs for a Porsche experiment, held 3rd ahead of the second Lancia, followed by the Rondeau of Spica and Migault and the Group 6 Osella-BMW. Mass led into the final lap, and the 56-second wait for the Lancia ended with the silent car cruising back down the hill to Eau Rouge, where Alboreto pulled off onto the gravel. Incredibly, it seemed he had run out of fuel, and he began to walk away. Thinking better of it, he then returned to the car, examined the reserve fuel tap, and discovered there were some six litres' worth of fuel still left in the tank. The organisers, however, deemed him to have abandoned the car, and could not be persuaded otherwise.

The 3.3-litre Cosworth DFV-engined Sauber SHS C6 of Hans Stuck and Hans Heyer came 9th overall in the 1982 Spa-Francorchamps 1,000km.

DEMISE OF GROUP B

The inaugural season showed that there was still a long way to go in terms of Group C being a viable series and sufficiently attractive to encourage other constructors and teams to participate. Having laid the foundations, the FISA needed to rethink the regulations for 1983. The Group B category had not been as successful as expected, and manufacturers were reluctant to commit to building cars to meet regulations that obliged their mostly private owners to compete for points in the same championship as the more potent Group C cars. The only alternative being for them to run in the Group C class had a huge disadvantage to the works cars in terms of building, running, development and general resources needed to run an advanced prototype car competitively so was not an attractive alternative.

The result of this was that Group C grids had been sparse, and virtually non-existent in Group B, apart from a single generally tardy car, which, in the shape of a 930, had caused a commotion by effectively winning the Makes' Championship for Porsche by scoring points in one race of the combined Group C and Group B categories.

Therefore, the Grand Touring Cup, a separate championship for Group B cars, was initiated at the beginning of 1983. At the same time, FISA introduced a completely new Group C junior category with its own championship. The decision to have a separate title for Group B cars was not ultimately very successful. FISA was rewarded with larger entries than before, although they could hardly have been much smaller than the previous year.

Group C Junior, referred to later as C2, was broadly based on the senior class rules, but gave teams with access to off-the-shelf smaller-capacity or less high-tech power units a chance to take part in the series. The fact that the junior title in 1983 was actually won by a car sporting a very advanced composite chassis powered by a multi-valve turbocharged engine meant that the F1 standard Cosworth-Ford DFL, which had been the main opponent to Porsche in Group C in 1982, very quickly became the required equipment in the C2 category.

DRIVERS' TITLE

Alongside the World Endurance Championship of Makes, FISA persevered with the concurrent Driver series, which was becoming increasingly prestigious. In addition, for 1983, they established a European Endurance Championship of Drivers, sharing many races of the World Series. The opening events at Monza, Silverstone, Nürburgring, Le Mans and Spa-Francorchamps counted towards both the World and Euro Series, with the two championships then going their separate ways, the World Series going to Fuji and Kyalami, and the European Series to Imola and Mugello. As well as the increase in entries hoped for by the implementation of the C Junior class, Porsche was doing its bit to boost the fields. Over the winter of 1982–83, it had implemented a chassis-building programme to supply customer teams with 956s. This was excellent news, not only for FISA but also for their loyal privateers who, in 1982, had been obliged to build and run their own Porsche Group 3 specials or else fall back on old 935s. The initial build of customer 956s was nine chassis by the end of the season, one of which was kept by the factory and used as a mobile test bed for the TAG Turbo Formula One engine. The remainder were sold to the private teams of Kremer, Jöst, Fitzpatrick, Lloyd and Obermaier in Europe, and the other two went to Preston Henn in the USA and Nova Engineering in Japan. Porsche's domination of the WEC in 1983 turned out to be almost total, the marque winning nine out of ten rounds, three of them by privateers, taking the Makes' crown, and the drivers' title going again to Jacky Ickx. They had learned the lessons that the fuel economy regulations had taught them in 1982, and simply done their sums better than anyone else and, just as importantly, had also built more capable cars.

After a year of circumventing the championship regulations with the LC1 'backdates', Lancia wholeheartedly entered Group C by constructing an entirely new LC2 aluminium monocoque chassis powered by a Ferrari twin-turbo V8. Although they enjoyed some limited success, taking pole in the Monza qualifying sessions, naturally to the joy of the native audience, and actually winning the Imola round later in the year due to the absence of any factory Porsches, the LC2s were generally too fragile to last the endurance distance.

EXIT OF FORD

Things were looking decidedly dismal at the British end of the WEC equation. After the poor performance of the Ford C100s in the WEC, the project was swept away by Ford's new European Motorsport director – and rallying connoisseur – Stuart Turner. This not only upset the personnel actively involved in running the WEC cars, but it also left Cosworth Engineering in limbo. They had always been heavily involved and were now committed to the conversion

The Le Mans 1983 race gets under way, with the Mazda 717C of Yojiro Terada, Yoshimi Katayama and Takashi Yorino pursued by the BMW M1 of Angelo Pallavicini, Prinz Leopold von Bayern and Jens Winther, and to the right, the 930 of Jean-Marie and Jacques Alméras that finished 15th.

of the 3.3-litre DFL to turbocharged units, as well as curing the inherent vibration problems of the larger 3.9-litre DFL by the installation of a balancer shaft. Gordon Spice had been contracted to build a new version of the C100, which would have been configured with full ground-effect and substantially lighter. However, Stuart Turner felt that that was throwing good money after bad, and although the Zakspeed-developed C1 managed to carry on for a while in the German championship, it was the end of Ford's desire to challenge for sportscar honours in the way it had done with the GT40 during the halcyon 1960s. There would be a reversal of sorts after Ford acquired Jaguar for $2.5 billion in 1990, but in 1982, closing the WEC team seemed like a bad call.

Meanwhile, things had also taken a downturn at Nimrod Aston Martin. Two teams running the cars had always been stretched for money, perennially short of sponsors, and effectively being personally financed by businessmen

The 1983 Nürburgring 1,000km was won by Jacky Ickx and Jochen Mass in 956 #005, here negotiating the Nordschleife's banked Karussel. German restrictions on tobacco advertising meant the Rothmans brand name could not figure in the 956's livery, a stipulation first imposed in 1973 on the JPS-Lotus F1 cars at the German Grand Prix.

Victor Gauntlett and Peter Livanos. The Robin Hamilton Works cars were obliged to leave Europe during the winter in the pursuit of dollars in the US IMSA championship, where #002 turned up as the Pepsi Challenger, only to be sold to American privateer Jack Miller to raise funds for the impoverished team to run the remaining car. Towards the end of the year, Hamilton was forced to liquidate his operation when cashflow problems became terminal. This left the quasi-works #004 car to be developed and improved in Ray Mallock's workshop for the WEC season. Despite a substantial facelift, both cosmetic and structural, for example, Mallock had discovered that the car's engine mounts had been allowing the V8 to flex in the chassis. The Nimrod was quite unable to overcome its inherent burden of weight and lack of power. A repeat of third place in the championship served to flatter and deceive, and that was only due to the total dominance of the Porsches and the lack of any other reliable opposition.

Peter Sauber's association with the Swiss Aerospace Company Seger and Hoffman – hence Sauber SHS C6 – had foundered during the off-season as well. This did not really affect the grid numbers during the early part of the year, because the existing C6 went over to the control of slot-machine millionaire Walter Brun and reappeared using a variety of power plants, including a BMW M88 3.2-litre single turbo, Ford 3.9-litre DFL, and even a Porsche 956, which never started a race. It was Brun's association with these cars that eventually led to his decision to become a Porsche 956 customer halfway through the season.

The main French hope, Rondeau, was in financial trouble, too. Although the interim M382C chassis, which was really only a lengthened version of the earlier Group 6 GTP M379 design, had been successful enough and had nearly won the Makes' Championship the previous year. Jean Rondeau had always pinned his hopes on the M482C wing car, which had been built with the ultimate intention of using Ford's promised DFL turbo engine. The team had always been pressed for funds, so when the Ford C100 project and its associated engine projects collapsed, followed by the retirement of a

Pictured in the pitlane during the 1982 Le Mans 24-Hours, the URD C81 of Michel Lateste, Hubert Striebig and Jacques Heuclin retired in the fifth hour when its 3.5-litre BMW engine failed.

three-car M482 entry at Le Mans, Rondeau decided to call it a day and concentrated his efforts thereafter on the construction and sale of Formula Ford chassis.

An interesting variety of cars filled the grids in 1983, in the shape of both C1 and C2 Juniors, including the debut of the Alba Giannini, which won the Junior Cup, the Mazda 717C, the Harrier RX83C, the Mazda CJ, the Cheetah G603 Cosworth, the Tiga GC83 Chevrolet, the Sauber BMW C7 and Steve O'Rourke's Tickford-powered EMKA Aston Martin C1, as well as a selection of Japanese C-specials when the series went to race at Fuji. The rebuilt and renamed ADA Ford 01 – previously the De Cadenet Lola T380 – was racing for the *craic* but was not really a contender. The most extraordinary entry was a Group B Ford Escort RS, which ran at the Nürburgring and finished ninth overall and third in class.

SARTHE STANDARD BEARER

So, taking Le Mans as the WEC standard bearer, held on 18 and 19 June, if anyone harboured any doubts about the pre-eminence of the Porsche 956, they had to think again. With eleven 956s entered and only two retiring, those nine survivors filled the top ten places at the finish. A solitary Sauber C7 BMW disrupted the whitewash by taking 9th place. Having lost a door and on the verge of a terminal oil leak, the slowing Rothmans number three car of Schuppan, Haywood and Holbert scooped the victory – narrowly – by a minute from the pursuing Bell/Ickx car. The result meant that Porsche thereby secured the Championship of Makes for the second year running, and there were still six of the ten rounds of the season yet to be run. The rest of the C1 cars either retired, including the Lancias, all three of the revised Rondeaux, the Nimrod Aston Martin, and the two Kremer CK5s. The C Junior honours went to one of the reliable Mazda 717Cs run by Silverstone-based Alan Docking Racing, crewed by Katayama, Terada and Yorino. ADA's 01 had moved down from the C1 class and led C2 briefly on Saturday afternoon, but slowed due to endless mechanical dramas. The Albert Giannini car expired during the night due to recurring electrical troubles.

The moon rises, twilight falls, and crowds disperse as one of the Mazda 717s speeds towards Indianapolis curve, Le Mans 1983.

THE 962 SUPERSEDES THE 956

The United States had its IMSA (International Motor Sports Association) series, with its myriad classes and categories, but in contrast to Group C where fuel consumption-restricted engines were used, IMSA had no such constraints. With the intention of ending the dominance of the Porsche 935 in 1982, IMSA introduced the GTP (Grand Touring Prototype) class. GTP was a modified Group C class with slight aerodynamic changes and the same tyre sizes on each axle. The 962's predecessor, the 956 with the bi-turbo engine, was not homologated, so, as the 956s were not permitted in the IMSA series they did see action in the Sports Car Club of America (SCCA) races. The sticking point was that the driver's feet – the pedal box – were ahead of the 956's front axle, so the car was permanently banned. Nevertheless, the interest from customer teams was so great that Porsche built an IMSA-compliant version of the 956, designated the Porsche 962. The chassis was extended slightly, and the cockpit was enclosed with a steel cage instead of the aluminium used in the 956. Besides this, the driver's feet were now behind the front axle. The front wheels and axle were moved forward, which resulted in a shorter front end, and, as a result, the 962 is 12cm longer in its wheelbase than the 956. Powered by an air-cooled single turbo 2.87-litre engine, 962-001 made its racing debut at the Daytona 24-Hours in February 1984, crewed by father and son Mario and Michael Andretti. But after just four hours of racing, Porsche withdrew the car due to engine cooling problems. Al Holbert claimed his first victory with the 962 in June 1984 at Mid-Ohio. The 2.87-litre 962 finished 2nd in each of the next four IMSA races. At the next race, Holbert replaced the 2.87-litre factory engine with an Andial-prepared 3.2-litre engine. Porsche understood that, in the IMSA championship, only this engine could compete with Chevrolet's powerful V8 engines and optimised the Andial engine accordingly.

To differentiate the 962s that participated in the North American IMSA championship from the cars that ran in the Group C World Sportscar Championship, Porsche designated the latter as the 962C. From January 1st, 1985, all new Group C sportscars had to be built to comply with IMSA rules, and at this point, Porsche switched from building the 956 to the 962C. At the start of the new season, it was clear that the older but perfectly prepared 956s of the customer teams were just as fast or even faster than the brand-new factory 962C.

I asked Jochen Mass whether the handling characteristics of the 956 and 962 varied from car to car. He explained:

> *They were always welded the same way, but sometimes different suppliers were used for the aluminium sheets used for the tub. So, the flexibility of sheeting varied, and that made a difference, too. Some cars were nicer and more pliable. We needed that degree of flexibility then, because the cars were quicker, even flexing a little more, but that's what we wanted. That's why sometimes the older models were faster than the brand-new ones. It was only later when aerodynamics became so proficient and so important that the chassis had to be rigidly stiff, and that's why the carbon chassis finally were far superior.*

So, the 962 evolution was pretty much the same as the 956, apart from the slightly longer chassis?

> *Yes, the 956 and the 962 only varied in terms of foot room, really, for safety reasons. The rules specified a sort of safety distance for the feet. In reality, it wouldn't have helped if you hit the wall or whatever, but all the rule makers thought it might be better, so there was a certain standard measurement from the front axle, which we had to comply with. But aerodynamically, the 962 wasn't much different – maybe it was a little less good in places, and maybe it was a little better in others. I like the 956 a little better than the 962, but it is such a small difference that I would hate to call it.*

VARIETY OF MATERIALS

Porsche built 91 examples of the 962C between 1984 and 1991, of which sixteen were works team cars, and 75 were sold to customers. Some 956s were rebuilt as 962s, while fresh chassis were created by Fabcar in aluminium for use in IMSA GTP in the USA, in carbon fibre by John Thompson and Kremer Racing, and in aluminium honeycomb by Richard Lloyd Racing. Other replacement chassis were made by Jochen Dauer and Chapman Chassis, while driver Vern Schuppan rebuilt probably five wrecked cars which subsequently returned to circulation.

The highlight of Le Mans in 1985 was a case in point. Joest Racing fielded their upgraded 956 in NewMan livery and aimed at overall victory, while the Porsche works team

THE WINNINGEST DRIVER

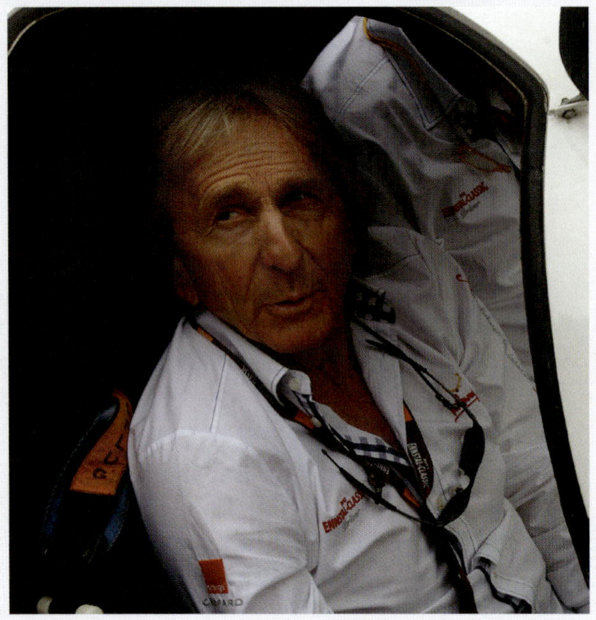

Snapped at Gröbming, Austria, during the 2012 Ennstal Classic Rally, Derek Bell was described by Porsche Engineering boss Dr Helmuth Bott as 'the winningest driver'.

Derek Bell never really stopped racing. His frontline competition career spanned over two decades, including an F1 stint at Ferrari and five Le Mans wins, culminating twice in the World Sportscar Championship title. That earned him the colloquial epithet from Porsche's Director of Engineering, Dr Helmuth Bott, as 'the winningest driver'.

In 1982, Bell was immediately successful with the 956, so what was the transition like from the 936?

Clearly, you've got a ground-effect chassis, and I remember it was a hell of a lot better, and we went a lot, lot faster. It was the same basic engine as the 936, it was the IndyCar engine that was configured to run on petrol rather than methanol that we used in 1981, and that engine we then used in '82 and '83, and the ground-effect during braking and cornering makes such an immense difference.

Was the 962 an especially different car from the 956?

Yes, it was a little different, because it was a 2½ or 3 inches longer wheelbase, but it did make a difference. It was for safety reasons, so the driver's feet were behind the front axle, and the difference between the two cars used in the WSC and IMSA was that the Group C car was twin turbo and that made a totally different sound to what we had in America, which was the big raw 911-type turbo engine in the back which looked like it had a windmill stuck on top of it, and we had up to 800+ horsepower. The IMSA 962 was a little higher off the ground for American regulations, so it didn't have quite as much ground-effect, but it was an amazing car.

Derek's first World Sportscar Championship title was won in 1985.

I would have been American (IMSA) champion too, but I couldn't compete both sides of the Atlantic at the same time because some of the races clashed, so I never became American champion because obviously it was more important that I won the World Sportscar Championship.

Derek's co-driver in 1985 was Hans Stuck, and they jointly won the World title. In 1986, he had Al Holbert with him as well as Stuck.

Yes, in '86, I was World Champion on my own without Stucky because of Porsche trying to play a trick on us and leaving me out of a couple of races, so I didn't get the points, and actually, I thought I'd lost the title to Jaguar and Derek Warwick, but in the last race at the Norisring somehow they didn't actually do as many laps as they had recorded. John Fitzpatrick lent me his old 962, because he spotted that Porsche were entering just one car as it was only two 1-hour race heats, and he said, 'It is pretty obvious they want Stuck to be World Champion on his own.' It was the only round that had one driver, and he was doing it in a rocket-ship of a car; everything was lightweight rather than doubles on everything to be reliable and, of course, because of that, he had problems and came 13th, and I was driving around slowly in 11th or 12th place, and I beat him to the title by one position, which was rather poetic justice.

So, was that mid-'80s period the halcyon years, as far as Derek's concerned?

Absolutely, yeah, from '81 on, once I got the 936, right through to 1990, that was the most amazing period of anybody's life, but we all have great periods, and I'm sure it really was for Stucky as well, to be honest. And don't forget that Al (Holbert) and I won Daytona and Le Mans, both in '86 and '87. I think I won 37 races in the WSC and IMSA, and Professor Bott said I was "the winningest driver in the history of Porsche" during the Group C era. I won more races than any other factory driver, and that includes the races I drove with Jacky Ickx and Hans Stuck.

Does he have a particular event that stands out as the best?

There is; we had some phenomenal races, but in IMSA at the Miami Grand Prix when I was leading the race with Al Holbert, and we had twelve laps to go, I was in the Lowenbrau 962, and David Hobbs and Darren Bradfield were in the Budweiser car, which was a Lola-Chevvy, which of course is perfect on a street circuit with that immediate power delivery, but the organisers wanted the American muscle cars to win, and there was a full course yellow, and when I went to restart it was firing on four cylinders instead of eight, and I got overtaken by the works Jaguar and also the Budweiser car, and it took me two laps for the engine to clear, and when it cleared I went after them, and I shot by on the inside at the last corner and went through to win the race. You could drive the 962 hard, and they were three- to four-hour races as opposed to five or six hours, and you could drive the pants off it because of the sort of tracks you were on, like around the streets of San Antonio where we also won, where you're drifting it through the corners and just missing the walls by inches. Whereas tracks like Silverstone are wonderful, but they didn't have the same drama to them because if you spin you might get it back eventually, but on a street track there was nothing but kerbs and walls. I think the most memorable WSC race that I didn't win was coming 2nd at Le Mans in '83 with Jacky (Ickx). He got hit on the first lap, and there was big pressure on fuel economy, and we had to really economise, yet we managed to take a lap off the whole field to get back into the lead without more fuel, which was pretty remarkable. Then, at 6 in the morning, we had a fuse box problem, and I had to change the electronics while stopped at Mulsanne. And then Jacky took over, and we had to work our way back up through the field, and we finished 2nd by about 26 seconds, and I think that was my best race at Le Mans, even though we didn't win it.

had similar ambitions – to win Le Mans with the 962C. Signs were auspicious when, during training and qualifying, Hans Stuck set a new lap record. Initially, the three factory 962Cs kept a low profile, but it turned out that this was not a speed problem but high fuel consumption. Joest Racing's 956 was unaffected and was able to continue on a tank for two laps longer, ultimately winning the 1985 Le Mans 24-Hours.

After a terrible debut season for the 962, Porsche set its sights on winning the 1986 Le Mans. Now, though, the factory team had to compete with increasingly strong privately entered Porsches as well as new teams, including Tom Walkinshaw's TWR-Jaguar operation, which in the early 1980s had developed a Jaguar for participation in the IMSA championship. Peter Sauber entered a Sauber-Mercedes, but it was not only incoming manufacturers who began to make life difficult for Porsche. Changes to the regulations presented new challenges. Sprint races were introduced so that Porsche could not count on the reliability of the 962, which was crucial, especially in long-distance races. Nevertheless, the Zuffenhausen marque managed to outdo both Jaguar and Sauber-Mercedes at Le Mans. After Jo Gartner's tragic accident on Mulsanne, a safety car period that lasted two and a half hours cooked several cars, amongst them the leading Jöst Porsche 956. The retirement of this leading 956 opened the door for the factory 962 and, after 24 hours of racing, 962-003, piloted by Hans Stuck, Al Holbert and Derek Bell, took the chequered flag for 1st place, followed by the privately entered 962 of Brun Motorsport. Not only did the factory squad win Le Mans, but they also lifted the Drivers' and Manufacturers' world titles. The team prize went to Brun Motorsport.

The 962C was also used in other national and international championships, including the Supercup in Germany and the All-Japan Sports Prototype Championship in Japan, where Porsche had to compete with Mazda, Nissan and Toyota. They debuted in Japan in 1985 with the 962 and won the championship in 1985, 1986, 1987, 1988 and 1989. The difference between the IMSA championship and JSPC in Japan was the duration of the races. While IMSA focused on short distances, the JSPC included 1,000km events, just as Group C did in Europe. Porsche dominated in Japan until 1988, when Jaguar and Toyota also won races. In 1990, the era of the Porsche 962 in Japan came to an end. In the period between April 1983 and December 1989, however, Porsche teams managed to win 31 out of 35 races in Japan with the 956 and 962C.

SUPER MARIO

Mario Andretti relaxes in the cabin of a 997 GT3 during a visit to the Donington Classic meeting in 2007.

Some of the best racing drivers in the world tried their hands at Group C. The season opener at the 1984 Daytona 24-Hours saw the debut of the 962 in the custody of one of them, Mario Andretti, partnered by his son Michael.

While his F1 exploits with Lotus, March, Parnelli and Alfa Romeo are well known, and most people are at least aware of his USAC, Can-Am, Sprint and NASCAR activities, Mario's forays into endurance racing are less familiar. Other racing commitments have taken precedence, and long-distance sports-car races have been more sporadic. With the Indianapolis 500 won back in 1969 and the Formula 1 World Championship under his belt in 1978, tantalisingly, he had yet to secure the final segment of motor racing's tripartite Blue Riband, the Le Mans 24-Hours, which would place him on an equal footing with Graham Hill – although Britain's Mr Motor Racing never wore the IndyCar crown, nor won Pike's Peak or the Daytona 500. Mario has actually made nine attempts at Le Mans. Despite a couple of high placings – 3rd in 1983 and 2nd in 1995 – outright success has proved elusive.

I was in the Ford Le Mans programme back in the mid-'60s. Although they often used seasoned drivers like Lloyd Ruby, Ken Miles and Bruce McLaren, I volunteered to do every test. We did several 24-hour runs at Riverside and Daytona, and that way I got plenty of road-racing experience.

Mario did not reappear at Le Mans until after his F1 career finished in 1982. If his subsequent Porsche outings at Le Mans were dogged by niggles that scuppered his chances, they were nothing compared with 1982, when he was due to race the Tiga-Mirage M12. Qualifying 9th, Mario was ordered off the grid on the pretext that the oil coolers were repositioned behind the gearbox post-scrutineering.

That was the first time Michael [his son] and I drove a sportscar like that. He was only 22 years old then. We did pretty well to qualify, as we'd only had limited testing in the States. There was a political tiff between Harley Cluxton (the entrant) and our friends (the Automobile Club de l'Ouest) at Le Mans, and they said, 'Out!' and that was that. I was physically hauled from the cockpit and the car pushed off the grid. They said we'd changed the position of the oil coolers, but Polaroid photos produced soon afterwards proved we hadn't. Jabby Crombac (the noted journalist) took up the case, but there was really nothing to be gained by pursuing it. We knew it was sketchy because they didn't want to hear an argument.

The following year, Mario was approached by Erwin Kremer to drive a 2.6-litre twin-turbo 956, and Mario proposed his son, Michael, as co-driver. They qualified 9th again. Mario recalls: 'I thought this would be a good time to bring in Michael, and we teamed up with Philippe Alliot. But we lost that race on the first stop,' he says ruefully. Group C regulations majored on fuel consumption and, much to the F1 Champ's frustration, he was constrained from going after the works' cars of Ickx, Mass, Bell and co.

You could only make 23 stops – so you had to have enough fuel to go at least nine laps. In the morning of the race we had a fuel pick-up problem. It wouldn't go onto reserve properly and we didn't have a chance to determine whether it was fixed. I was expecting the reserve light to come on after nine laps, but on the seventh lap Manfred Kremer called me in. I said: "No, the reserve light is not on yet; we must do at least nine laps, otherwise we will have to sit idle in the pits and we will not have enough fuel to finish the race. It was the weirdest rule. And he's screaming: 'Obey, obey! Stop, stop!' and we had to sit in the pits for two laps. It turned out that the reserve light was perfectly okay, and we could have done the whole nine laps of that fuel window. After that, we had no hope of winning the race.

It was not just the team director who blundered. Phillipe Alliot earned a rebuke from Andretti for spinning the car a couple

Contentiously, the John Horsman-designed Tiga-built 3.9-litre Cosworth DFL-powered Mirage M12 of father and son Mario and Michael Andretti was taken off the grid at Le Mans 1982 because of an alleged misplacement of an oil cooler. Indignant, the Harley Cluxton-run Mirage never returned to La Sarthe.

of times during the night, though without doing any damage. Mario dumped the whole debacle on the team, though:

> *At one point in the race we had to sit in the pits for four minutes – that's like a whole lap – while they changed the brakes and things they didn't need to change. By the end of the race, the factory cars were overheating and a door and the undershield fell off one of them – and we could have beaten them. I always held that against them (Kremer Racing) – if it hadn't been for those pit stops, we would have won. I told them: 'You lost us the race. That was the stupidest call I ever saw.' With all their experience, that really had me baffled.*

Mario Andretti and his son Michael (3rd and 4th from right) ran a 962 in IMSA's GTP class, including the 1984 Daytona 24-Hours.

Despite that, the Andretti/Alliot 956 still came 3rd overall.

Mario was not so impressed by the IMSA-spec single-turbo Porsche 962 prototype that he drove at Daytona in 1984. An evolution of the 956, the wheelbase was extended by 12cm at the front to place the driver's feet behind the front axle line, and the 935/76 flat-six's turbocharger was mounted above the gearbox. A steel roll-cage and 120-litre fuel tank, plus bodywork changes, completed the picture.

> *The main difference was that the 956 had twin turbos and was much more responsive. The 962 had a huge single turbo, at least for the IMSA races, and that made it a bit of a dog. This huge turbo was right on top of the gearbox – and that extra weight located there made it oversteer. Basically, the 956 is an understeering car, and so now we had a car that oversteered and understeered. The 956 was much nicer to drive, more responsive. It was good out of the box – anyone could drive it and be competitive. That's why they were so successful.*

Norbert Singer in conversation with Bob Wollek and Hans Stuck during the 1986 Silverstone 1,000km meeting. Wollek's teammate was Jochen Mass, sidelined with transmission issues, while Derek Bell teamed with Stuck for a 2nd place finish.

Bob Wollek, Derek Bell and John Andretti's Miller High Life/BF Goodrich 962 won the 1989 Daytona 24-Hours, the first round of that year's IMSA series' GTP class. Chassis #108C was the replacement for #108B, built by chassis-maker Chapman – the original car having been written off at Daytona in 1985 and again damaged at Sears Point in 1988.

Blanking off the louvres for the 962's air-cooled flat-six secured Mario the Daytona pole in 1984 by two seconds. He established a healthy lead but, during Michael Andretti's first stint, the car developed serious gear selection problems. Over a long pit stop they deduced that the enormous heat dissipated by the turbocharger sited above the gearbox had fused the internals together. Repairs took an hour and a half, putting them out of contention. At first they blamed Michael, thinking he was a young man flying too high. But there simply was not enough heat protection over the gearbox.

Strategies in play

Mario Andretti paints a vivid picture of strategies in play during the fuel consumption-led Group C era.

At Le Mans in 1988, it was Michael and my nephew John and myself, and the regulations meant you had to maintain a certain fuel mileage. Norbert Singer was manning our car, and he was the best. Hans Stuck and Bob Wollek were lead drivers in the other two cars, and Singer said: 'Don't worry about them, they'll be fighting each other – and by 1am they'll be deficient of 30 litres of fuel.' And that's exactly what happened. We maintained our pace and, by one o'clock (in the morning), we were solidly in the lead. The Jaguar was also in deficit, so they kept having to slow down. The rain helped, but all of a sudden we dropped a cylinder. That was too bad. Another one we could have won – but there was nothing we could do on five cylinders.

Nevertheless, the Andrettis finished 6th. Mario ran at Daytona three times with a 962.

The last one was '93 – that was Michael, Jeff (his younger son) and myself. Michael had to leave early to do a McLaren F1 test, so Jeff and I had to do the rest of the race ourselves. I did a double stint because Jeff wasn't feeling too good, and I was knackered 'cos the car was so hot! We finished the race 5th or 6th, but the turbo seized and things like Mustangs were coming by us!

There was success within the family at Daytona: in 1989, nephew John Andretti won the 24-Hours, partnering Bob Wollek and Derek Bell in the Jim Busby 962.

So, back at Daytona '84: with the help of a set of qualifying tyres, Mario placed the car on pole for the Florida enduro and, despite a brief skirmish with Van der Merwe's March 83G, Porsche looked set to walk away with a win when the gearbox played up, and finally, the car was forced out with camshaft failure. In common with its 956 counterpart, this prototype chassis 962-001 never raced again, and was kept by the factory for testing purposes and display thereafter. Although it failed on its debut, the car's potential was obvious, and by the middle of 1984, a rash of customer chassis had appeared in the Championship, which is just what Porsche had wanted, and there was little to touch them.

None of the three Lancia LC2s entered at Le Mans in 1983 went the distance, two succumbing to engine failure – including the Nannini/Andruet/Barilla car pictured here – and one to transmission problems.

The Joest Racing New Man 956 was driven to 9th place at the 1984 Brands Hatch 1,000km by Volkert Merl, Dieter Schornstein and 'John Winter'.

962 IN DECLINE

As the Group C World Sportscar Championship underwent rule changes in 1992, the number of participating 962s sharply declined. Nevertheless, Porsche felt that the 962C could still compete for overall victory at Le Mans despite being subjected to new LMP regulations, which led to a drop in performance. German protagonist Jochen Dauer created a road-going 962, using revised 962 carbon-fibre and Kevlar panels. Norbert Singer and Jochen Dauer worked together to create the Dauer 962 Le Mans, a road-and-race car based on the Group C 962C, and two cars were built. The racing version used the water-cooled type 935 3.0-litre flat-6, equipped with a pair of KKK – Kühnle, Kopp & Kausch – turbochargers developing 720bhp and a top speed of 405km/h.

At Le Mans 1994, the Dauer Porsches were not able to compete with the fastest Group C cars – Courage and Kremer Spyder – and started 4th and 5th on the grid, having recorded lap times twenty seconds slower than Oscar Larrauri's, set in 1990 in a 962C. In 1994, speed differentials in the GT1 class in which the Dauer Porsches were entered were enormous. Yet, 24 hours later, the #36 Dauer 962 Le Mans of Yannick Dalmas, Hurley Haywood and Mauro Baldi took the overall win, with #35 Dauer 962 Le Mans of Hans Stuck, Danny Sullivan and Thierry Boutsen finishing 3rd, a lap behind the winning car.

CONTROLLING BODY CONTACT

Perversely, 1984 was the year in which March-Chevrolet took the IMSA Camel Championship for Makes title by virtue of a string of victories and high placings. Before the new customer 962s had been shipped across the Atlantic, Hans Heyer, Stefan Johansson and Mauricio de Narvaez had given the 935 its last major international victory in the Sebring 12-Hours. The Group 44 Jaguar XJR-5s staged a fine one-two podium finish at Miami. After that, it was March Chevrolet or Porsche 962 all the way. All in all, it was a good year for IMSA and one that marked a turning point, in stark contrast to the FISA series, which had well and truly come under the domination of Porsche and was already beginning to look a bit stagnant. Possibly aware that this was happening, and after an early season visit to Daytona, FIA Chief Jean-Marie Balestre returned to Europe to announce in March that it had been decided that the fifteen per cent reduction in fuel allowance that had previously been announced in 1984 would now be scrapped, and C1 car weights would be increased immediately from 800kg to 850kg. Moreover, IMSA GTP cars would now be allowed to compete in the WEC, although constrained to the same fuel regulations as everybody else. Then, in July, the FISA's technical commission decided that the fuel consumption rules that had provided the backbone of the Group C championship were to be scrapped entirely for 1986. These moves were certainly a signal that FISA wanted to bury the hatchet and link up again with the Americans, but were, perhaps, also a move to curtail the increasing dominance of Porsche in the WEC.

Even before July's revelations, the German firm's reaction had been understandably swift and emphatic. Porsche had spent three years and much money on designing and developing cars to run to fuel efficiency parameters, only to see their baby about to be thrown out by FISA. As a mark of protest, and while negotiations went on in the background, the factory withdrew from Le Mans, leaving the field clear for Porsche privateers at this, the premier event of the season. Lancia was upset as well, and for the same reasons, but decided not to be too upset to see that this also gave them their best chance of winning the prestigious Le Mans enduro. In the event, the fifteen per cent reduction was implemented as planned, but now, just for the 1985 season, the idea of ending the fuel formula was shelved, and FISA never dropped it. In the WEC, 1984 still turned out to be a season of Porsche versus Porsche, despite, or perhaps because of, the uncertainties cast by the organisers. You could, when all was said and done, count on a 956 or 962C being reliable and competitive.

The works cars won all but one round that they entered, the exception being at Imola, where their singleton car destroyed its experimental PDK gearbox four times in one weekend, and the Jöst, GTi Engineering and Brun teams took three of the remaining four races, the last going to Lancia at Kyalami when a dispute over travel expenses led to a boycott by most teams, handing the Italians a hollow victory. This meant that the Makes' title went to Germany again, as well as the Drivers', with Stefan Bellof fulfilling the promise he had shown from his first drive for the factory in 1983. He took the title from fellow works pilot Jochen Mass, with Jacky Ickx and Derek Bell third and fourth, making it a complete Rothman's works whitewash. To strengthen their hands, Porsche had built four B-specification 956s, chassis 114 to 117, for sale to the Jöst, Brun, Kremer and Fitzpatrick teams, which the works considered to be their emergency race backup squads. These cars featured lighter chassis and bodywork, and better steering geometry.

TECHNICAL DESIGN TWEAKS

Naturally enough, the works cars retained enough technical design tweaks to be able to keep these customer cars behind them under most circumstances. The last 956, chassis 118, was sold to Japan, and thereafter, production commenced of the customer-spec 962 in anticipation of the enforcement of the IMSA foot-box regulations and the entry of IMSA GTPs into the WEC. Apart from Lancia's continued but generally abortive efforts, the challenge was so small as to amount to virtually nothing at all and, indeed, was so underwhelming that Group C2 cars filled the third to seventh places in the overall manufacturers' championship. This merely served to reinforce the opinion of many observers that, in terms of real growth, variety and technical advancement, the WEC made no meaningful progress in 1984. There were signs, though, that the Porsche privateers were making positive progress to close the development gap that the works contrived to maintain over them. The building of the first clone 956 chassis by GTi Engineering – AKA Richard Lloyd Racing – and the increasing use by most teams of aerodynamic aids through the season was evidence of that.

John Fitzpatrick Racing's 956 #110 won the 1983 Brands Hatch 1,000km, helmed by John Fitzpatrick and Derek Warwick, beating the two Rothmans works cars by one lap.

Lancia, however, continued to fly the flag for Italy. Early in the season, they lost their longtime chief engineer to the Alfa Romeo F1 team. His place was taken by the head of Abarth, Pierre Paolo Messori, who devoted considerable energy to cleaning up the Lancia C2's aerodynamics and developing the enlarged 268/C 3.0-litre engines that were used from then onwards. It was all to no avail, as the Italians had an even more dismal year than before. Their best results were the inconsequential win in South Africa and third place

The 2.6-litre twin-turbo Ferrari V8 engine powering the Lancia LC2 of Alessandro Nannini, Paolo Barilla and Jean-Claude Andruet at Le Mans 1983 gave up in the 14th hour.

At Le Mans for the 1984 race, Martini Racing's Lancia LC2 driven by Mauro Baldi/Hans Heyer/Paolo Barilla sported the deep yellow livery of main sponsors Malardeau; its 3.0-litre Ferrari V6 turbo engine lasted 117 laps.

at the opening race at Monza, although they were still very fast in practice, deploying 700bhp in qualifying trim, and usually managing to get a car to the finish. Inadequate preparation and mechanical failures conspired to let them down throughout the year, prompting sceptics to question their commitment. Even talented wheelmen such as Riccardo Patrese and Sandro Nannini were unable to redress the balance, and in view of the clear advantage enjoyed by even the privately entered Porsches, it was strange that Bob Wollek, having proved his worth as a driver of talent and intelligence with Jöst in 1983, chose a career move to Lancia for 1984, where he found himself driving a succession of LC2s that were fast in practice but failed in the races.

Sauber and Rondeau had already stepped back from the WEC, though Sauber C7s were campaigned in IMSA through 1985 and '86, and would re-emerge with the C8 and Kouros backing and Mercedes engines in 1985. Rondeau, meanwhile, continued to be represented in WEC by private entries. The Nimrod Aston Martin project came to a sad end when both the Viscount Down and Bovis-sponsored C2 Bs were destroyed in the same horrific shunt during Saturday evening at the Mulsanne kink. One of the drivers, John Sheldon, was badly injured, and a marshal was killed. The team was left with neither the motivation nor the resources to continue.

JAGUAR COMEBACK

The Le Mans epic also provided a platform for Jaguar's much-hyped reappearance, with the entry of two of Bob Tullius's IMSA GTP XJR-5s. Despite the advance publicity, the enthusiastic British crowd, and immaculate preparation, the cars proved a disappointment. They never looked likely to challenge in terms of sheer pace. One was eliminated by accident damage, and the other hobbled unclassified to the finish on a seized gearbox.

Having run a Cosworth DFL-powered Cheetah G603 to 8th and 9th at Mugello and Imola in 1983, Chuck Graemiger presented his new Aston Martin-powered G604 for its debut at Spa, employing a full carbon-fibre chassis and the driving talents of Ray Mallock and Bernard de Dryver. The car had a clear power-to-weight advantage over the previous Nimrod compatriots, but a lack of testing and development showed. Most interest in 1984 was to be found in the C Junior class, which by common consent was now called C2, where the Alba Giannini managed another win, mainly because the Zingonia-based team were the only one to contest the whole series, except for the boycotted South African race, and because they had sold their 1983 car to a private team, who had a more successful year than they did. The previous year, Alba had been in the position of being the most effective engine chassis combination in relatively small or very small fields consisting of cars with even worse reliability. In 1984, the balance had changed, in that 31 cars with 21 different chassis and eleven different engines ran in the championship at various times. This exposed the Alba Giannini's reliability issues under pressure and led to a much closer contest.

Aussie Neil Crang's C1 Tiga Chevrolet was updated and converted over the winter to accept Cosworth power and entered in C2 with Crang, Gordon Spice and Ray Bellm driving. They provided the bulk of the opposition to Alba throughout the season. Roy Baker abandoned the Harrier and opted instead for a Tiga, the new GC284 chassis with a 1.7 litre Ford BDT Turbo engine. ADA Engineering gave their old faithful #01 its last international run at Le Mans and, from Sandown, opted to campaign one of the new German Gebhardt chassis.

A name from 1950s sportscar racing reappeared, as Ecurie Ecosse commissioned Ray Mallock to modify an old De Cadenet Lola T380 chassis for C2. The resulting Ecosse Cosworth looked like a scaled-down version of the Nimrod that Mallock had vainly been trying to develop over the past year. However, in contrast to the larger car, the smaller blue car looked competitive at Monza, Silverstone and Le Mans, until it was destroyed mid-season in a non-championship race at Brands Hatch.

The Brands Hatch race on 29 July 1984 was the British round of the championship, the British Aerospace-sponsored 1,000 kilometres. A crowd of 25,000 basked in the hot sun, watching the Canon Porsche of Jan Lammers and Jonathan Palmer storm to a copybook victory, albeit a slightly empty one. No fewer than ten of the 38 cars posted had failed to turn up. Second was the Jöst car of Jochen Mass and Henri Pescarolo, and the JFR Boutsen/Keegan/Edwards 962 came third. Strangely, the Rothmans works Porsches were not entered, but their drivers were released to be able to drive for the customers, so Bellof drove for Brun with Harald Gröhs, and Jochen Mass joined Reinhold Jöst's team.

Less concerned with the drivers' title than before, both Bell and Ickx decided to moonlight in the USA for the weekend, and Bell shared driving duties at the Portland IMSA

The 2.0-litre BMW M12/7-engined Gebhardt JC842 #840-1 of Jan Thoelke/Frank Jelinski/Gerry Amato rounds Druid's Hairpin at Brands Hatch during the 1984 1,000km, sidelined by fuel pump failure.

The Lola T610, powered by a Ford-Cosworth DFL 3.3-litre V8, entered by John Bartlett and driven by Roger Anderson, Steve Kimpton and Max Cohen-Olivar, came 14th in the 1984 Brands Hatch 1,000km.

round with Al Holbert. Understeer was a big headache for all the teams. The previous year at Brands Hatch, John Fitzpatrick Racing had come up with a special hairdryer tweak to squeeze extra grip out of their car, and this time it was the Canon GTi Engineering/Richard Lloyd Racing 956, whose winning car sported a high downforce nose with an auxiliary aileron on it. Lancia tried their own variation in the form of longitudinal fences along the tops of the LC2 wings, though that did not seem to help much because they hardly featured at all over the weekend.

Rounding Mulsanne corner during Le Mans 1982 is the Primagaz team's 3.0-litre Cosworth DFV-powered Rondeau M379C, driven into 10th overall by Pierre Yver, Bruno Sotty and Lucien Guitteny.

Winners of the 1984 Brands Hatch 1,000km by two laps were Jonathan Palmer and Jan Lammers in the Richard Lloyd GTi Engineering 956 #106.

The Roy Baker Racing Tiga GC285 C2 of Will Hoy, Paul Smith and Nick Nicholson receives attention in the pits during the 1985 Le Mans weekend. This 1778cc Ford BTD turbo-engined Tiga came 21st in the 24 hours.

Bob Wollek was only able to claim fourth on the grid, nearly two seconds adrift of the Lammers/Palmer Porsche and finished seventh in the race, having switched to the Martini Racing LC2 of Mauro Baldi after Barilla had stuck his original mount in the catch fencing. Porsches therefore filled the first six places of a rather processional race, and the Crang/Bellm Tiga, bereft of the driving talents of Gordon Spice, pushed out the Albas again in C2. Other new C2 cars debuting during the year were the Mazda 727C, which looked a much sleeker and more stable proposition than the 717C and was derived from the BF Goodrich-backed Lola T616 Mazda; the Lyncar MS83 from Costas Los; the Alba AR3 Cosworth run by Kelmar Racing; the Arundel C200; Ark Racing's Ceekar 83J with a Cosworth BDA-derived engine; the BDX and the Rondeau M379C.06 of Jean-Philippe Grand, which found a new lease of life in the junior C2 class, as did other Rondeaux. The older Grid S1 had been sold to Gil Baird, who dropped into the Junior class and made a single appearance at Brands Hatch, giving the regulars a bit of a shock with its pace until stopped by a broken throttle linkage. The Autobeaurex-Lotec BMW won C2 at Fuji with a crew of local drivers, placing sixth overall. Having campaigned his BMW M1 in Group B and won the Touring Car Cup virtually single-handed, Jens Winther realised that the class was just about finished and decided late in the season to use his Castrol sponsorship to purchase the old Harald Gröhs URD C82 BMW for the last race at Sandown Park. Winther immediately made the car run better than anyone had managed previously until the suspension collapsed.

Running in C2, the 3.0-litre Cosworth DFV-powered Ark Racing Ceekar 83J of Lawrie Hickman, Max Payne and Chris Ashmore finished 17th overall in the 1987 Spa-Francorchamps 1,000km.

BMW M1 GLUT

The demise of Group B was inexorably slow. The class now had to rely mainly on the re-homologated Group 4 BMW M1s, which swamped the class to the exclusion of all else, despite various Porsche 924 Carrera GTs, 928s and 911 derivatives trying to get in on the act. A new four-wheel-drive Porsche had been promised for Group B homologation, but

Just after the start of the 1985 Le Mans enduro, Bob Wollek's Lancia LC2 surged from the second row of the grid, taking the lead from the two works 962Cs, here followed by Klaus Ludwig in the Jöst 956B, Jonathan Palmer in the Canon-Richard Lloyd Racing 956, and Sarel van der Merwe in the Kremer 956B.

when the 961 did appear sometime later – a racing version of the twin-turbo 959 supercar – it only raced twice, both times at Le Mans and then in the IMSA GTX class. A new Ferrari GTO was also expected to save the category, but none ever appeared in the WEC. The enormous initial purchase price, much the same as for a turnkey C2 car, and the investment potential as road cars persuaded anyone wealthy enough to become an owner to reconsider. The expectation that Le Mans, held on 16 and 17 June, would be won by Porsche privateers – and give the marque its ninth victory in fifteen years – kept the Porsche factory team away, declaring their withdrawal from Le Mans as a protest at FISA's fiddling with the Group C rules, which was a breach of FISA's own stability rule. Not for the first time, Le Mans' organisers, the ACO, found themselves being used as a punch bag in someone else's squabble. The punch bag was, on this occasion, swinging between Stuttgart and Paris. In the meantime, Lancia contrived to be equally piqued but recognised that it was the perfect time to seize the day.

It turned out to be one of the best 24-Hours of the modern era, up to that point in time, and it also marked the return of Jaguar, in the shape of the Bob Tullius Group 44 Jaguar XJR-5s, chassis number #006 of Brian Redman, Bob Tullius and Doc Bundy, and #008 of Claude Ballot-Lena, John Watson and Tony Adamowicz, who had made their way across the Atlantic especially for Le Mans. Meanwhile, Cesare Fiorio, the boss of Lancia, naturally hoped his team would be the centre of attention, having just completed exhaustive endurance trials at Mugello and Monza and, for once, seemed to have got its act together. But the catalogue of petty failures that had dogged the LC2 since its debut meant that few people expected the cars to last, the weak link being the

The John Fitzpatrick Racing 956B of Jo Gartner, David Hobbs and Guy Edwards sits beside its garage in the Le Mans pitlane – along with a spare nosecone – during the 1985 event, when it finished 4th overall.

transmission, and for fans, the best to be hoped for would be for the Lancias to lead the race for as long as possible.

True to form, Bob Wollek took pole position in practice, and Mauro Baldi took second in the sister car, both utilising the older 2.6-litre power plants before changing over to the new 3.0-litre 680 horsepower V8s for the race. Come the race, the dramas started to unfold immediately. It was a hot afternoon, one of the hottest ever at Le Mans, apparently. Roger Dorchy's WM took the lead on the first lap by overtaking the slower Porsches on the Mulsanne Straight and then out-braked Wollek's Lancia for the lead into Mulsanne corner. WMs had been racing at Le Mans for a few years, but this was probably the amateur team's greatest moment. It lasted but briefly, as Wollek took the lead back on lap two only to lose it again to the French car in lap three. On the fourth approach to the Mulsanne corner, the pace told on the WM as its brakes overheated, locked up, and sent the unfortunate Dorchy into the barriers.

A semblance of normality returned as the fierce battle joined at the front between the German and Italian cars, with nine different leaders. So intense was the fight that the normally reliable Porsches started looking decidedly brittle, and virtually no one escaped problems. The Wollek/Nannini Lancia led the longest, notching up 137 laps in front until being delayed by the anticipated drivetrain bothers and eventually scoring an honourable eighth place. Their teammates led for 29 laps, leaving the battle with a blown engine. Then the Jan Lammers/Jonathan Palmer Canon Porsche led for two laps until suffering suspension maladies.

After the WM, undoubtedly the fastest along the Mulsanne Straight was the Kremer Kenwood 956 of Alan Jones, Vern Schuppan and Jean-Pierre Jarier, thanks to the loan of a works engine, which kept it in front for 55 laps, falling back after a mid-race coming-together with Dorchy's WM. Another leader to visit the barriers was the second New Man Jöst Porsche of Johansson/Schlesser, which led for eleven laps. Eventual winners were Klaus Ludwig and Henri Pescarolo in the second New Man Jöst Porsche 956, making it the French veteran's fourth Le Mans win.

ANOTHER WEC TITLE FOR PORSCHE DRIVERS

The 1985 season saw Porsche's continued dominance of Group C to the almost total exclusion of every other marque. In mid-season the new Tom Walkinshaw Racing TWR Jaguar XJR-6 arrived, and a Joest Racing 956, #117, won Le Mans, while Derek Bell and Hans Stuck jointly won the world drivers' crown. Their combination of experience and driving flair was hard to beat, but only after the factory team overcame early-season fuel consumption problems. Although Bell's skills and ability to read a race were a major factor, it was Stuck's good-humoured, press-on-regardless attitude that sealed the title for the pair. Walter Brun's decision to ditch the Sauber and buy a Porsche 956 for the second half of 1983 gave Stuck a chance to show his real ability as a sportscar driver on a regular basis, and so impressed the Rothmans team management that they offered him a works contract for 1985. After the factory's virtual abandonment of the World Sportscar Championship in the late 1980s with only sporadic forays at Le Mans, Stuck was lost to the regular championship and earned his living driving Audi 90s in the IMSA GTU class and their Group A cousins in the ADAC DTM series.

The Lancia LC2 of Mauro Baldi, Bob Wollek and Andrea de Cesaris came 3rd in the 1985 Brands Hatch 1,000km. Concerns over the safety of the Porsche 956 tub in the wake of Bellof's death at Spa meant Porsche privateers stayed away, and no points were awarded for the Teams' championship.

RACING IS ALSO THIS

Another who invariably drove fast and competitively was Stefan Bellof, the 1983 WEC Drivers' champion. With Bellof's Formula 1 career burgeoning, he was unable to commit to a full season of sportscars, and thus, paradoxically, it was his seat at Porsche that Stuck secured. It was tragic that Bellof should be driving Water Brun's 956, chassis # 116, at the Spa 1,000km when he attempted an impossible overtaking manoeuvre on Jacky Ickx in his Rothmans 962. Bellof was trying overexuberantly to regain the lead when his and Ickx's cars touched, and Bellof went off and struck the barriers at Eau Rouge head-on. The cabin folded up in the massive impact, and Bellof died shortly after being cut from the wreckage.

Earlier in the weekend, Jonathan Palmer had been very badly hurt, trapped by the legs when his Canon 956 left the track on a fast downhill sweeper, thumping the barriers and destroying itself. And three weeks earlier at Mosport, Manfred Winkelhock had a similar shunt and had to be cut from the crushed cabin of his Kremer 962 #110, and he died later in hospital. Three Grand Prix drivers, three Porsches, and three similar high-speed accidents; it was Group C's bleakest period.

Although it is unlikely that any chassis could have survived the enormous impacts involved in those accidents any better than Porsche's, it reduced the willingness of F1 teams to allow their expensive protégés to compete in the WEC. These were the first issues of real import that the newly formed Organisation for Sports Car Racing – or OSCAR – had to deal with, having been mooted as a liaison between teams and sponsors and an apparently disinterested FISA who, having framed the regulations for Group C at the start of the 1980s, had now, apparently, no further interest in promoting the championship. OSCAR had plans to raise the profile of the class, but its lack of political clout became obvious in the middle of the season when FISA started juggling with the F1 calendar in the wake of the cancellation of the Belgian Grand Prix at Spa. Already upset that the Canadian Grand Prix clashed with Le Mans, thus denying them the services of several high-profile drivers at the WEC's key event, they now found that the newly rescheduled Grand Prix calendar clashed with the Fuji and Brands Hatch rounds, and were thus unable to field all their contracted Grand Prix drivers, which had obvious implications for the teams, affecting not only their competitiveness but also their sponsorship commitments. OSCAR threatened to boycott the Fuji and Brands Hatch races, but FISA was unfazed, pointing out that the Japanese organisers were contractually bound to their date by the television companies.

The Brands Hatch round was moved one week as a sop to the teams, but it was a small concession, and the German privateer squads elected instead to race in their national sportscar championships that weekend. Grand Prix racing's influence on sportscars extended still further during the year. In 1985, the delayed fifteen per cent reduction in fuel allowances was finally implemented, and some of the larger teams were offered the use of specially developed fuels that overcame some of the extra limitations. It was a classic case of Colin Chapman's 'unfair advantage'.

The 5.3-litre Michael Caine Racing-built EMKA Aston Martin C83-B of Steve O'Rourke, Tiff Needell and Nick Faure finished 11th in the 1985 Le Mans 24-Hours.

SYNTHETIC FUEL

Basically, these fuels emerged from research carried out for Formula 1 and featured additives such as toluene and naphthalene, which are dense aromatics, slower-burning than petrol, and ideally suited to a fuel economy formula, particularly when used in high-temperature-operating turbo engines. They were also entirely legal because they were hydrocarbons rather than alcohols or nitrate compounds, which were specifically excluded by Group C rules and, in fact, excluded throughout FISA's various formulae since 1958, so as to preclude the use of methanol and nitromethane fuels. Neither did they increase the octane rating of the fuel when subjected to the standard FISA laboratory test in use at the time. The growing use of high-aromatic fuels in the WEC represented a worrying trend because they had been sourced from F1, in which a limit on fuel allocation had been used to restrict engine outputs. In Group C, however, the fuel regulations were envisaged to create a formula in which the engine outputs were already effectively controlled, and which allowed a wide variety of atmospheric and forced induction engines to compete on fairly equal terms. The fact that aromatic additives favoured turbo engines upset this basic premise and led to their eventual exclusion from the WEC – or WSPC as it was by then – in 1987. Twenty years later, incidentally, Lotus produced a road-going Exige prototype fuelled by Bioethanol, the fastest car they made at the time. This synthetic fuel was even available from Morrisons' supermarket pumps, and we thought the future had actually arrived.

All of this was quite irrelevant during what was probably the best race of the year, Le Mans, where all the cars were obliged to run on fuel supplied by the organisers from a central reservoir. Joest Racing's trio of Klaus Ludwig/Paolo Barilla/John Winter silenced the pundits and the other teams, including the factory Rothmans team, by simply strolling away from the field after an early slipstreaming tussle with the Canon Porsche of Jonathan Palmer and James Weaver. Despite using bigger 3.0-litre engines for the first time in practice, which allowed them to dominate the grid, the factory cars did not feature at all in the race, and their problems were worsened by a rash of gearbox and wheel bearing problems.

Despite mutterings from Jöst's opponents about special Motronic chips and other technical trickery, the win was largely based on experience gained the previous year with the same chassis, with instructions to Klaus Ludwig, 'John Winter' (real name Louis Krages), and Paolo Barilla to tread lightly on the gas pedal, change up early, downshift late and tackle the turns as gently as possible. The Rothmans cars' problems were not confined to Le Mans, and the team had an unusually fraught year using the new 962Cs.

TITLE CHANGES

Rule changes from a 'Makes' to a 'Teams' championship meant that all teams were now scoring points for themselves rather than for the make of car they were using, so there was added pressure on the works Rothmans squad, now without the cushion of the Porsche privateers to back them up in the championship. Added to this, they were uncharacteristically muddled during the first half of the year, apparently unable to find the correct electronic chip for the new fuel allowances to make the delicate balance between power and economy. Stuck and Bell ran out of fuel at Mugello, having led, and were disqualified for exceeding the maximum time allowed for their last lap – 400 per cent of the pole position time. However, Ickx and Mass rescued the win for the factory team. At Monza, Stuck was lucky to escape a practice fire caused by a fuel leak, which destroyed his 962C. He was luckier still to place 2nd in a replacement car built up overnight from a 956 tub with a 962C rear grafted onto it.

There was worse. At Hockenheim, the Rothmans' pit became engulfed in flames during a fuel stop, and four

Lancia Corse employed some of the best drivers, including Riccardo Patrese and Bob Wollek, pictured here in discussion with engineer Claudio Lombardi (centre), who oversaw both the Lancia Rally and Group C projects and subsequently went to Ferrari and then designed the Aprilia V4 motorcycle engine.

mechanics, engineer Helmut Schmidt and team manager Norbert Singer were badly burned, the latter's injuries necessitating a lengthy stay in hospital.

The fifteen per cent fuel reduction had precluded the use of a new 3.0-litre flat-six engine for all but qualifying, especially given the problems with engine management. So, the old 2.6-litre unit was retained as race equipment for another year. With an improved challenge from both the privateer teams and the Martini Lancia LC2s, the performance gap was closing, and Weissach breathed a huge sigh of relief at the end of the 1985 season, with the championship secured again.

Lancia had plenty to do to remain viable in Group C after three dismal seasons that yielded virtually nothing, so they elected to conduct a Europe-only campaign, entering just seven races using unmodified versions of their existing LC2s. A new chief engineer, Claudio Lombardi, instigated a number of changes, including a wider track on redesigned suspension, front and rear, 16-inch diameter wheels all round, with Michelin radial tyres and aerodynamic refinements to the top surfaces and underbody. Furthermore, improved

Two of the three Lancia LC2s entered for Le Mans 1984 were fastest in practice – Bob Wollek took pole by 3.0 seconds, winning his own weight in Champagne. Wollek was partnered by Alessandro Nannini, and the other Martini LC2 was driven by Mauro Baldi/Hans Heyer/Paolo Barilla. A third car driven by Pierluigi Martini/Beppe Gabbiani/ Xavier Lapeyre raced in the yellow livery of the Malardeau-sponsored Jolly Club team.

Weber-Marelli engine management was also being used on Lancia's 3.0-litre power plant, yielding some 640bhp in race trim and giving a clear early-season fuel advantage over the Porsches. They looked like a serious threat and were still quick, but despite a win in the shortened Spa-Francorchamps round, reliability was, as ever, Lancia's weak point, though it was notably improved over 1984.

The fuel consumption advantage disappeared by late season as Porsche got their electronics dialled in. Patrese, Wollek, Baldi and Nannini again loyally formed the driving team, although test driver Lucio Cesario, Henri Pescarolo and Andrea de Cesaris made appearances during the year as operational requirements and F1 commitments dictated. This surfeit of driving talent was unable to overcome the inherent fragility of the car's design, and by the end of the year, there was a lot of internal pressure on the Lancia management in Turin to cancel the Group C project and concentrate on rallying – at which they were virtually invincible, with ten WRC manufacturer wins logged in 1974, 1975, 1976, 1983, and, subsequently, 1987, 1988, 1989, 1990, 1991 and 1992.

The Lancia LC2 of Bob Wollek and Mauro Baldi came 12th in the 1985 Silverstone 1,000km, while its sister Martini Racing LC2 of Sandro Nannini and Riccardo Patrese placed 3rd.

ENTER TWR

Perhaps the most significant single event of the season was at Mosport, where the long-awaited Jaguar XJR-6 made its race debut and led the early laps before being overhauled by the Rothmans cars. In 1984, Jaguar was newly privatised and in desperate need of a boost to its reputation. What better way to put the leaping cat back on the map than a return to sportscar racing? Tom Walkinshaw Racing (TWR) were a successful but relatively unknown race preparation company. I had known Tom when he was doing Formula Atlantic in the John Player-sponsored championship in 1974, and he was diffidently determined. In 1976, he established TWR Racing, sharing a BMW3.5 CSL with John Fitzpatrick to win the Silverstone Six Hours, and ran Jaguar XJS V12s in the ETCC, winning the title in 1984. This led to a contract to develop a works Jaguar prototype for Group C, and the 6.2-litre V12 XJR-6 made its debut halfway through the 1985 WSC series at Mosport, Canada. One car had been subjected to a few track tests beforehand, but the sister car arrived in Canada without having turned a wheel on track and its initial shakedown was pre-race practice and qualifying. Despite a lack of seat time, Brundle was immediately on the pace, claiming 3rd on the grid, a fraction slower than Hans Stuck's pole-position 962. At the start of the race,

The winning Jaguar XJR-6 V12 of Derek Warwick and Eddie Cheever at the 1986 Silverstone 1,000km finished two laps ahead of the 2nd place Rothmans 962C of Bell and Stuck.

Running in the IMSA/GTP class at Le Mans 1985, the Group 44 Racing Jaguar XJR-5 V12 of Brian Redman, Hurley Heywood and Jim Adams retired with transmission failure.

Brundle shot past both Porsche 962s from the second row to take the lead into the first corner. He held this lead for nine laps, but the car was forced to retire at twelve laps due to wheel bearing failure. The sister car of Jean-Louis Schlesser and Mike Thackwell took 3rd place, which was an incredible achievement on the weekend of its first shake-down. Nevertheless, TWR had a lot of work to do to ensure that the cars had the reliability and durability needed for endurance racing. Accordingly, several changes were made before the next race, including alterations to the nose to counter understeer and new measures to prevent wheel bearing failure.

The next round was at Spa-Francorchamps, where the XJR-6 scored 5th place. However, this race was overshadowed by the tragic death of Stefan Bellof in a horrific crash at Eau Rouge. Brands Hatch was the third race for the XJR-6

The second Jaguar XJR-6 V12 was crewed by Jean-Louis Schlesser and Gianfranco Brancatelli at Silverstone for the 1986 1,000km, finishing in 7th place.

and the first in front of a home crowd. Alan Jones qualified in fifth, but throttle issues causing engine damage meant the car had to retire after twenty laps. Following earthquakes and heavy rain at Fuji, which prompted all the European teams to withdraw before the race, the Selangor 800km was the last race of the season. With several upgrades having been made throughout the season, all eyes were on the XJRs for their final outing. Mike Thackwell qualified fourth quickest and maintained a steady pace throughout the race to finish the season with a 2nd place. This was an impressive performance for a brand-new design.

The XJR-6 was based on a carbon composite chassis designed by Tony Southgate. It had advanced suspension and ground-effect aero achieved with massive underbody venturi. It ran the latest Dunlop tyres. It was powered by a 6.2-litre race version of the stock-block Jaguar V12 engine, allied to a March-developed transmission.

TOP-HEAVY V12

TWR lined up prodigious driving talent, too, employing Martin Brundle, Hans Heyer, Jean-Louis Schlesser and Mike Thackwell. However, in the wake of the Mosport (Winkelhock) and Spa (Bellof) tragedies, Brundle was barred by his F1 boss, Ken Tyrrell, from taking any further part in the TWR-Jaguar project. Alan Jones and Jan Lammers were drafted in, followed by John Nielsen and Gianfranco Brancatelli. During a short season of races using the slightly underpowered two-valves-per-cylinder version of the V12, some of the team gained three points-scoring finishes, including 3rd at Mosport and 2nd at Shah Alam in the hands of Jan Lammers. A four-valve head existed but was judged too weighty for the already top-heavy V12 power plant, even though it was more efficient in terms of power and economy.

TONY SOUTHGATE

Designer Tony Southgate's pedigree reached back to 1960s' Eagle, 1970s' BRM, Shadow, Lotus (Types 78 and 79 ground-effect F1 cars), and Arrows F1 cars, with input into the Ford C100 Group C car and RS200 Group B rally car. His designs won the Indianapolis 500 (Eagle TG2), the Monaco Grand Prix (BRM P160B), and Le Mans 24-Hours (Jaguar XJR-9 and XJR-12), a rendering of motorsport's 'Triple Crown'. Southgate left TWR in 1990, working for Toyota (TS010 1991–93), Ferrari (333 SP 1993–95), Lister, Nissan (R390 GT1 1996–97), and Audi (R8R and R8C).

In total, six XJR-6s were constructed. The initial couple of chassis, serial numbers #185 and #285, had been created with some urgency early in 1985 and finished in dark British Racing Green livery with white panelling on the engine cover and nose. From their third race at Brands Hatch in September 1985, front brake cooling ducts were added on each side of the central radiator intake in the nose, and cockpit cooling ducts would later be sunk into the horizontal door panels. Initially, these XJR-6s suffered from insufficient rear-brake cooling, causing premature retirements as axles and bearings overheated. Periscope brake cooling ducts attached to the top of the hollow suspension uprights were then adopted as standard. For short-distance races, the cars carried biplane rear wings supported by a pair of alloy plates bolted vertically on the gearbox tail casing. The XJR-6 wing endplates tapered towards the front and had a

Martin Brundle explains a point at Silverstone during the 1991 430km. He and Teo Fabi and Derek Warwick did two stints each that season, and Brundle drove both cars but did not score points because the other two were the nominated main drivers. Brundle put Teo Fabi's car on pole at Silverstone but started Warwick's car from second place. Then the team decided to put Warwick in Fabi's car so they could both share points, leaving Brundle to drive the entire race on his own, finishing 3rd.

DUTCH COURAGE: FROM PORSCHE TO JAGUAR

Jan Lammers raced in most single-seater formulae, including F1 and winning Le Mans in 1988. Subsequently, he drove in the BTCC and the Dakar Rally, set up Racing for Holland and A1 GP and became sporting director of the revived Zandvoort circuit.

Netherlands star Jan Lammers' first ride in a Porsche was in a 917 at Le Mans. How do you follow that? Well, you could always go on to win Le Mans in a Jaguar XJR-8 and race a 956 and 962 along the way.

In 1983, Lammers joined Richard Lloyd's Canon Porsche team, racing 956s in long-distance Group C events with Lloyd, Thierry Boutsen, Tiff Needell, Keke Rosberg and Jonathan Palmer. There were several podiums and 8th at Le Mans in 1983, Jan coming 5th and 7th in the '83 and '84 World title rankings.

> *I spent two and a half years racing 956s and 962s, and at somewhere like Daytona, that was thrilling. But there were also dark days, like when Bellof had his accident at Spa and Gartner at Le Mans.*

What were the Porsches like to drive?

> *The 956 was an impressive car; a lot of power and mechanical grip. At high speed everything had to come from the geometry and the mechanical side – tyres, dampers – so that meant that you needed arms like Mike Tyson. Shifting was all mechanical too, and when I did Le Mans with Jonathan Palmer it took me a week to recover!*

The 956 represented a breakthrough for sportscar aerodynamics.

> *When Richard Lloyd, Jonathan Palmer and I dominated Brands Hatch '84 with the double wing on the front, it was the first time we beat the factory Porsches. That was the first signal that sportscar racing had gone ground-effect. Aerodynamics were a big issue, especially at Le Mans with the fins on the Jaguars and the Rondeaus. The Porsches had ducting, which sucked cooling air in from underneath the car, but we realised that if we shut off those vents, the engine would run a little warmer, but for a few laps, you would have great grip, so we made a big step forward. After that the Tony Southgate-designed Jaguars went a stage further, and then the Toyotas, Peugeots and Sauber-Mercedes raised the bar even higher. As the aerodynamics developed over the years and you got more aerodynamic assistance, you could take some of the stress off the mechanical side so we could run with a little less castor because the aerodynamics were taken care of. A bit of a fight but still very enjoyable.*

Mid-decade, sportscar chassis metamorphosed from aluminium monocoque hulls to honeycomb and carbon fibre. Jan did six years with Tom Walkinshaw's Castrol Jaguar and Silk Cut Jaguar in the WSC in Europe and IMSA in America, with wins in '87 at Jarama, Monza and Fuji in the XJR-8 and victory at Le Mans in 1988 in the XJR-9 with Andy Wallace and Johnny Dumfries.

He was aboard the winning XJR-9 at Daytona in 1988 and the XJR-12 in 1990, and subsequently ran for TOM'S Toyota in the TS010. Lotus and Nissan drives followed in BPR Global GT Endurance and FIA GTs and drove GTP Toyota Eagles with Eddie Irvine and Jacques Villeneuve in Japan. 'From a performance point of view, the Toyota TS010 was impressive – the grip, power and braking ability of that car was phenomenal.'

In GT2, Jan shared Roock Racing's 996 and 997s with Claudia Hürtgen and Mike Hezemans, and there were also IndyCar forays with Dan Gurney's All-American Racers, and a season of F3000 in Japan, while in the UK he is probably remembered best for his exploits in the zany TWR Volvo 850 R Estate in the 1994 BTCC. He laughs:

> *I hold these silly records. I made the biggest comeback ever, because I'd left F1 in 1982, and ten years later in 1992 I did another two races for March in Adelaide and Suzuka. In qualifying in the rain (at Suzuka) I was 6th fastest – with Prost, Mansell, Schumacher and Senna all in the frame. Unfortunately, in the race, the clutch failed. And then March went broke.*

In the absence of Sauber-Mercedes, the 3.5-litre turbo V6-engined TWR Jaguar XJR-11s of Martin Brundle/Alain Ferté and Jan Lammers/Andy Wallace took 1st and 2nd at the 1990 Silverstone 480km, beating the privateer Porsche 962Cs of Jöst, Kremer and Brun Motorsport.

In the pitlane during qualifying for the Silverstone 1,000km, the Silk Cut Jaguar XJR-6 of Derek Warwick and Eddie Cheever would go on to take the race victory.

vertical trailing edge. Adjustment slots were provided within each plate to facilitate the selection of the incidence angle of the upper wing. All XJR-6 chassis ran on sand-cast one-piece five-spoke Speedline magnesium wheels, 17-inch diameter at the front and 19-inch at the rear, shod with Dunlop Denloc racing tyres. The XJR-6 front headlamp recesses accommodated a single headlamp and indicator light only. Sponsors throughout the latter part of 1985 were Jaguar Cars and Castrol Oil. Chassis #185 and #285 were not raced again after the end of the 1985 season, but both were tested extensively at Estoril, Portugal, in February 1986. Chassis #285 was the first to be re-liveried in 1986's Silk Cut Jaguar colours of mauve, gold and white, reflecting a new sponsorship deal with Gallaher International. Mobile 'fag packets' were still very much to the fore: Gallaher was the third largest of the three major British tobacco groups after British American Tobacco and Imperial Tobacco, the latter's iconic John Player Special branding about to be dropped by John Player Team Lotus in favour of R. J. Reynolds' yellow Camel livery for 1987. As we know, Rothmans sponsored Porsche in Group C from 1982 to 1987, as well as Prodrive and Subaru in Group B rallying.

Meanwhile, the XJR-6 chassis was considerably re-engineered for the upcoming 1986 season, including the adoption of a 6.5-litre version of the V12 engine and other mechanical and bodywork improvements. Cooling louvres were cut into the side panels for the engine oil heat exchanger, battery and engine bays, and engine air intake scoops appeared on the cars' roofs.

SEASON THREE: 1985, PART TWO

Shah Alam might seem a strange choice of venue for the WEC, but after the cancellation of the Sandown Park round because of financial problems and subsequent aborted negotiations to transfer it to Surfers Paradise, FISA decided very late in the year – and actually made the decision after the ninth race at Fuji – to experiment with the circuit near Kuala Lumpur as the season-closer of its ten-race calendar. Run in Malaysian steam heat, the race attracted an understandably small entry, and the track was never used again for the WEC. Of the ten races, all counted towards the drivers' championships, C1 and C2, and several teams scored points in the new Teams' titles, again split as C1 and C2, which replaced the long-established Manufacturers' championship.

In C1, another Aston Martin-based project, the EMKA, was revived and appeared at four events. Encumbered by excess weight and a lack of power, Steve O'Rourke's brainchild delighted its owner and the crowd at Le Mans.

Driver change, refuel and spruce up during Le Mans 1985 for the 5.3-litre EMKA C83B Aston Martin of Steve O'Rourke, Tiff Needell and Nick Faure, which finished 11th.

It's Le Mans 1984, and the Primagaz Cougar C02 3.3 DFV of Yves Courage, Michel Dubois, John Jellinek and Alain De Cadenet is pursued by the Lola T610 3.3 Cosworth of François Migault, François Servanin and Steve Kempton, and flanked by the 930 of Claude Haldi, Altfrid Heger and Jean Krucker, which finished 16th.

Tiff Needell led briefly during the first fuel stop sequence and ultimately finished 11th, ahead of the surviving Group 44 Jaguar XJR-6, which was making its last European appearance.

Disillusioned with his C2 Lyncar, immediately after Le Mans, Costas Los bought the Kreepy Krauly IMSA GTP March 84G-Porsche that had finished 22nd in the 24-Hours, and shifted his aspirations up to C1. Although an ex-IMSA car, the 84G had run in France under Group C regulations and was, therefore, effectively a turn-key proposition. Other occasional C1 entries were the WM-Peugeots that ran at Le Mans, and Richard Cleare's modified Kremer CK5, plus the Cougar C12 Porsche with finishes at Spa and Le Mans. Brit Tim Lee-Davey's efforts to bring a new lease of life to the Cosworth 3.9-litre DFL engine in his ex-Gordon Spice Tiga on the basis that new fuel allowance rules would make it competitive again in C1 proved mistaken. It also ran once in C2 at Le Mans, running a smaller 3.0-litre DFV, but it was clear that the DFL's future was in C2, and then almost exclusively in its reduced 3.3-litre configuration.

There was the by now predictable glut of Japanese specials at Fuji and Rondeau Cosworths at Le Mans, and it was here that Peter Sauber presented his new C8 model with a turbocharged 5.0-litre Mercedes V8. This looked promising in practice until John Nielsen got airborne at the Mulsanne hump, back-flipping twice and destroying the car, though happily, Nielsen himself walked away. Plans to race the repaired car later in the year were shelved when a full Sauber-Mercedes programme was announced for 1986.

C2 ENTERTAINS

Group C2 was in its third season and provided much of the racing interest, so it was deemed worthy of attention in its own right and not simply there to make up the numbers. There was now a separate championship for drivers in the 700kg/330-litre division. However, despite a decent variety of cars at most events, there was growing evidence of a widening gap between the front-runners – Ecosse, Gebhardt and Spice – and those who were definitely not front-runners – Alba – a reflection that C2 was conceived as a budget formula.

Having had its Lola-based Ecosse C284 written off in a mid-1984 British Thundersports event, Ecurie Ecosse appeared with a new car clad in the same sleek bodywork, covering a purpose-built monocoque assembled by Ray Mallock using DFL power and enjoying sponsorship from Bovis Homes.

Entered for Silverstone's 1,000km '85 by Castrol Denmark and driven by Jens Winther, Margie Smith-Haas and David Mercer, the URD C83 was powered by a 3.5-litre BMW M88 six-cylinder engine, classified 24th, but DNF. Built in Stürtz, Germany, URD produced sports-prototypes from 1976 to 1998, with Harald Gröhs and Gerhard Berger among the URD drivers in Group C2.

Ray Mallock, David Leslie and Mike Wilds shared the driving, and the combination tended to win on the occasions when the Spice and Tiga did not, taking three first places and several second places overall in the championship. C2 winners were the newly formed Spice Engineering, led by Gordon Spice and Ray Bellm, who took five C2 wins and two 2nd places running the 3.3-litre Cosworth DFL-powered Tiga-Spice GC85, based at Silverstone with designer Graham Humphries and team manager Jeff Hazell.

The magic of racing at night-time: Arnage corner during the 1986 Le Mans 24-Hours.

PLY WARS

The tyre war expanded during 1985, with more manufacturers vying for honours in C1. Michelin came on the scene for the first time, supplying their radials to Lancia and Cougar. Yokohama supplied Fitzpatrick Racing and Costas Los's Cosmic March team, while Goodyear had contracts with Richard Lloyd Racing, Kremer Racing, and Obermaier, who were using cross-plies before moving to radials mid-season. Dunlop was also heavily committed to radial tyre development, using the Japanese championship for testing and persevering with their boltless Dunlop cross-plies in the WEC, supplying the works Rothmans Porsche team as well as Brun Motorsport, Joest Racing and the new TWR Jaguars. Avon exclusively targeted the C2 class, having created almost a seller's market for their range of cross-plies, which was specifically designed for the 'junior' category. The lighter weights in play and the 750-kilogramme class meant that using typical C1 compounds carried a disadvantage because they never attained optimum operating temperature. As the other companies were throwing all their resources into C1, Avon cleaned up and took nine of the ten rounds in the championship, the only exception being at Fuji, where the Lotec shod with Yokohama rain tyres repeated the previous year's C2 win.

THE 1986 WORLD SPORTS PROTOTYPE CHAMPIONSHIP

A three-way manufacturers' battle for the newly named World Sports Prototype Championship – the WSPC – was eagerly anticipated for the 1986 season as Porsche, Jaguar and Lancia vied for C1 honours, with Spice, Ecosse and Gebhardt contesting C2 glory. The Japanese makers were also represented, with Nissan, Mazda and Toyota in the picture too. The Porsche factory Rothmans squad was backed up – numerically at least – by an army of privateers, most familiar names by now, in the shape of Brun, Jöst, Kremer, Richard Lloyd Racing, John Fitzpatrick and Obermaier.

Brun and Jöst hounded the works Rothmans team 962Cs during the year, both taking wins and each outpacing the Rothmans cars on at least one occasion. Good preparation and, therefore, reliability, combined with aggressive driving by their star turns, Oscar Larrauri and Frank Jelinski, ably backed by their co-drivers Jesús Pareja and Walter Brun in person, enabled Brun Motorsport to take the C1 Team's title at season's end. All this was achieved by the customers using the standard specification 2.85-litre turbo engines, while the works cars generally found it acceptable to run their larger 3.0-litre engines. These were not yet for sale, though, and after the unexpected pasting they took during the year, they would not be available until the works team withdrew from the WSPC in the middle of 1987. The private teams were under more pressure from the Works' decision

Notwithstanding the banning of grid girls in modern F1, a feature of endurance racing in the 1970s and '80s was the posse of Hawaiian Tropic models, seen here at Le Mans '86. As if drivers' hearts were not racing enough already…

The Brun Motorsport 962C driven by Walter Brun and Frank Jelinski finished 9th in the 1986 Silverstone 1,000km, ahead of both its sister cars of Oscar Larrauri and Jesús Pareja, placed 10th, and Thierry Boutsen and Massimo Sigala in 11th.

Photographer Nigel Barrett captured the start of the 1986 Le Mans from a bird's eye view above the pits, as Klaus Ludwig in the Jöst 956B and Thierry Boutsen in the Brun Motorsport 956 outflank the works 962Cs of Mass and Bell for Ludwig to grab an early lead.

to restrict its actions to a programme that concentrated only on the five rounds counting towards the Teams' championship. This also made it harder for the factory drivers to score in the season-long Drivers' championship.

Paradoxically, although Rothmans Porsche failed to take the Teams' title, Derek Bell managed to secure the Drivers' championship, but only after confusion about the results at the last race in Japan.

The Brun Motorsport and Joest Racing teams were hampered by Weissach's desire to use the new PDK double-clutch semi-automatic gearbox throughout the season. An exception was made for Le Mans, with the prospect of achieving 24 hours' reliable running time rather than six hours; even so, a third 962C was entered fitted with PDK transmission, which boosted the Rothmans 962C's average weight to over 900 kilogrammes. The Rothmans squad had also suffered fairly major disasters mid-season, as its two regular 962C chassis were wiped out in the same multi-car accident at the Nürburgring WSPC round. As Hurricane Charley swept across Europe, the Eifel Mountains got their fair share of rain, and an accident involving two C2 cars brought out the pace car, though such is the adverse effect of spray at the Ring that not all drivers were aware of the crash circumstances, and several of the quick cars, including race leader Thackwell in the Sauber, Mass and Stuck in the works 962Cs, and Baldi and Weaver in the Richard Lloyd cars all collided into the queue lined up behind the stationary pace car. It is a wonder similar accidents do not happen more often, such are the vagaries of weather in the Eifel region. For example, at

Sporting LH (Lang Heck) long-tail rear end, the Joest Racing 956C of Klaus Ludwig, Paolo Barilla and 'John Winter' (real name: Louis Krages) that won the 24-Hours the previous year dropped out of the 1986 race in the 13th hour with engine failure due to overheating in the safety car period following Jo Gartner's fatal accident.

the Nürburgring 24-Hours in 2024, fog, rather than spray, caused the race to be red-flagged at eight hours because the marshals' posts could not see from one to another to monitor the race progress. Back in 1986, whilst the written-off remnants were sold off to Vern Schuppan and Reinhold Jöst, this left Rothmans with an old 962 #002, which was unpopular with both crews, and another car hastily assembled around a brand new monocoque, #006, to enable them to see the year out. They were obliged to use a retired 956 #009 as the training car.

Kremer Racing endured a bleak year, especially with the loss of Austrian ace Jo Gartner at Le Mans, whose death was understandably a blow to teams and fans alike. His accident was never properly explained, though there was a theory that oil had leaked from his 956's gearbox, which had then seized up as he accelerated along Mulsanne and flicked him into the barriers. In spite of which, as race teams mostly do, Kremer carried on going and built a new car on a John Thompson-made honeycomb tub, their new 962 making its debut at Spa-Francorchamps.

The Tom Walkinshaw-built and run Jaguar XJR-6s increasingly posed a threat to the Stuttgart makes (Mercedes-Benz engines now being in the mix). Their carbon-fibre chassis had been refined and lightened and were now powered by an enlarged 6.5-litre V12 producing 700bhp. Sponsorship for 1986 was from Silk Cut Tobacco, the cars liveried accordingly, and a strong driver line-up included Derek Warwick, Eddie Cheever, Jean-Louis Schlesser, Jan Lammers, Gianfranco Brancatelli and occasionally Martin Brundle and Win Percy. The purposeful TWR squad looked to have the potential to rain on the Weissach parade. The Jaguars' Le Mans spec featured a sleek, aerodynamic long tail, lower downforce wing and rear wheel spats. These changes all worked to reduce drag and ensure that the XJR-6 was competitive with the blistering top speed of the Porsches on the Mulsanne Straight. At the pre-race test session for Le Mans, things looked positive for #385 as Schlesser managed the second fastest time, and Cheever in #286 clocked the highest speed down the Mulsanne Straight at 221mph. In the actual 24-Hours, Cheever battled up to 8th place within the first hour and maintained a consistent pace going into the night, passing several of the favoured 962Cs and 956s, and was in 4th place with fifteen hours left to race. However, soon after midnight, a broken driveshaft with Win Percy at the wheel ended the race for car number 53. So, although the Jaguars had the pace to worry the mighty Porsches, their reliability was proving an issue, and not a single Jaguar finished the race that year. The initial Cheever-Warwick driving partnership was strong, but became marred by both drivers making errors and a growing rivalry between them. A catalogue of mechanical problems and driver error conspired to thwart TWR's challenges throughout the season, exemplified at Jerez, where all three Jaguars pitched each other off on the first corner, leaving the pair of Brun Motorsport Porsches to run away with the poorly supported race. Then, miraculously, an emphatic win at Silverstone consolidated support from thousands of Jaguar fans for the rest of the year. But Silk Cut-TWR could and should have won more races than they actually managed.

The third dedicated manufacturers' team in 1986 was Martini Lancia, the Turin-based operation still running derivations of the original 1983 LC2, mildly modified over every closed season and now presented in LC2-86 specification. The fact that they had not contrived to design and build a new chassis in advance of the 1987 IMSA foot-well regulations coming into force was an indication of indecision rather than indifference, given the attraction of the World Rally Championship. Just a single car was slated to run a foreshortened '86 season, an indication that time was running out for Lancia in Group C. And yet, at the same time, and perhaps as a way to maintain its involvement in sportscar racing, the factory had sold one of its older LC2s #003 in 1985 specification to Gianni Marzotto's Turbocar racing team, which appeared a couple of times during the year after being refitted to 1986 spec and sporting Sponsor-Geest livery, but to no good effect, falling victim to a massive Interserie crash at Zeltweg when it was totally destroyed and terminating Marzotto's campaign. Turin had also been negotiating with Jean Rondeau regarding his purchase of two other LC2 chassis, but, appallingly, Rondeau was killed when his Porsche got stuck on a railway level crossing near his home at Le Mans.

Mauro Baldi and Paolo Barilla brought their Martini Lancia LC2 home in 3rd place at the 1984 Monza 1,000km.

Starting 5th on the grid for the 1986 Brands Hatch 1,000km, the Lancia LC2 of Andrea de Cesaris and Bruno Giacomelli retired with gearbox problems.

Meanwhile, De Cesaris and Nannini's LC2-86 raced at Monza, Brands Hatch and Silverstone and was as competitive and as fragile as ever. There were corporate pressures for the company to focus on its increasingly successful rally programme, and the death of development driver Giacomo Maggi in an accident at Lancia's La Mandria test facility set the final seal on the situation. Soon after the Norisring street race, centred on Nuremberg's spectacular Zeppelinfeld (the Albert Speer-designed edifice inspired by the Panathenaic stadium of classical antiquity), Lancia announced its withdrawal from the championship.

SAUBER GAINS PACE

Meanwhile, the Sauber-Mercedes C8 was not yet considered an official Works effort, although Stuttgart-Untertürkheim helped from behind the scenes. Peter Sauber's outfit was run as professionally as any in the pitlane. The car was immaculately presented, and high-profile sponsorship came from the Kouros Cosmetics company, which funded the championship as a whole. Nevertheless, it was something of a surprise when Mike Thackwell and Henry Pescarolo won the Nürburgring race. Until then, the design had lacked the outright pace and efficient ground-effects of the Porsches and Jaguars. This all changed at the rain-swept German venue, where the Sauber turned out to be the best package for the conditions and was competitive and well driven enough to stay out of trouble to take the laurels. Despite the sponsorship and professional approach, regular success was still some way off and would really only come with the arrival of concerted Mercedes-Benz factory backing for the project. Of the rest of the C1 contenders, there was Costas Los and his Cosmic Racing March APE 4G-01 Porsche twin-turbo, fitted – unusually – with Avon tyres, which ran the full season, driven by Los and sponsored by Metaxa Brandy. Tiff Needell raced it four times, and Los notched up three top ten finishes. Richard Cleare had the IMSA APE-5G version of the same car, chassis #06, using a single-turbo Porsche flat-six, and appeared five times in the GTP category, winning that class at Le Mans and coming 14th overall. The other GTP contenders were Mazda, who had now turned their attention to C1 with a new triple-rotor Wankel engine, which gave prodigious output in the 767 chassis, running just at Le Mans, where they retired. Most of their efforts were concentrated on the Japanese Championship, like the Nissan-March and Toyota-Dome C1 teams. Other intermittent entries included Yves Courage's Cougar Porsche and the WM Peugeot, which looked fast at Le Mans. Sigi Brunn and Ernst Schuster's Joest Racing Porsche 936C placed 6th at Le Mans. Tim Lee-Davey continued to experiment with the intractable Cosworth DFL turbo engine in his Tiga GC83/86, while another Tiga GC 83/85 masqueraded as a Lamborghini Countach QVX powered by Sant 'Agata's 5.7-litre V12, which Tiff Needell took to fifth place in its only outing, at the final non-championship race at Kyalami.

SPECIAL BUILDER

Veteran racers Vern Schuppan and Richard Attwood were on hand to demonstrate various Porsches at the 2022 Le Mans Classic meeting. Attwood scored the marque's first win at La Sarthe in 1970 in a 917, while Schuppan notably won the 24-Hours in 1983.

One of the highlights of Aussie Vern Schuppan's two decades at the top of the motorsport tree was his 1983 Le Mans victory. Yet, it so nearly did not happen…

On the face of it, things came gift-wrapped to Vern, like his 1983 Le Mans win when, despite the door of his Porsche 956 falling off, the car took the chequered flag and promptly expired 200 metres later. 'Those final ten minutes were possibly the most nerve-wracking I can ever recall,' laughs the action man, who did his own Le Mans repairs trackside. Vern's first taste of endurance racing was in 1972, although he did not actually drive for Porsche until 1981. 'I'd finished third at Indy in '81 with my own M24 McLaren, and I was formally asked by Porsche if I could drive a 936 at Le Mans. I said OK, and that was the start of it all.' In the meantime, Vern built an impressive record in endurance racing with the JW Automotive Gulf-Mirages in a strong driver line-up that included Ickx, Bell, Hailwood, Wisell, Watson, Jaussaud, Jarier, Schenken and Ganley. 'I'd had seven seasons in various versions of the Mirage from 1973 to 1979, and that was a very long stint,' he muses. Results manifested in third at Le Mans with Jaussaud in 1973, fifth in 1976 with Bell, and second in 1977 with Jarier. Vern's first full year with Porsche was 1982, and Weissach quickly gained a stranglehold. Vern was not involved with the development of the 956, though: 'It was already in the pipeline, and only Ickx and Bell did the testing. The first time I drove the car was at Le Mans in 1982, placing 2nd with Jochen Mass, and then I carried on driving in World Endurance races.'

Vern highlights the quantum leap between the tube-frame 936 Spyder and the closed, ground-effect 956:

> *There was a noticeable difference in cornering speed. The thing that struck you, apart from the ground-effects, was that the first 956's steering was very heavy. In fact, it was so heavy, combined with the ground-effects that, going through some high-speed corners, you wondered how the tyres could stay on the rims. Eventually, they redesigned the suspension geometry to get rid of that very heavy steering.*

Vern's finest hour at the wheel of a Porsche was Le Mans 1983, sharing a works Rothmans 956 with Americans Al Holbert and Hurley Haywood. They took the lead in the course of refuelling and were never headed thereafter. Ickx and Bell came second in the number one car, but fell foul of the stringent fuel consumption rules that bedevilled Group C's early years.

The 1983 Le Mans 24-Hours was won by Vern Schuppan, Al Holbert and Hurley Haywood in 956 #004, covering 3132.9 miles (5042km), averaging 130.7mph (210.34km/h). The following car is the 4.0-litre Cosworth V8-powered Brun Motorsport Sehcar, driven by Jacques Villeneuve, Ludwig Heimrath and David Deacon.

It was not quite a done deal, though. In the small hours, Vern's passenger door came adrift. 'It flew right off into the night,' he recalls dryly, 'which was alarming enough at maximum speed. But I also thought that the cabin could depressurise to the extent that the rear bodywork could let go, as well, so I spent a long and draughty six laps, circulating while they looked for a spare door so I could bring it into the pits and get a new one fitted.' The repair was quickly carried out, and he kept the lead. With about half an hour to go, he handed over the car to Al Holbert.

> *By that stage, it was a reasonable assumption regarding the finishing order for the top three cars, so the organisers came down to our pit and escorted Hurley and me to the podium tower. We were up there, watching the last few minutes on the monitor, and couldn't believe our eyes when we saw smoke coming from the left-hand exhaust. It dawned on me that, after leading for over nineteen hours, not only might we not win, but we might not even finish. I felt sick! But when Al crossed the line with a seized engine, just 50 seconds ahead of Bell and Ickx, it was total euphoria! Who cared that poor old Al couldn't enjoy the final parade lap: we were on cloud nine. But, it was a bit of a close call.*

For the rest of the decade, he raced factory Porsches and for Erwin Kremer internationally, bowing out with 13th at Le Mans in 1989 in his Team Schuppan 962 and serving as reserve driver for a couple of seasons thereafter.

TAKE IT TO THE LIMIT

Convinced of the potential market for road-going Group C cars, evidenced by the Jaguar XJ220, Vern geared up to take the 962 supercar into limited production and, in 1992, the Schuppan 962CR was announced. A fabulous, gaunt-looking car, with no decals to blur its purposeful lines, its chassis and carbon-fibre bodywork were produced independently by Schuppan, with final assembly at Modena Cars at High Wycombe. Power came from a detuned version of the race car's 600bhp IMSA-spec twin-turbo 3.3-litre flat-six, enabling 0–60mph in 3.5 seconds and a 230mph top speed.

In another time, another place, it might have taken off like the Ascari, Mosler, McLaren, Koenigsegg brigade, but worldwide recession doomed it as much as the $2m price tag – two Japanese buyers allegedly reneged on payment after delivery – and the project floundered with just five cars built.

Vern Schuppan, Hurley Haywood and Al Holbert won the 1983 Le Mans 24-Hours in 956 #004, despite losing its left-hand door in the closing stages, and a terminal oil leak on the last lap made it expire just 200m after crossing the finish line.

Teammates in the Rothmans Porsche squad at Le Mans 1987, Hans Stuck, Vern Schuppan and Derek Bell, ahead of the race. The Stuck/Bell/Holbert 962C #006 won, but the Schuppan/Wollek/Mass 962C #008 that started from pole failed to finish due to holed pistons caused by poor fuel quality.

SPICE OF LIFE

Having discarded their Tiga chassis, Spice Engineering were now building their own cars, two initially to the order of General Motors for the IMSA Camel Lights Championship. The resulting Spice Pontiac Fieros were out-and-out ground-effect machines and were constrained in terms of body shape to look at least a little like the production vehicle that they were named after, and this accounted for their rather dumpy slab-sided aspect, albeit with exceptionally low drag. The finished Fieros were sent to America ready for the installation of the 350bhp Super Duty Pontiac 3.0-litre engine. A third chassis was set aside for the Silverstone Company's defence of the WSPC C2 Championship by Gordon Spice and Ray Bellm and was built to take a 3.3-litre Cosworth DFL V8, a totally new design from the team who were busy developing the C285.02 and similar C286.03 during the winter of 1985–86. Spice was also turning a Tiga into the Lamborghini Countach V12 QVX for Portman Lamborghini.

The Spice Fiero SE86C was quick and competitive, but Ecurie Ecosse won the C2 Makes' title, while Spice and Bellm jointly won the C2 Drivers' championship. Ecosse boss Hugh McCaig decided to power the new C286 car with the relatively unknown quantity of the Austin-Rover V64V engine, which had been developed for the Group B Metro 6R4 rally car. Designed by ex-Cosworth employee David Wood, the V64V engine was a 90-degree V6 with four valves per cylinder (hence V64V) with belt-driven twin-overhead camshafts per bank producing 250bhp in 'Clubman' form or 410bhp in 'International' tune. It was the first-ever engine explicitly designed for rallying, and the project proved something of a white elephant in that Austin Rover Motorsport built 200 Metro 6R4s for Group B homologation, and at the end of 1986, FISA banned Group B supercars from the World Rally Championship, leaving the manufacturer with a lot of redundant high-tech rally cars in the company carpark. In a Group C2 context, the 3.0-litre V6 was never going to be a match for the Cosworth DFL V8s and turbo engines elsewhere in the class, but when installed in Ray Mallock's aerodynamic flat-bottomed design, the Ecosse won out on

The Spice SE86C was powered by the 3.3-litre Ford-Cosworth DFL, driven to 14th place by Gordon Spice and Ray Bellm at the 1986 Silverstone 1,000km.

PORSCHE 961 GTX

An interesting one-off was the experimental Porsche 961 GTX four-wheel-drive car, which ran at both Le Mans test day and the race itself. It was based on the steel monocoque of the production 959 supercar that had originally been intended for GTO Group B homologation. The car was now mooted as the prototype for a series production of IMSA GTO customer cars that the works was planning. This plan did not ultimately come to fruition, but this sole example ran well in the 24-Hours, finishing 7th, driven by René Métge and Claude Ballot-Lena, and took the GTX class. The crew felt that if it had rained, the 961 would have been a contender for overall honours, but it did not, so it was not.

The Porsche 961 was the racing derivative of the roadgoing 959 Supercar, given chassis number #WP0ZZZ93ZFS010016 and powered by the twin KKK turbocharged 2849cc Type 961/70 F6 4v DOHC flat-six. Driven at Le Mans 1986 by Claude Ballot-Léna and René Metge, it came 7th overall and 1st in the GTX class, 47 laps behind the winner.

In the pitlane during 1989 Le Mans is the Spice-Fiero SE86C of John Hotchkis, John Hotchkis Jr and Richard Jones, powered by the Hart 418T 1873cc S4 turbo, which succumbed to an oil leak at 86 laps.

top speed and fuel economy. Ecosse C286.03 – dubbed 'Reggie' – ran well throughout 1986, and scored four class wins by season's end. The older C285.02 DFL-powered car ran once at Le Mans and scored points for the team there driven by a trio of North Americans.

This turned out to be a bonus in terms of points because Mike Wilds crashed the newer car in the middle of the night, though it was repaired, and then was crashed again by David Leslie, repaired again and subsequently disqualified for allegedly receiving outside assistance.

Team ADA had another good year with their Gebhardt wing car and led the championship for the latter half of the season, losing out at the last round in Fuji to both Ecosse and Spice by having to conserve fuel. The car had been rebuilt over the winter with a new suspension system designed by former Fittipaldi designer Richard Divila, but their budget would not cover electronic engine management like the other front-runners. Nevertheless, Ian Harrower, Evan Clements and Tom Dodd-Noble scored a comfortable C2 win at Le Mans and came 8th overall. But, going into the crucial last round with a single point lead over Spice, and not even having a fuel gauge in the car, pursuing the Spice in vain all afternoon in the burning heat of Jerez, they ended up with 2nd place.

The other works Gebhardt Cosworth took C2 wins at Monza and the Norisring during the early part of the season driven by Frank Jelinski and Stanley Dickens. Roy Baker persevered with his Tiga GC285 and GC286 VDT turbos. He did not have much of a budget, but for a while, he was running three cars, renting out cars to pay drivers, of whom the best was Thorkild Thyrring. Chamberlain Engineering joined the WSPC with a Tiga TS85 that had run for a year in the British ThunderSports Series, fitted with a roll-cage and roof to turn it into a C2 car, powered by an F2 1.8-litre Hart four-cylinder turbo engine. In the hands of Will Hoy, this car was extremely quick but proved unreliable.

FUTURE SHOCK

FISA's original twelve-race series turned out to be nine rounds. Four races disappeared from the calendar, replaced by a single 360-kilometre sprint race at Jerez, and there were two other sprints, the Monza 360 kilometres and the Norisring 180 kilometres. All nine rounds counted towards the Drivers' championships in C1 and C2, but only Silverstone, Le Mans, Nürburgring, Spa-Francorchamps and Fuji were qualifying rounds for the Teams' title.

THE LONG-DISTANCE RUNNER

In the cabin of a 935K3 at the 2014 Goodwood Festival of Speed, John Fitzpatrick's career is almost entirely synonymous with Porsche, with several titles to his credit earned in 911 derivatives during the 1970s. Between 1981 and 1984, he managed his own Group C and IMSA GTP Racing team, running 956s and a 962.

One of the Skoal Bandit-sponsored 956s, that of Guy Edwards and Rupert Keegan (left), poised in the pits ahead of the start of the 1984 Silverstone 1,000km, in which it finished 3rd.

One Group C exponent whose career transcended several epochs, including IMSA, is John Fitzpatrick, founder of the eponymous Fitzpatrick Racing Team. From tin-top title-winner in a Ford Anglia in 1966, John Fitzpatrick forged a great career in BMWs, works Fords and Porsche 911 RSRs, winning the European Touring Car Championship in 1972 and '74 driving for Kremer Racing. By the end of the 1970s, he had joined Georg Loos's GELO Racing, handling 935s in IMSA and the WSCC. Assisted by Kremer, he formed his own team in 1981, running the 935K4. But it is his involvement in Group C and IMSA with 956s and 962s that earns his place here.

Fitz moved to San Diego in 1980 to drive for Dick Barbour Motorsport. 'That first season I won the IMSA championship and the Porsche Cup, driving his 935.' Fitz was also fastest in practice at Le Mans that year and ran a commanding race, partnered by Barbour and Brian Redman, finishing 5th overall after engine problems late in the race. Unexpectedly, Dick Barbour shut up shop at the end of 1980, leaving Fitz with four years of his contract left to run. He took the plunge and assumed Barbour's Sachs sponsorship to go it alone. 'I bought my own car – a 935 – and ran my own team in California till '86. Guys like David Hobbs drove with me a lot and Derek Bell did the odd race.'

Fitz never quite managed to win Le Mans outright, but nevertheless, the 24-hour enduro is a consistent barometer of car and driver performance. Fitzpatrick and David Hobbs finished 4th overall in 1982 in the tube-frame 935 IMSA/GTX car. The following year Fitz got a new sponsor, the US tobacco firm Skoal Bandit, which backed him for a couple of years.

The team was running 956 and 962 Group C cars by now and had a base at Silverstone from which to cover European races. In chassis 956/102, Fitzpatrick, Guy Edwards and Rupert Keegan placed 5th overall at Le Mans 1983, the car proving thirstier at 50 litres per 100km than the works Rothmans 956s that returned 44 litres per 100kms. Fitz recalls:

> *One of the highlights was the 1,000km at Brands Hatch in '83 when Derek and I beat all the Rothmans cars fair and square. This very rarely happened because they had Hans Stuck and Jacky Ickx. It was wet but our tyres were better.*

A long racing career like Fitz's has its share of highs and lows, and the team was devastated by the death of one of his oldest associates. 'Rolf Stommelen was killed in one of my cars at Riverside in April '83, which was pretty heavy and put a damper on the whole thing.' Their friendship went back to 1965, but the Riverside Six Hours was the first time the German had driven for him. Paired with Derek Bell in one of the tube-frame Jöst-built 935s, Stommelen started from the front row, but halfway through the race when lying 2nd, the rear bodywork came loose, pitching the car sharp left into the barriers at close to

The 956 of John Fitzpatrick and David Hobbs is fettled in the Silverstone pitlane ahead of the 1983 1,000km, when it finished 8th.

200mph. Bell and Hobbs won the race in Fitzpatrick's other 935 without knowing that Stommelen had died in hospital. At the end of the season, Fitz stopped driving to concentrate on running the team.

High placings demonstrated how good Fitzpatrick Racing were. Their 956 came 3rd at Le Mans in 1984 crewed by Hobbs, Philippe Streiff and Sarel Van der Merwe, and in 1985 the 956B placed 5th at La Sarthe with Hobbs, Edwards and rising star Jo Gartner at the helm. The following year, Fitzpatrick Racing entered two cars in the French epic. The 4th-placed 956 ran under the Danone Porsche España banner with Emilio de Villota, Fermin Velez and George Fouché driving and Philippe Alliot, Paco Romero and Michel Trollé handled the 10th-placed 962C. And that was about it. The writing had been on the wall for a couple of seasons.

My sponsors went over to F1 because for the money it cost to do a season in Group C – $2–3 million a year – you could get on the back of the F1 grid for the same amount. So I spent a couple of years picking up sponsors here and there and then decided to knock it on the head. I sold the cars and everything else at the end of '86.

Fitz handled the Group C cars often enough to know them inside out:

We bought and sold five cars over three or four years, two 956s and then three 962s. The 956s were fabulous cars. They did everything well, everything was good and reliable from a private entrant's point of view. You couldn't really tell the difference between the 956 and 962. The 962 had a slightly longer wheelbase so it was never quite as good as the 956. The short-tailed version, the high-downforce version of the 956, was more driveable than the 962, no question about that, but they changed the rules so you had to have the driver's feet behind the front wheels. The year Derek won the World Endurance Championship for Porsche, it wasn't just the long races that counted; some of the short ones, like the Norisring, counted too. He was neck and neck with Stuck and Bellof for the title, but Porsche weren't doing that race. So, he took my third car to the Norisring and he got one or two crucial points which won him the World Championship.

Fitz's favourite car is a special 935 built by his own team.

I bought a K5 from the Kremers, which was one of two tube-frame cars they made, took it to the States and completely rebuilt it. I used it in IMSA and beat the GTP prototypes. It had a 3.5-litre twin-turbo intercooled engine, and on full boost it had 950 horsepower. We used to run 750–800bhp all the time and it had fantastic downforce. Of the Porsche customer race cars, the 956 was a sensational car, and the RSR was great back in the '70s. They were all very nice, good handling and reliable. Porsche were conservative with their race cars; they had great designs but they never developed them right to the limit, it was the private owners who tended to take them that little bit further. Reinhold Jöst was one of those. He'd get a new car from Porsche, strip it down and start again because, being near the factory, he had a lot of factory mechanics who worked for him at the weekends so he'd get all the right bits.

John regrets giving up front-line racing when he did, given that some contemporaries carried on for at least the rest of the decade, but he is nevertheless still very much a presence on the historic racing scene.

Fitzpatrick Racing's 935 Kremer K5, driven by Bob Wollek, John Graham, Hugo Gralia, Preston Henn and Al Holbert, started 6th and finished 6th in the IMSA GTP Sebring 12-Hours, 1984.

Rounding La Source hairpin at Spa-Francorchamps, the 962C of Hans Stuck and Derek Bell came 3rd in the 1986 1,000km.

The concept of including sprint format races was proposed by the entrants' organisation, OSCAR, who theoretically put it forward as an effective way of making sportscar racing more marketable and attractive to the public. Despite an adverse reaction from the punters, FISA persevered with refining the format, and it became clear that this was a harbinger of the way the championship would be heading, and, as it turned out, 1986 was a pivotal year in the history of Group C. In October, FISA put forward their own proposals, which actually amounted to a diktat for a wholesale restructuring of the regulations, and which provoked an immediate response of anger and frustration from the teams, not specifically because of the content, but because it seemed that FISA had already made up its mind without any consultation with the entrants – a measure of how seriously OSCAR was taken by FISA. The broad content of FISA's proposals was to scrap the original concept of Group C entirely – based on fuel regulations, ground-effects, and aerodynamic devices – and the teams were not impressed. So powerful was their reaction that FISA was forced to enter into discussions, and eventually, a think-tank was set up to stabilise the rules while at the same time phasing in reasonable and positive changes.

There were no such problems in the USA, where IMSA was running sportscar racing as a benign dictatorship, with no significant upheavals implemented in 1986, apart from reining in the ultra-successful Porsche 962s. The main impact of this was felt by Porsche works representative Al Holbert and privateers using the 962. In 1985, most teams had been using the 3.2-litre Andial-tuned engine, which had been developed in America, and it was largely this that made the 962 so dominant, winning all but one round. In 1986, those wishing to carry on using the Andial 3.2-litre engine carried an extra weight penalty of 43 kilogrammes, but the 962s remained the pace of the field, with Al Holbert Racing winning six of the seventeen races, including the Daytona 24-Hours, and Holbert lifting the Drivers' crown for the second year running, and his usual co-driver Derek Bell finishing third. Of the private Porsche teams, Rob Dyson's was the most successful, taking three wins with Price Cobb behind the wheel at Riverside, Charlotte and Sears Point.

CHAPTER 4

JAGUAR JAMBOREE 1986–89

In 1987, Tom Walkinshaw's Jaguar XJRs finally came good, but on the other hand, it was not a particularly good year if you happened to be racing in Group C running anything other than a Kidlington-built Jaguar. Jaguar easily won the Teams' championship, and its drivers filled the first four slots in the Drivers' Championship, with Raoul Boesel taking the top spot. The XJR-8 followed on from the XJR-6 used in the 1985–86 seasons and was designated the XJR-8 because the XJR-7 nomenclature was already applied to the Jaguar IMSA GTP race car by Group 44. After extensive winter development, the XJR-8 was packed with upgrades to maximise performance and combat previous reliability issues. The most notable change was an even larger 7.0-litre V12 engine, which pushed power output up to 720bhp. There were also some minor modifications to the bodywork, as well as a revised Silk Cut livery. TWR-Jaguar had found the right balance with the XJR platform, winning the WEC with the XJR-8s scoring eight wins, including victories on home turf at both Silverstone and Brands Hatch. However, there was one fly in the ointment: the XJR-8s did not succeed at Le Mans, which was probably the most important race of the season for the Silk Cut team, which had its sights set on scoring the first Jaguar Le Mans win since 1957. In C2, Spice narrowly beat Ecurie Ecosse to the 1987 Teams' title, head and shoulders ahead of the rest. Also in C2, Tim Lee-Davey continued working with the Terry Hoyle-prepared Cosworth DFL turbo engine, now concentrating on using the new Tiga GC87 chassis, which was not ready until late in the year, so that he was obliged to rent a drive in John Bartlett's Bardon C2 at Le Mans.

In 1987, Porsche originally intended to run only a restricted programme of WSPC races for the works cars. By Monza, they had changed their minds and said that they would now compete with a two-car team for the rest of the year. So, it was even more stunning when they dropped a bombshell at the Norisring, announcing the immediate cancellation of any further regular works participation in the Championship and leaving the task of beating off the Jaguar challenge to the private Porsche teams. The only real relief from the Silk Cut Jaguar whitewash in 1987 was Baldi/Palmer's win for Brittan-Lloyd Racing in the 962 at the Norisring, and at Le Mans, where Bell, Stuck and Holbert triumphed in the factory 962C, with Lässig/Yver/De Dryver in 2nd for Obermaier, with Raphanel/Ragout/Courage 3rd in the Porsche-engined Cougar C20-01, and Kremer's 962C of Fouche/Konrad/Taylor 4th, and the sole remaining Jaguar out of the three entered finished a distant 5th. Weissach had certainly proved the durability of their creations, but the now old 962 design was lacking in outright speed compared with the Silk Cut Jaguars. At season's end, TWR topped the Teams' listings with 178 points, with Porsche squads filling the next five slots.

On the grid ahead of the 1987 Spa-Francorchamps 1,000km, Volker Weidler, Franz Konrad (reserve driver), and Kris Nissen share a joke. Their Thompson-chassis'd Kremer Racing 962C #110CK did not finish due to an accident on lap 78.

CALLING TIME

Porsche's reasons for retiring from the series were diverse. Weissach's hard-pressed racing department was focused on three separate strands of development, starting with the design and construction of the TAG Techniques d'Avant Garde F1 engine for McLaren's title-winning MP4 series; then, designing and developing an IndyCar challenger based on a March chassis for the CART series, plus servicing Group C and IMSA customers. Keeping a weather eye on its commercial markets and recognising that the most media exposure was to be had from competing successfully in F1, it was the Group C 962Cs that they pulled the plug on. Additionally, FISA's vacillation surrounding Group C, manifested in its proposals at the end of 1986 to effectively scrap the Group C formula, did not impress Porsche, even though they were probably best equipped to deal with these vagaries. So, when Jaguar started dominating the early part of the 1987 series, it seemed a perfect time for Porsche to withdraw gracefully. Also complicating matters for the teams was the full implementation of the IMSA-style foot box regulations, which at a stroke made the 956 obsolete. This led directly to teams such as Kremer building new cars on John Thompson's TC Prototype 962 honeycomb-cloned monocoque instead of buying the standard sheet-aluminium Porsche version.

There was also a ban on aromatic fuel additives, such as toluenes, and a mandatory reversion to commercial-grade fuels of no more than 97 octane. This ban, which took effect on 1 January, caused most teams problems. However, it had a particularly devastating effect at Le Mans, where a spate of piston failures wiped out half the Porsche fleet in the first hour of racing. This was initially blamed on the allegedly poor-quality fuel supplied by the AC de l'Ouest, but the survivors' stops to change to a different Motronic engine management chip indicated that Porsche had been caught up in events. Porsche's withdrawal was not potentially the bad news it might have seemed for its clients, and might even have been considered a boon, since the factory, guided by Jürgen Barth, still provided full customer support. Immediately after Le Mans, the 3.0-litre, fully water-cooled, flat-six engine that the Rothmans cars had been using in 1986 became available for purchase. Most teams chose this option for their first-string cars, although Obermaier Racing was a notable exception.

Paradoxically, Brittan-Lloyd Racing, formerly Richard Lloyd Racing and GTI Engineering, were the only Porsche-equipped team to score a victory while still using the standard 2.8-litre unit at the Norisring, and this, after having had to completely rebuild 962-106B when it burned out two weeks earlier at Le Mans. Overall, Brun Motorsport had the most successful year in terms of points, although they were matched at most venues by Jöst, who had a string of top-five placings in the second half of the season after a poor first half. Missing from the Porsche ranks, incidentally, was John Fitzpatrick Racing, which withdrew from the championship at the end of 1986.

NEW JAGUAR POWER PLANT

TWR's engine division, led by Alan Scott, had now refined the stock block Jaguar V-12 to such an extent that they were able to equip the sophisticated carbon-fibre chassis XJR-8 with a larger, by 695cc, power plant, using a long-stroke

The Liqui Moly Equipe 962C #106B came 2nd in the 1987 Brands Hatch 1,000km, driven by Mauro Baldi and Johnny Dumfries.

Pictured during practice for the 1987 Silverstone 1,000km, the 7.0-litre Jaguar XJR-8 that would take the win was driven by Eddie Cheever and Raul Boesel.

The victorious 7.0-litre Jaguar XJR-8 #TWR-J12C-287 of Raul Boesel and John Nielsen heads Kremer Racing's John Thompson's Thompson Composites chassis 962C, driven to 6th place at Brands Hatch by Kris Nissen and Volker Weidler.

Kouros Racing's Sauber-Mercedes C9 5.0-litre V8 was driven to 7th place at the 1987 Spa 1,000km by Mike Thackwell and Jean-Louis Schlesser.

crankshaft of 99mm bore and 84mm stroke, instead of the earlier 78mm stroke. The result was additional torque, which meant less gear shifting and lower fuel consumption. The new engine only gave an extra fifteen to twenty brake horsepower at peak revs, but 45bhp lower down the rev range where the power was mostly needed. This, combined with some 64 changes to the complete package including chassis, engine, aerodynamics and a new Dunlop Kevlar carcass tyre, was the key to Jaguar's success. In addition, TWR developed a specific Le Mans project car, the XJR-8LM, endowed with low drag, short-tail bodywork, and a compromise on the usual high-downforce underbody aerodynamics. This was tested on chassis #186 at the Silverstone 1,000km and on the Le Mans test day before the 24-Hours, where it performed surprisingly similarly to the standard configuration. TWR's regular drivers for the season were Raoul Boesel, Eddie Cheever, John Nielsen, Martin Brundle, Jan Lammers and John Watson, joined by Win Percy and Johnny Dumfries occasionally. Percy was unlucky enough to validate the inherent strength of Tony Southgate's chassis design when he ran over some debris on the Mulsanne Straight, burst a tyre, and was launched airborne into the woods. The car was a mess, with all four corners and most of the bodywork missing, but Win Percy emerged unscathed, and the monocoque was barely damaged.

After providing one of the big shocks of 1986 by winning the rain-drenched Nürburgring race, Peter Sauber's lightly blown, 5.0-litre, Mercedes-powered cars were now running in C9 trim, based on the same Leo Ress designed, bonded sheet-aluminium monocoque, still backed by Kouros Aftershave. The cars now had improved torsional stiffness and better ground-effects and were using the experimental Motronic 1.7 engine management system. Sauber prepared two cars, both of which ran at Le Mans, with Johnny Dumfries going well in practice and the early part of the race, and taking the lap record in the process. However, Sauber was limited by finances to doing just five rounds of the championship and was plagued by transmission failures, never featuring when the flag fell. Dumfries, Thackwell, Pescarolo, Heidi Okada and Chip Ganassi shared driving duties.

ENCOURAGING MOVE

Yves Courage took his Cougar-Porsche 2.6t up a step, in C20 trim, to record 3rd place at his final outing of the year at Le Mans in June. It was a decent reward for the Le Mans garage owner's small team and his loyal sponsor, Primagaz. Designed by Alain Touchas, the conventional sheet-aluminium monocoque was well prepared and performed

Powered by the VG30ET 3.0-litre twin-turbo V6, the NISMO-entered Nissan R85V of Takao Wada, Masahiro Hasemi and James Weaver came 16th at Le Mans in 1986.

On the grid for the Spa-Francorchamps 1,000km in 1987 is the Spice SE86C, driven to 10th place overall and 1st in C2 by Fermín Vélez and Gordon Spice.

well at Monza and Silverstone before its short season ended in France.

Other contenders at Le Mans included WM-Peugeot; Nissan – via NISMO Nissan Motorsports – with their V8 March 87G, also using one of the 1986 V6-powered March 86G Nissans; Toyota with the Dome-built 87C; and Mazda, the latter winning the IMSA. The Japanese makers naturally took in the Fuji round as well but spent most of the year concentrating on their national Group C championship. There was also another incarnation of the Porsche 961 four-wheel-drive prototype, now in Rothmans' colours. Its potential development into a series-production GT racer for IMSA was abruptly shattered when Kees Nierop crashed and burned out the car on the Sunday morning. It is currently resident in the Porsche Museum.

Frenchman Noël DiBello bought an ex-works Sauber-Mercedes C8, chassis 86C 802, raced at Le Mans in 1986 by Thackwell and Nielsen, and competed three times without success. Meanwhile, Gianni Massato reconstructed his Lancia LC2-86.003 from the previous year's Zeltweg Interserie wreck, designating it as 003B. He took it to Norisring and Kyalami, with Bruno Giacomelli driving. Richard Cleare took his IMSA March-Porsche 85G to Silverstone for its last international outing, and James Weaver and Andrew Gilbert-Scott won the GTP class and came 9th overall.

SPICED UP

Using the same SE86C chassis 001 that had been campaigned in 1986, and later, a new SE87C 003, Gordon Spice and new co-driver, Fermín Vélez, jointly won the C2 Drivers' title, Spice for the third consecutive year, and the Teams' title after a protracted struggle with the Ecosse outfit. The cars were still known as Spice Fieros, in deference to their original patron, General Motors, who had commissioned the design from Spice Engineering as a silhouette version of the Pontiac Fiero for General Motors' assault on the IMSA Camel Lights Championship. The C2 version even sported Pontiac logos embossed on the bodywork behind the cabin. But unlike the Camel Lights cars, which ran with the 3.0-litre Pontiac engine, the works C2 used a standard Cosworth 3.3-litre DFL power unit. Spice and Vélez contested all ten constituent rounds, joined at Le Mans by the Franco-Swiss fashion designer Count Philippe de Henning with his Dianetics Scientology sponsorship. Later in the year, De Henning also drove the Charles Ivey Tiga GC287 Porsche and featured again in the Spice at Kyalami after Costas Los had sold his Tiga GC287 Cosworth and purchased the Le Mans C2-winning car. Los and De Henning won the C2 class at the non-championship Kyalami race at the end of November and took 2nd in the C2-only event there the following weekend. The other Spice chassis in the series was Hugh Chamberlain's freshly built SEH6C.002, into which a sleeved-down version of the Brian Hart 420 Formula 2 engine was installed, turbocharged by a single Holset turbo. The 418T four-cylinder made the Chamberlain Spice a potent machine, particularly when in the hands of Nick Adams, who ran the factory version close during the early laps at its Monza debut until sidelined by a blown turbo. Adams then led C2 at Silverstone until punted out by Arenberg's Porsche. He then took class pole at Le Mans and finally finished unclassified after several problems.

NORWEGIAN WOOD

Norwegian rallycross star Martin Schanche's Lucky Strike-sponsored Argo JM19B Zakspeed, with Will Hoy co-driving, notched up seven C2 pole positions in nine events. However, the team was dogged by mechanical failure and a couple of race-ending shunts, such as at Le Mans, when Schanche went backwards into the Dunlop Chicane barriers during the first hour due to a puncture. By the following season, the team switched from Zakspeed to DFL power. Also swapping engines, Hugh McCaig's Ecurie Ecosse team lost the engine deal with a disinterested Austin-Rover Group and embraced the Ford-Cosworth DFL. That meant C285.02, known as 'Henry', the 1985/'86 DFL car was pensioned off, and C86.03, nicknamed 'Reggie' was converted to Cosworth V8 power, while a completely new C286.04 DFL, called 'Pat', a tidied-up and lightened version of the same design was built by Ray Mallock, the latter winning its first race at Silverstone. Both 'Pat' and 'Reggie' raced in cheery SwiftAir Royal Mail colours for the remainder of the season, with one more win at Brands Hatch, and Ecurie Ecosse then pulled out of the WSPC, joining forces with Aston Martin in the 1989 AMR1 C1 project.

The Ecosse C286 of Marc Duez and Mike Wilds is poised on the grid for the start of the 1987 Spa 1,000km. Mike Wilds (then bearded) leans against the pit wall Armco ahead of the fray, in which they finished a lap ahead of their Ecurie Ecosse teammates Ray Mallock and David Leslie.

BURNING BRIGHT

Tigas outnumbered every other make in the C2 class, and, remarkably, there were sometimes more Howden Ganley-built cars than Porsches on the grid. Despite this, it was a disappointing year for the marque, fraught with a series of broken suspensions and gear linkages. Costas Los had a tie-up with Roy Baker Racing early on, but soon moved on to Keith Greene and Dave Pruitt's newly formed team Cosmic GP Motorsport. Tiga racer Roy Baker was disenchanted with Ford BDT Turbos and swapped over to standard Cosworth DFL V8s. One of his GC2H6 chassis, #335, was sold off in BDT form at the start of the year, but he retained GC286.336, which he took to the first two Florida IMSA races at Daytona and Miami Beach. Towards the end of the season, Los elected to buy the works Spice SEH7C.003, only five races old, ready for 1988. Noted Porsche entrant Charles Ivey ran a similar Tiga, powered by a 956 engine, powerful but thirsty, driven by Tom Dodd-Noble, John Cooper, Max Cohen-Olivar, Philippe de Henning and John Sheldon, the latter ending the season with pole and fastest lap at Kyalami. Thorkild Thyrring's rally-engined Ford BDT-E turbo was backed by the Tiga works and ran in a detuned state for most of the year in the interests of fuel economy but was nevertheless dogged by mechanical mayhem. On the plus side, he ended up being the leading non-Spice or Ecosse driver in the final reckoning. Perennially short of funds, ADA had a setback when team owner Ian Harrower badly damaged the Gebhardt 843 DFL at Jerez. A new car, ADA 02, debuted at Brands Hatch, where Tiff Needell led the field early on, shadowed by Gordon Spice despite his screen becoming spattered in oil from the ADA's DFL engine, and Needell and Harrower retired later with its steering awry.

The season's final denouement was FISA's twelve-race series, which fizzled out after the scheduled Australian round was cancelled. A standalone sprint round planned as part of a Japanese double-header at the end of the calendar was also cancelled after the teams arrived in Japan, supposedly because of the lack of a circuit licence. For the first time, all rounds in the WSPC counted towards the drivers' and teams' titles in the C1 and C2 categories. However, for the Drivers' Championships, only the best seven scores were counted for the final totals. In the Teams' titles, all race scores were included at the end of the season.

THE GOLDEN ERA

With so many works teams and manufacturers represented, the 1988 Le Mans 24-Hours ranks for some as the pinnacle race from this golden era of sportscar racing. Porsches had won six consecutive Le Mans – that is every single one since the Group C category was introduced in 1982 – and going into 1988, they were still very much the marque to beat.

At this stage, Jaguar was still playing catch-up and even though its TWR-run cars had enjoyed significant success, victory at Le Mans had still eluded them. For 1988, they fielded a fleet of five V12 XJR-9s – a volume of cars harking back to the mid-1960s when there were as many as twelve Ford GT40s on the grid and almost as many Ferraris. Of course, there were also a great many Porsches lined up in 1988 – eleven at Le Mans that year. But it was not just the giants of Germany and Britain. The Japanese were also keen to get in on the action, and both Nissan and Toyota each sent a two-car team – not to mention the three-car Mazda team in the GTP class. In broad terms, 1988 was TWR-Jaguar's most successful year. After two earlier abortive attempts, they finally won Le Mans, which was always the main reason for the Jaguar marque's return to sportscar racing: capitalising on its 1950s heritage and gratifying the fans. Later, after a season-long struggle with the unexpectedly fast, reliable, and well-driven Sauber-Mercedes, they were able to retain both the Teams' and Drivers' titles, Martin Brundle winning the latter. The icing was laid on the cake at Le Mans.

The previous year, TWR's success had been achieved by almost completely dominating the championship from start to finish, and their loyal fans and the sport's cognoscenti gave them due credit. However, in terms of column inches, the 1987 performances were almost completely ignored in the media, and it was only when Jaguar scored its victory at Le Mans that the publicity machine went into overdrive. This confirmed just how essential the French enduro was, and always had been, to the continued health of the Championship, a point inexplicably lost on FISA during 1989 and 1990.

IDENTITY CRISIS

TWR had now also entered the IMSA fray, picking up where Group 44 left off. On both sides of the Atlantic, Tony Southgate's development of his original XJR-6/8 composite design now designated the XJR-9, was used. Similar though different power plants based on the same Coventry factory-made aluminium V12 block were used. As far as the chassis was concerned, evolution, not revolution, was the name of the game. The same basic configuration was in use pretty much as it had been in 1985. For example, the car placed 4th at Le Mans 1988, #TWR-J12C-186 was built at the start of 1986 as an XJR-6 and was kept as a training car for most of that season. It was wheeled out in anger a couple of times, though, and driven at Le Mans by Hans Heyer, Brian Redman and Hurley Haywood, retiring at 53 laps with low fuel pressure. Derek Warwick also drove it to 3rd place in the Norisring street race sprint. It was modified sufficiently over the following winter to qualify for a fresh chassis plate, designating it as an XJR-8 built in February 1987. In this identity, it had another quiet twelve months, with Brundle and Nielsen using it at Silverstone to test TWR's new Le Mans low-drag package, with the same pairing running it at Le Mans, going out at seven o'clock on the Sunday morning with a cracked cylinderhead. For 1988, #186 was reconfigured as an XJR-9 IMSA car, given yet another chassis plate, claiming it had been built in January 1987, but returning to Europe in June for another run at Le Mans in Group C trim, now helmed by Derek Daley, Kevin Kogan and Larry Perkins, and finishing 4th.

For the 1988 FISA series, fundamentally the same 7.0-litre engine that had been used in 1987 was installed, with the chassis lightened where possible and subtle changes to the exhaust system releasing more power and torque at a higher rev limit, developing 750bhp at 7,200rpm and producing over 600lb ft of torque at 5,500rpm. Seeking even more power for 1989, the four-valve heads were finally tried experimentally at the Brands Hatch 1,000km, producing 800bhp. However, as expected, the additional weight on top of the already top-heavy engines seriously affected handling. Nevertheless, Jaguar might have been forgiven for thinking that its defence of the WSPC crown would be reasonably straightforward, since Porsche was now out of the picture with Weissach concentrating on the IndyCar CART project and their committed privateers also beginning to struggle with a six-year-old design.

IMSA RUNNERS

Despite now enjoying official Mercedes-Benz works status, Sauber still had not done enough on a regular basis to command respect. So, there were some raised eyebrows at Kidlington when the Swiss-German team snatched the first round at Jerez and then proceeded to harass the Silk Cut cars for the remainder of the year. Despite this, and being well beaten on several occasions by Sauber-Mercedes,

TWR-Jaguar and its vast array of driving talent – including Brundle, Lammers, Nielsen, Cheever, Wallace, Dumfries, Watson, Boesel, plus guest appearances by Price Cobb, Larry Perkins, Derek Daley, Danny Sullivan, Henri Pescarolo, and Davy Jones – were able to sweep aside the Porsche 962s and to finally withstand Peter Sauber's AEG-sponsored onslaught for the new IMSA season. Changes to the regulations had reduced the maximum displacement of GTP Group I engines from the 7,000cc that had been permissible in 1987 to 6,000cc. This regulation change was announced very late in the day, causing frustration at Kidlington, where they had anticipated being able to use a virtually unchanged Group C engine. To meet the revised regulations, TWR's engine division produced a unit based on the same basic block, sharing as many common components as possible with the Group C version. This was done to extract maximum power from the smaller displacement and the unlimited and higher-octane fuel that was allowed. Engine Division manager Allan Scott concentrated on gaining higher revs, using a short stroke, 72-millimetre crankshaft, titanium conrods, a repro profile camshaft, and a higher 13.5:1 compression ratio. This enabled a 7,800rpm rev limit, with maximum power of 670bhp, coming in at 7,500rpm, with maximum torque of 536lb ft at 6,250rpm. This, and the sophisticated aerodynamics and high downforce of the chassis-body package that had been refined over the previous two WSPC seasons, meant that the XJR-9 GTPs were immediately competitive and generally able to overpower the Porsche 962, which until then had been the pacesetter of the IMSA championship.

Leaning on his TWR Jaguar XJR-8, Eddie Cheever does a grid interview ahead of the 1987 Spa-Francorchamps 1,000km, where he and John Nielsen finished 4th.

PORSCHE MARKS TIME

None of the Porsche teams had much to cheer about in 1988, and the Holbert Racing Team suffered a hammer blow when Al Holbert was killed in a light aircraft accident when flying into the race at Columbus, Ohio, in October. Holbert's team was dissolved soon after that. Nevertheless, the sheer weight of 962 numbers made up for the paucity of victories and despite being unable to match the Jaguars and Nissans for pace, their proven durability and consistent point-scoring finishes paid off for Weissach, amazingly allowing them to retain the World Championship for Makes again. Indeed, most of the interest lay with the Porsche teams, who made up for the shortfalls in the ageing 962 design by developing ingenious aerodynamic and electromechanical refinements for the growing number of clones and factory-made chassis. Most of the big teams had at least one of the more rigid honeycomb clone monocoques, mostly fabricated by John Thompson TC Prototypes. The major exceptions were Jöst, who stuck faithfully to factory tubs, possibly because they were being groomed to take on a quasi-works role the following year, and Obermaier, who already had a factory chassis and insufficient money or reason to change. Richard Lloyd Racing built its own honeycomb chassis and, having sold off a spare to Rob Dyson in America to raise funds, was ready for the new season with an all-new car with super-slippery melted-jelly-style bodywork. Unfortunately, its main sponsor withdrew only days before the start of the championship, which obliged it to restrict its schedule to a limited number of races.

Both Kremer and Brun tried major aerodynamic changes throughout the year, but the basic bodywork configuration was usually found to be the best for the majority of venues.

GERMAN MOTORSPORT LEGEND

Over a good-humoured lunch in a Frankfurt restaurant in 2012, Hans-Joachim 'Strietzel' Stuck described his days as a Porsche 956 and 962 test driver and racer.

Two-time Le Mans winner Hans-Joachim Stuck was a key player in Porsche's domination of the FIA World Sportscar Championship during the 1980s.

He is unusually tall for a professional racer, fast-talking, cheerful and unfailingly enthusiastic with a twinkle in his eye. He began racing in 1969, aged eighteen, following in his famous father's tyre tracks graduating from touring cars to Formula 2 and Formula 1 in 1975.

In 1984, Hans joined the Swiss entrant Walter Brun when he bought a Porsche 956.

My first race with Brun was the Spa 1,000km with Harald Gröhs, and we came 3rd. That was the start of my third career in motorsport. Walter Brun gave me the chance to drive the customer Porsche and I won in Imola with Stefan Bellof. I thought that Porsche was a cool car, and I knew Stefan was on the way to a full-time contract with Tyrrell, so I called Professor Bott (Dr Helmuth Bott was Head of Development at Porsche) and said, 'I am free for the next year so maybe I can drive for Porsche,' and he said, 'I thought you had a lifetime BMW contract!' So, I went to see him and within ten minutes we made a handshake agreement for racing.

Hans speaks warmly of his 'third career'.

I learned so much in my years with Peter Falk, and having Derek Bell as teammate was like heaven on earth. Nobody could beat Porsche as they were so perfect with their preparation, with their development and on-track race strategy. He had a major role at Weissach, signing off every customer 962 they built. Absolutely fantastic! Peter Falk calculated that I was the driver who'd clocked up the most kilometres in track time with Porsche 956 and 962 because I did almost all the testing in Weissach. I did so many kilometres. Sometimes I was asked to do a 500km test and at 3 o'clock the mechanics would fill up my car with 90 minutes left and then go home, and then it would be just me and the ambulance and the fire tender there, and I would finish the test, put the car in the workshop, close the door and drive home! They just left me to it!

With a few exceptions, every 962 produced after 1984 was signed off at Weissach by Hans.

From late November '84, I drove all the cars on the track at Weissach. I didn't have any influence on the construction of the chassis, because they built chassis after chassis with the same hand-riveted system. No customer car left the premises without having a shakedown, which was my job as I was the only driver living close to Stuttgart. I was living in Garmisch at the time, which was two hours away, but Jochen Mass was in South Africa, Derek was in England and Wollek was in France, so I was the closest one available. For the amount of kilometres I was doing I was very lucky. I had some big crashes too but always to the back of the car. Crashing with the front meant you were history. Gartner, Bellof, Winkelhock – they were unlucky.

One of his biggest rivals was Kremer Racing:

I drove for them only once, and it was sort of a one-off deal because it was the first 962 'convertible'! They cut the roof off, so it was an open-top 962 Spyder, and I drove it at Le Mans in '88 with Dominic Lacaud. I raced against Kremer, of course, and we met on the weekends regularly, and it was funny because there were two or three of these main actors in Germany – Kremer, Jöst, Brun, Obermaier, Loos, running private race teams – and Kremer was very innovative, he made and adapted a lot of things.

Hans also highlights the fundamental difference between the 956 and 962:

In the 956 the pedals were ahead of the front axle line, and for safety reasons, they had to move the pedals behind the axle line. This is why the 962 was 10cm longer. That was it.

The IMSA version of the 962 used a single turbocharger. 'There was much longer throttle lag and then an explosion of power like the BMW 320tc touring car. The sound was nicer though. Power output was a little higher in the single turbo version as it used a bigger turbocharger and could handle a bit more boost.'

In 1984 there were one-off outings in a Porsche 944 Turbo and a 935.

Jürgen Bath who was Porsche's customer sports representative called and said that Bob Akin was looking for a driver in IMSA, and this was my first race for him. And the 935 is like a hammer, as it has a very light front end with only the gas tank, and the engine's at the far back. It was such a difference between empty and full tank: when the tank was full the handling was nice, when it was empty it was terrible. It was a fantastic car, the engine, the brakes and so on, but it was a bugger to drive, I tell you!

It's a generation thing, but most racers who have experienced them cite either the 917 or the 962 as their favourite Porsche. Hans is no exception:

The 962 was a good configuration, and the combination of downforce, tyre width and power was the best I had ever driven. Those things had so much to give. The faster you made a corner, the more downforce you got. That was down to Norbert Singer's design. Underneath the front of the car was a bubble and this created the suction. This bubble accelerated the air beneath the car and the diffuser in the back sucked the car onto the ground. One of the greatest moments was having a Porsche 962 in 750bhp qualifying set-up, with qualifying tyres and full wing. The only car that had more downforce was in Formula 1 in 1979 when we had the ATS wing car, but this was more like a cannonball as nobody knew whether the sliding skirts would work or whether they would jam.

No surprise that the Nürburgring Nordschleife is Hans's favourite European circuit. He rationalises his next choice because it's not been 'Tilkered':

My second favourite is Sebring in Florida because it is fast and has not been destroyed by punishing chicanes and tarmac run-offs. The new circuits like Malaysia, Shanghai or Dubai (where he won a 24-hour race) are so boring. It's different times; you cannot land a jumbo jet on a grass strip, and you cannot do F1 at the Nordschleife, but the tracks that Hermann Tilke built do not require big balls any more. If you do something wrong and go onto the 50m tarmac run-off area like at Eau Rouge, if your turn-in doesn't work, you open up the throttle a bit more and go straight. But when you speak to guys like Montoya or Hamilton, they say it is nice, but the sheer driving pleasure was different when it was not like this.

He regards his two Le Mans wins (1986 and '87 with Bell and Holbert) and Sebring twice (1986, '88, Gartner, Akin and Ludwig) in a Porsche 962 as his greatest achievements. After taking part in the 2011 Nürburgring 24-Hours with his sons Ferdinand and Johannes in a Lamborghini Gallardo P600, Hans declared time on an illustrious racing career, handing the baton to the next generation of Stuck racing drivers.

The winning 962C of Hans Stuck – at the wheel – Derek Bell and Al Holbert about to leave after a pit stop during 1986 Le Mans 24-Hours.

Kremer Racing's Porsche 962C of Harald Gröhs and Kris Nissen in the pitlane for the 1987 Silverstone 1,000km. It retired after 72 laps with engine failure.

Derek Bell in the 962C #010 he shared with Hans Stuck and Klaus Ludwig, which, but for a malfunctioning reserve fuel tank, would have won Le Mans 1988, instead of coming 2nd.

Most of the biggest aerodynamic changes were hidden from view, on the underbody layouts. The most radical advance, though, was a new release of Bosch Motronic management software, version 1.7, a prototype version of which had been developed on the Sauber Mercedes in 1987. This found its way onto the three Shell-sponsored factory Porsches, for what had originally been planned as the Works' sole excursion into the championship in 1988.

LAST ORDERS

So, 962 #010 was the last works 962C to be built; it was not a repainted '87 Rothmans car but a brand-new chassis full of trick lightweight parts and a special high boost engine giving out 880bhp, and constructed specifically to win Le Mans in 1988. Driven by Hans Stuck, Derek Bell and Klaus Ludwig, in qualifying, Stuck's lap of 3min 15.6sec was 3.0 seconds clear of #007 in second place. With the race seemingly under control, #010 ran out of fuel under Ludwig's tenure, because the ten-litre reserve did not operate. Klaus managed to jerk the car back to the pits cranking it on the starter motor. Even so, it seemed possible they might actually win because it then started to rain, which meant that fuel consumption was not an issue, enabling the Porsche to challenge Lammers, who was leading in the XJR-9LM – with only 4th gear available to him as the Jaguar's transmission faltered. Hans Stuck was at the wheel of the 962C by now, and while everyone else dived into the pits for wet tyres, Hans stayed out on slicks. However, the rain abated, and so #010 finished second – amazingly on the same lap as Lammers/Dumfries/Wallace's winning Jaguar.

At the same time, Weissach borrowed Nissan's idea of electronic control of the turbocharger wastegate and applied it to the now fully water-cooled 3.0-litre flat-six engines. Both innovations substantially increased horsepower without any apparent loss of fuel economy. Strangely, however, they were not released to the private teams until well after the French Marathon, a possible tactical error that could have cost the German cars their chance of winning the Le Mans classic.

Unexpectedly, the Porsche Works team attempted another foray at Fuji, with a single car in Omron colours, chassis #008, possibly to bolster their score in the Teams' championship and make a showing in the all-important Japanese market. Other Porsche 962Cs were raced by Antoine Salamin, Jochen Dauer, Walter Lechner and Vern Schuppan, and a pair of Japanese-owned cars were at Fuji. At the start of 1988, Tim Lee-Davey carried on with his Tiga Cosworth DFL turbo concept, only to see it totalled in a conflagration at Brno. He then joined the mainstream and bought what he imagined would be the last 962 to be made, chassis #138, partly as an investment, although 962 production was subsequently restarted. In any event, for the first time in many years, Porsche failed to win a single round of the World Sportscar Championship. This left sporadic appearances by small, under-financed teams to make up the numbers. Jean-Pierre Frey's Dollop Racing Lancia LC2-003, acquired from Gianni Massato, ran at a few events, and Frey packed up after just one season. Yves Courage ran his Cougar-Porsches only at Monza and Le Mans, although at the all-nighter he brought two cars, a C-20 and a C-22. Also at Le Mans, Noël Del Bello returned briefly for a short season with his ex-works Sauber-Mercedes C8, and WM-Peugeot made their annual pilgrimage, Roger Dorchy's small amateur team fielding two of the Objectif-400 cars, the P-87 from the previous year, and a new P-88, both powered by Peugeot PRV twin-turbo 3.0-litre engines. Both were configured expressly to break the 400km/h record on the Mulsanne Straight, with the result that their handling was compromised almost everywhere else on the circuit. The older P-87 finally managed to hit the magic 400km/h during the mild Saturday evening with Roger Dorchy driving, after which the car underwent what cynics saw as its annual pitlane rebuild.

THE SUN ALSO RISES

Meanwhile, the Japanese manufacturers were making progress, although they refrained from contesting their cars in the whole championship arena. Both Toyota and Nissan were developing 3.0-litre 32-valve turbocharged engines, Nissan on the somewhat outdated March 87G chassis, and Toyota on a neat Dome-built honeycomb and carbon-fibre tub. With no direct challengers, Mazda carried on racing with the GTP 757 and 767, using three- and four-rotor Wankel engines. All three marques attended Le Mans, and Mazda won the GTP class with ease, getting all its cars over the line – 15th, 17th and 19th overall. Toyota chose the safe option at La Sarthe, and raced with older 2.1-litre 3S GTM, inline-four, single-turbo power plants. They finished 12th, while Nissan came 14th. At Fuji, it was the same story, with the result sheets dominated by TWR-Jaguar in 1st place (Cheever/Brundle) and a raft of 962s down to 8th place, broken up by a Sauber-Mercedes C9 (Mass/Acheson/Schlesser) in 5th.

SAUBER GOES BIG-TIME

12 January 1988 was a momentous day for the Sauber équipe because the Daimler-Benz board made a landmark decision. After 33 years of absence, they decided officially to return the Mercedes name to motorsport. And while they pondered

The Kouros Sauber-Mercedes C9 turbo 5.0 V8 of Jochen Mass/Jean-Louis Schlesser leads the 7.0-litre Jaguar XJR-9 of Martin Brundle and Eddie Cheever into the Castrol S complex on a damp Nürburgring at the start of the 1988 1,000km. The race was staged in two heats of 500km or 3 hours each, with the Sauber beating the Jaguar by one lap on aggregate.

their long-term strategy, the board elected to provide full factory support to Peter Sauber's WSPC team, which had already been receiving low-profile help from the factory. There had been little regular success on which to base their decision, apart from a freak win at a wet Nürburgring in 1986, coupled with a string of promising performances since, so, actually, it was an act of faith on Mercedes's part.

For the first year, the sponsorship was from AEG Olympia Office Equipment, a subsidiary of Daimler-Benz, ostensibly to negate the corporate downside effect of any adverse results should the Saubers fail to perform as expected. Daimler-Benz could scarcely have expected the immediate and dramatic results of official backing when, at the first round in Jerez, a single Sauber C9, still basically in 1987 trim, romped away to win from the start from the TWR Jaguars. Daimler-Benz management and Sauber's team were surprised and exultant. Jaguar and TWR were shocked, and it was the prelude to a tough and increasingly bitter season-long struggle that panned out with Sauber-Mercedes taking five victories to TWR-Jaguar's six. Jaguar had taken two years to undermine Porsche's stranglehold, so the speed with which Mercedes achieved similar competitiveness was hard to countenance.

For the first three rounds, an older C9-87 chassis updated to 1988 specification was used, while the new C9-88 cars were being fabricated. It seems that the new cars were not designated C10, because such an application is apparently very difficult to pronounce in German. The C9-88 was built to the same Leo Ress-bonded sheet-aluminium design as before. Where the big improvement was made, was in the durability of the lightly blown five-litre V8 engine, and its temperamental transmission train. The engines and their KKK turbos, which had previously been looked after in Heini Mader's workshops, were developed in the Mercedes R&D facility under the supervision of Herrmann Heireth for improved economy and power and were now prepared by a full-time, four-man team of technicians from the factory.

Technical assistance was also given on strengthening the Hewland VECG gearboxes, using new internals designed jointly by Mercedes-Benz and the British firm Staffs Silent

In August 1988, Jean-Louis Schlesser won the Diepholz Supercup in the Sauber-Mercedes C9, with Mauro Baldi 2nd in the second C9. Close behind are Walter Brun in the 962C, who came 7th, and Bob Wollek in the Jöst 962C, who came 3rd.

Refuelling, tyre swap and driver change for the 3rd place 5.0-litre V8 turbo Sauber-Mercedes C9 of Mauro Baldi and James Weaver during the 1988 Silverstone 1,000km.

Round 4 at Brands Hatch, July 1989, and Kenny Acheson in the winning Sauber-Mercedes C9 shared with Mauro Baldi leads the 10th-placed 962C of the Alméras brothers into Druids hairpin.

Gears. After Jerez, Jaguar hit back with three consecutive wins, but the Saubers were always in the frame, taking second at Jarama and Monza, then 2nd and 3rd at Silverstone. Their first big setback came at Le Mans, where Klaus Niedewidtz's car suffered a high-speed blowout on the Mulsanne Straight during first practice. Visions of the awful 1955 accident crowded in, which claimed the lives of over 90 people, prompting the withdrawal of Mercedes-Benz from motor racing for over three decades – though, of course, the circumstances were very different – and discussions ensued with Michelin, who were unable to provide any explanation or guarantees in the short time before the start of the race, so it was decided to withdraw the two-car entry, in the interests of safety.

TYRE DOUBT

Later, it transpired that tyre overloads generated by the enormous downforces induced along the newly resurfaced and more abrasive surface of the top-speed straight were also affecting the Jaguars and other cars in the same way. But while the Jaguars, which used Dunlop cross-plies, could cure this by adjustments to the suspension geometry, Sauber-Mercedes, who were using radials, could not alter the carcases to a sufficient extent to dial the problem away. However, Sauber-Mercedes did fit heat shields around the rear dampers to negate the effects of heat build-up from the engine bay.

Jochen Mass and Jean-Louis Schlesser took the next race at Brno in July for Sauber-Mercedes, with Mauro Baldi and James Weaver coming in fourth behind the two Jaguars. But there was further drama at Brands Hatch when Mass was punted out by a spinning C2 car, leaving the other entry, which only narrowly avoided the carnage to recover at the restarted race, for third place. Two wins followed at Nürburgring and Spa, and by this time, it was clear that Jean-Louis Schlesser stood an excellent chance of winning the Drivers' title by virtue of an impressive run of top-three finishes. Martin Brundle was his nearest challenger, but when the Brit won the next round at Fuji, with Schlesser and the surviving Sauber C9 only able to manage 5th, the title slipped from the Frenchman's grasp.

Nevertheless, AEG Sauber-Mercedes finished their impressive debut season with a one-two victory at Sandown, Australia. However, the non-start at Le Mans and the other races, where Jaguar were always ready to pounce when things went wrong for the Swiss-German outfit, meant that the Silk Cut Jaguars were able to take the Teams' title by quite a comfortable margin. Mass, Schlesser and Baldi were the key Sauber drivers, with variously Stefan Johansson, James Weaver, Kenny Acheson, Klaus Niedzwiedz and Philippe Streiff all filling the role of fourth driver, but none shone in unfamiliar machinery.

SPICE DISHES UP

Back in the European Group C2 category, 1988 was a year of nearly total domination for Gordon Spice's cars. Indeed, for the first time, the Silverstone works ran a two-car team, one SE88C for Spice and Ray Bellm, another for Thorkild Thyrring and Almo Coppelli and, later on, Eliseo Salazar. Between them, they were able to take ten out of the eleven

The winning Sauber-Mercedes C9 of Jean-Louis Schlesser, Mauro Baldi and Jochen Mass leads the Jaguar XJR-9 of Martin Brundle and Eddie Cheever, plus the Spice SE88C of Thorkild Thyrring and Almo Coppelli at the Jerez 800km in April 1988.

races on the calendar. This secured the teams' title by an enormous margin and filled the first four slots in the drivers' championship, the proprietor himself scoring his fourth consecutive drivers' title in the process, sharing with Ray Bellm, who took his third. There was a win at the Nürburgring two-parter for Kalmar Racing, who had retired their old Tiga GC85 at the start of the year and bought two GC288 Tigas, still using 3.3-litre DFLs. Team owner Pasquale Barberio shared the driving with Vito Veninata, Ranieri Randaccio and Maurizio Gellini. The GC288s featured all-new bodywork with enclosed rear wheels and proved a handful, with a tendency to scrape their noses along the track under heavy braking. But by Nürburgring, the Kalmar mechanics had both chassis dialled in properly. The GC288 ran strongly as the rest of the field drowned in the torrential rain of the first heat, and Ray Bellm in the works Spice made a rare mistake and hit the Armco in the rain-swept darkness. This left Kalmar looking as though they might take an overall C2 one-two at the finish, but Gellini and Randaccio suffered their own damp-induced electrical issues near the end of heat two, which left Barberio to take the win with Veninata. Two more 3rd places at the end of the year rounded off the season. Charles Ivey entered his 956-engined Tiga chassis 332 at Le Mans, where Tim Harvey, John Sheldon and Chris Hodgetts led C2 until broken CV joints dropped them to 4th. Roy Baker ran his GC286.336 with a 3.9-litre DFL engine, now pink-painted, whose high point was a 6th-in-class finish at Le Mans, although at Brands Hatch, Steve Hynes spun in front of both Sauber C9s going to Clearways, putting Jochen Mass into the barriers and stopping the race.

Throughout 1988, Sauber-Mercedes grew stronger, despite withdrawing from Le Mans because of the dramatic tyre failure on Klaus Niedzwiedz's car on the Mulsanne Straight during practice, and it was clear that they would represent the biggest threat to Jaguar in 1989. In C1, the excitement generated by the extended season-long struggle between the Jaguars and the Sauber-Mercedes masked the lack of variety and innovation, with the Porsche brigade now outpaced and making up the numbers. The Japanese had still been studiously avoiding any extended rivalry with the

European Group C teams except where they were obliged to do so, geographically at Fuji, or commercially at Le Mans. By season's end, though, the Japanese manufacturers were beginning to take an interest, as the lure of beating Porsche, Jaguar and Mercedes attracted them as a way of proclaiming the quality of their cars. Mazda had been running their rotary-engined cars at Le Mans since the 1970s, but 1989 saw the first concerted efforts to take on the big European makes in Group C. Nissan now dived in with their Lola-designed car, driven by IndyCar star Mark Blundell and former Sauber-Mercedes helmsman Kenny Acheson, and the Nissan showed well throughout the 1989 and 1990 seasons with a well-designed chassis and powerful turbo V8 engine. However, Nissan never quite broke into the triumvirate of Porsche, Mercedes and Jaguar to score a win, despite signs of optimism on occasion. Toyota, on the other hand, always seemed somewhat half-hearted about Group C until, ironically, it was too late as the new 3.5-litre rules took their toll. The main thrust for the Japanese, however, was always Le Mans, and it was long-time contender Mazda who became Japan's first winner of the French epic. In 1991, Mazda gave the responsibility of running their entry to the French team Oreca – subsequently better-known for running the works Dodge Vipers in the FIA GT2 category. With F1 and F3000 drivers Johnny Herbert, Volker Wiedler and Bertrand Gachot, they took a well-judged win ahead of three Jaguar XJR12s.

All smiles on the victory lap at Le Mans 1991 from Mazda's Bertrand Gachot, Volker Weidler and Johnny Herbert.

CHAPTER 5

SAUBER SUCCESS 1989–90

The WEC retinue starts lap 2 of the 1989 Spa-Francorchamps 1,000km, with the eventual winning Sauber-Mercedes C9/88 of Mauro Baldi and Kenny Acheson leading out of Eau Rouge towards Raidillon, pursued by the second C9 of Schlesser/Mass which retired after 69 laps, the XJR-11 of Lammers/Tambay which lasted sixteen laps, and the 962C of Wollek/Jelinski which finished 2nd.

In what was intended to be a pivotal year for the WSPC, the early signs in 1989 indicated that changes in the championship were positive, suggesting that sportscar racing was about to enter a golden age of growth as new rules kicked in. Gone was the option for teams being able to pick and choose their races according to how well they thought they would do; they now had to register for the whole series and then appear at every race, or at least at scrutineering, or face a hefty $250,000 fine for every no-show. There was a new free fuel class for C1's 750-kilogramme normally-aspirated cars with 3.5-litre racing engines, though teams that wished to continue using cars conforming to the earlier rules could do so, albeit for two more seasons only, to the existing fuel regulations and with an increased weight of 900 kilogrammes.

DEMISE OF C2

The C2 category was meant to run for two more seasons, by which time it was assumed that existing junior teams would have prepared for the programmed 750-kilogramme atmospheric regulations. In fact, the strategy was so appealing that most C2 teams had already made the transition. A year ahead of schedule, the class was scrapped entirely, making 1989 the last year of Group C2.

Also dropped was the long tradition of 1,000-kilometre events, interspersed over the season with two or three 360-kilometre 'sprints'. Now, all WSPC counting races were to be 480 kilometres in length, except for Le Mans. FISA promised greater commitment, rule stability and better promotion to present a highly saleable, almost corporate image for a championship that was centrally controlled and administered, very much like the way the Formula 1 World Championship had been developed in the 1980s.

Full-time officials, including a new series administrator, John MacDonald, and technical man Charlie Whiting, were present at every race. New, too, was the F1-style Longines/ Olivetti timing and, more controversially, FISA laid claim to ownership of all television rights. These last two points led the FIA into an extended struggle with the ACO at Le Mans, who predictably had their own ideas on those matters. MacDonald and Whiting made their presence felt immediately when they decided to approach the Group C rule book from an outsider's point of view. Whiting read the regulations and started applying them strictly. At Suzuka, where he had to deal with the WSPC cars for the first time, he pointed out features on the cars that did not comply with the letter of the law. One of his main concerns was the basic rule that stated that the car body must cover all mechanical components so that when viewed from above, no parts of the chassis, engine or running gear should be visible. That sounded simple enough, but in the case of the Porsches, the radiators in the side pods on either side of the cockpit had always been visible, and on a Jaguar, the engine could be seen through the air intake. This inevitably caused grief amongst the teams, who pointed out in no uncertain terms that it had been this way since 1982. But Whiting was insistent, and teams were given until the Dijon round to carry out the modifications, supposedly with sheet aluminium and a pop-rivet gun or suitably reinforced fibreglass. For TWR-Jaguar, at least, this meant a major bodywork redesign.

FANS EXCLUDED

There was more: FISA's control extended further into the paddock than before in other ways. Previously, areas that had traditionally been accessible to the public, affording fans the opportunity to get close to the cars and drivers, now became forbidden zones, allowing access only to the crews and the chosen few, thus removing at a stroke one of the long-established privileges of the sport.

The move to standardise race distances to 480 kilometres was deliberately aimed at encouraging increased television coverage, something that had always been missing from Group C, the WEC and the WSPC. The roughly three-hour duration of these races would theoretically make it easier to package them into edited highlights or even broadcast them in their entirety without losing the attention of the viewing public – unless they happened to be race fans, which, of course, many of us were and still are.

Paradoxically, however, the only FISA-sanctioned sports-car race that enjoyed worldwide media coverage continued to be the 24-hour Le Mans, and the major national TV companies studiously ignored the rest of the WSPC. Nonetheless, the scenario had looked very promising at the start of the season, but the move to shorter race distances alienated many of endurance racing's paying cognoscenti without attracting more ephemeral sports fans. Indeed, there was the simple question of whether or not the 480-kilometre WSPC distance could still be regarded as endurance racing in any case.

One success of FISA's dictum came as a direct result of the requirement that teams should contest all races, obliging the Japanese makers to contest every WSPC round, rather than just running at their domestic races and at Le Mans. This suited their publicity machines admirably, as Nissan, Toyota and Mazda now had to take the full schedule on board. Accordingly, both Nissan and Toyota refined their V8 turbo engines throughout 1989 and 1990. Nissan chose

Roy Baker Racing's 3.3-litre Cosworth DFL-engined Spice SE87C of Philippe de Henning and Dudley Wood came 18th at the 1989 Donington 480km, though they were unclassified, having completed the last lap too slowly.

The Group C field bursts off the Brands Hatch grid for the start of the 1989 480km, with the Sauber-Mercedes C9 pair of Acheson/Baldi – eventual winners – and Schlesser/Mass who came 3rd, with the Jaguar XJR-11s of Lammers/Tambay and Jones/Ferté alongside, plus the Nissan R89C of Bailey/Gilbert-Scott to the right.

to move to an all-new Lola-built composite monocoque instead of the dated March aluminium monocoque used before. Mazda continued on the Wankel route, which FISA had no plans to allow in 1991, merely adding extra rotors for increased power.

THERE MAY BE TROUBLE AHEAD

Trouble lay ahead, and it started brewing in October 1988 when Le Mans organisers *L'Automobile Club de l'Ouest* declared themselves alarmed by FISA's plans. Unsurprisingly, the two main sticking points were the ownership of television rights and the use of Longines-Olivetti timing. The ACO had always marketed worldwide television coverage of 'their' race and had rather naturally been the main beneficiaries of the funds thereby accruing. Also, Le Mans used its own established Siemens ALGE timing system. So, the stage was set for a dispute that rumbled on through that winter of 1988–89 and into the new season, leading to the race being removed entirely from the championship. This did not please the race teams and particularly their sponsors, who saw the race with its massive media coverage as one of the prime reasons, and indeed, for some, the only reason, for being involved in the WSPC in the first place.

Fortuitously, FISA imposed the embargo on the 24-hour epic only after the appropriate race and circuit licences had been granted and after entries for the event had closed. So, the race went ahead anyway, and little apart from Championship status was lost. However, things would get messier as the battle of French wills continued into 1990. After the dropping of the 24-Hours and the traditional close-season date swapping, just eight rounds remained on the Championship calendar. Notable absentees were Fuji, which was replaced by a season-opener at Suzuka, and Silverstone, which fell victim to circuit owner Tom Wheatcroft's ambitious plans to turn Donington Park into a world-class motor racing venue. After years of lobbying, Wheatcroft finally succeeded in securing a FISA World Championship race for his circuit, and it was judged that Britain did not merit three rounds in one year. Silverstone had to be content with hosting a round of the German ADAC Super Cup Sprint Championship, which turned out to be well-organised but a poorly supported event.

The Lola-based works-entered Nissan R89C of Julian Bailey and Mark Blundell came 3rd overall, beating most of the fancied runners in the 480km Donington Park round of the 1989 WEC.

The Spice SE86C-Cosworth of Swiss driver Pierre-Alain Lombardi and Bruno Sotty departs the Donington pits during the 1989 480km, classified 20th, though they retired on lap 107 out of 120.

RACING ROYALTY: TRIPLE LE MANS WINNER KLAUS LUDWIG

Snapped by Sarah Hall, the author interviews Klaus Ludwig at Le Mans Classic in 2018. He won the 24-Hours in 1979 in a Kremer 935 K3, and in 1984 and '85 in the same Joest Racing 956B. He entered Group C in 1982, driving the Ford C100 for Zakspeed-Ford, then Joest Racing from 1983 to 1986, and works Porsche 962C in 1988, placing 2nd at Le Mans.

Klaus Ludwig was so successful throughout his five-decade racing career that his fans regard him as racing royalty. They do not come a great deal more successful than Ludwig: three Le Mans wins – plus one 2nd place; victor of his native German DTM Championship, as well as forays Down Under to Bathurst and across the pond for the Trans-Am and Camel GT IMSA series. Klaus Ludwig has enjoyed success driving top-line cars, not only for Porsche but for Mercedes-Benz and Ford as well. He started off racing BMW 2002 and Ford Capri touring cars in 1969 and, having done F2 with Willy Kauhsen in the mid-'70s, his first successful Porsche drive was at the 1976 Monza 6-Hours in a Tebernum Racing Team 934, claiming the win with Tim Schenken and Toine Hezemans. He drove Georg Loos's 935 alongside John Fitzpatrick and Hezemans in 1978, winning at Mugello, Hockenheim and the Nürburgring 1,000km, and for 1979 was enlisted as number one driver in the Kremer Racing 935, in which he had a spectacularly successful season, notching up eight wins. Highlight was the Le Mans 24-Hours, supported by Americans Bill and Don Whittington. They finished 1st, an amazing result for a private team, in a race beset by heavy rain. Three years later, at the wheel of the Joest Racing New-Man 956, he won again, scoring back-to-back victories in 1985 and '86. There were numerous outright successes in Porsches throughout the '80s and '90s, as well as finishing 2nd at Le Mans in 1988, partnering Hans Stuck and Derek Bell in a 962. Having retired in 1999, he could not resist some 'hobby racing' at the Nürburgring 24-Hours, placing 2nd in the Alzen brothers' 997 GT3 in 2006.

Klaus moved from Ford to Porsche in the mid-1970s. 'Yeah, from a saloon car to a coupé, and later, in '82, I came from Ford C100 Group C prototypes to Porsche 956 prototypes, so that was about the same, speed-wise.' That placed him with Reinhold Jöst, driving his 956.

Actually, I didn't know him so well at the time, but I was doing some prototype racing with the Ford C100, and then Porsche asked me if I wanted to drive for Reinhold Jöst, who at that time was a pretty small operation, about fifteen people and two cars, but very professional, good guys and very good mechanics. The car came from Porsche, and it wasn't over-engineered, and we didn't do too many things to it, like what happened later when they built their own chassis, like the Thompson chassis and trick suspensions, but that was pretty much a standard long-tail Le Mans 956 from Porsche, on Dunlop tyres the first year. That was the Marlboro car in '83, and we (Ludwig, Johansson and Wollek) were very unlucky that year because we were good for 2nd place for sure, but I lost it at Arnage because there was a big oil spill and no flags, and we spent a long time in the pits repairing it, so we only finished 6th overall.

Then, a year later, we came back with a New Man Jöst 956, and Pescarolo, Johansson and I won, and a year later, we came back with the same New Man Jöst 956, and we won again, this time with Barilla. The year after that, I came back to Le Mans again in Jöst's Blaupunkt car with Goodyear tyres, and we were really dominating the race, using less gas – and the gas consumption was a secret – and the tyres were less roll-resistant because they had a lot of chemical grip, and at the time nobody really recognised that. But we knew that we could run a little bit less downforce or wing on the straight, so we were very quick, we used very little gas and that was wonderful. So, we (Paolo Barilla and John Winter) were dominating the race – until the engine blew up because of the pace car situation after Jo Gartner's dreadful crash. That meant it was not running hot enough, and we were running no thermostat in the cooling system, so when the water temperature went down to 35 degrees and the oil temperature was at 35 degrees, the oil pressure went up to

The winning 956 at Le Mans 1984 was entered by New Man Joest Racing and driven by Henri Pescarolo, Klaus Ludwig and Stefan Johansson, covering 3,044.89 miles (4,900.27km) at an average 126.87mph (204.14km/h)

eleven, and then I think a bolt flew out of the oil pump, and that was it! It was very sad because that year was our year; we would have won.

Recalcitrant fuel pump

In 1987 and 1988, Klaus Ludwig was handling the 962C:

I was also driving with Mass and Wollek, Dieudonné and Winter, and I came back to Le Mans in '88 in a factory car with Stuck and Bell, and we were flying again. But we couldn't make use of the reserve tank because the fuel pump was full of the yellow foam from the tank. It was a new car, and we didn't know that, and when I came in from my first stint I was surprised that the pump wasn't working, so we had to push the car and we lost some time. We fought back, though, and Stuck did a wonderful job during the night in the rain, and we were leading again, easily. And then a water pipe broke, and we had to stop for another seven minutes, then we fought back again, this time against the Jaguar. But we couldn't overtake it, and so the race was over, and we finished 2nd behind the Jaguar. That was one of the hardest fights we ever had, and Stuck and Derek Bell did a great job. I was the first one to experience that problem with the fuel pump; the system in the Porsche was very straightforward to handle: a white light came on to warn you that the main fuel tank is now empty, so now you have to switch over to the reserve, but you could carry on going until the engine started to cough because it was starved of fuel. So, I passed the start/finish line, went down the Mulsanne Straight, and at the end of the straight came the first cough, and I pressed the reserve switch but there was nothing happening because the pump was clogged up and wouldn't deliver the gas. I managed to limp back with the dregs of the normal tank, as far as the last chicane, but the engine then cut out and I covered the last 100 metres jerking it with the starter motor! That was very lucky because it was only 100 metres to the pits; if it had been 400 metres I wouldn't have made it. After that we could only use the main tank's 90 litres, but it was ok because we just did one lap less so we didn't run into a problem. It was really a shame, though, because we could have won that time, because after the race I spoke with Jan Lammers who was in the Jaguar, and he told me the Jaguar was dead, complete transmission failure with the gearbox groaning and nothing working any more. So maybe with just one more lap, they would have stopped on the straight, and we might have overtaken them. That's how it goes; they were very lucky, and we were a bit unlucky. At the time, I thought that was good for the sport, Jaguar winning at Le Mans in front of 100,000 English people; they loved it.

LE MANS HIGHLIGHT

In 1989, Sauber-Mercedes ruled the WSPC and the Le Mans 24-Hours. The centrepiece was Le Mans, where the team dominated when conventional wisdom said they needed at least another year to do it. The driver roster notably included Mercedes Junior team member Michael Schumacher, who displayed the talent that would shortly make him the world's greatest driver by lapping at speeds that alarmed the Sauber-Mercedes team management but still enabled him to eke out extra laps per stint. Jaguar, by contrast, lost out in the escalating power battle with Mercedes's turbo V8. In response, Jaguar produced the V6 turbo-powered XJR-11. This was markedly faster than the outgoing V12 XJR-9 but was fragile and not as quick as the C11 Sauber-Mercedes. In fact, in 1989, the most promising British Group C car was Aston Martin's AMR1. At Brands Hatch, the XJR-11's maiden event, the AMR1 took 4th place ahead of the surviving Jaguar, and it picked up several other good placings throughout the year. As 1989 ended, the Proteus team had built a 1990 spec AMR1, which was considerably lighter than the original car. However, the Ford Motor Company purchased Aston Martin – as well as Jaguar – and saw no need to have two of its marques fighting each other, and the Aston project was folded – which was a shame, as Jaguar had gained considerable kudos from its Group C programme, and the same could have happened back then for Aston Martin.

RETURN OF THE SILVER ARROWS

With the arrival of the Japanese teams, the new Aston Martin AMR1 and the small number of C1 atmospheric cars, there was more variety on the grid and, on paper, a greater challenge to the Jaguars than presented by the now reliably competitive Sauber-Mercedes. But in 1989, Jaguar fumbled the ball, and Sauber neatly caught it, leaving everyone else wondering how to even get into the ballpark. The Saubers were now running in full traditional Silver Arrows Mercedes-Benz livery instead of the dark blue AEG backing seen the previous year, and pundits were not slow to draw comparisons with Mercedes-Benz's mega-successful silver-hued racing cars of the 1930s and 1950s. The same C9 87/88 honeycomb and sheet-aluminium Leo Ress-penned chassis was retained for 1989, but the big technical change was the introduction of a new 32-valve V8 engine, designated the M119. This had been tested over the winter, and it proved very fuel-efficient and, significantly, made the previous lumpy power characteristics of the car out of slow corners much more predictable for the drivers.

These included Jean-Louis Schlesser, who was 2nd in the title standings in 1988 and who would be Drivers' World Champion in 1989 and 1990, together with Mauro Baldi, who was booked in for the lead car. Jochen Mass was retained to drive the second car, joined by new fourth seat

It is hot at Jarama in June, and hotter still driving a Group C car, as Jochen Mass reveals in the Sauber-Mercedes pits in '89, while Jean-Louis Schlesser heads out in the winning C9, and John Nielsen passes by in the TWR Jaguar XJR-9, which came 6th.

A Le Mans pit stop for the Sauber-Mercedes C9 of eventual winners Jochen Mass, Manuel Reuter and Stanley Dickens reveals the car's Mercedes-Benz M119 5.0-litre twin-turbo V8.

The two works Sauber-Mercedes C9s of Kenny Acheson/Mauro Baldi – eventual winners – and Jean-Louis Schlesser/ Jochen Mass, who finished 3rd, lead the way down Graham Hill into Cooper Straight on the first lap of the 1989 Brands Hatch 480km. It's mighty crowded up at Druids.

Nephew of 1960s' F1 driver Jo Schlesser, Jean-Louis Schlesser drove for several Group C teams in the '80s, including Rondeau, Fitzpatrick, Jöst and TWR-Jaguar. He joined Sauber-Mercedes in 1988 and won the World Endurance Championship in 1989 and 1990 – sharing the Drivers' title with Mauro Baldi in 1990. Subsequently, he was also very successful in off-road rallying, such as the Paris–Dakar.

The Sauber-Mercedes driver roster for 1990 included Young Turks Karl Wendlinger, Heinz-Harald Frentzen and Michael Schumacher.

driver, Irishman Kenny Acheson, who proved perfectly able to run at the pace of his compatriots and frequently faster. Gianfranco Brancatelli, Stanley Dickens, Alain Cudini, Manuel Reuter and Jean-Pierre Jabouille were hired to do just Le Mans, which saw them and the four regular drivers humiliate the opposition by taking 1st, 2nd and 5th places.

At Suzuka, Acheson was obliged by Mass's illness to start in the middle of the grid and drive the whole race on his own, but he still managed to overhaul the entire field and take the lead before being ordered to fall back into line behind Schlesser and Baldi for the finish. It was all the more surprising that, at the end of the year, he was deposed to make way for Austro-German junior team drivers Schumacher, Wendlinger and Frentzen for 1990. There were more odd personnel changes. The hugely experienced former racer and team owner Dave Price had joined Peter Sauber's ensemble in 1988 as pit manager and technician, working directly for Max Welti. Price succeeded in rounding the rough edges off the Sauber-Mercedes package, using his wealth of knowledge to hone the team's racecraft and turn it into an unbeatable combination. However, Dave Price would join Kenny Acheson at Nissan at the end of the 1989 WSPC season.

PORSCHE BACK IN THE HUNT

With this all-round, in-depth strength, Sauber-Mercedes easily took the 1989 WSPC Teams' title, winning every round except Dijon, where Bob Wollek and Frank Jelinski gave Porsche its only win of the year in the semi-works Joest Racing lightweight 962C #011, on Goodyear tyres, while the Sauber-Mercedes C9s struggled with a lack of grip from their Michelins. It was not surprising, then, that Porsche chose Joest Racing to be its official representative for a fresh attempt on the WSPC, with factory employees including Norbert Singer conspicuous in the Jöst pits garages, Singer later taking over one of the team management positions and coordinating fresh chassis and the latest factory-prepared engines and electronics, so that he Blaupunkt-sponsored 962Cs were, to all intents and purposes, works entries.

However, Wollek and Jelinski's Dijon success, which raised hopes of a Porsche revival, proved to be a one-off. At all the other races, the old 962 spec had finally found the limits of its development. Except for the Jöst car, which was always quick – though not really quick enough to threaten the Sauber-Mercedes – any other placings that came the Porsche teams' way tended to be down to durability rather than outright speed.

Joest Racing took 3rd place at Le Mans, Suzuka and Mexico, came 2nd at Brands Hatch and Spa-Francorchamps, and very nearly won on the Nürburgring's GP circuit but managed to run out of fuel. Brun Motorsport, featuring Walter Brun, Oscar Larrauri and Harald Huysman, and sponsored by Hydro Aluminium, also overcame the 962's limitations with some great drives and placed 2nd in Mexico and 3rd at Jarama. Kremer Racing built and campaigned the first all-composite 962 to wring more performance from the ageing 962 design, although the best result for 962 CK6/2 was 3rd in Germany. And yet, as testament to the enduring qualities of the 962 design and spec, several other teams also elected to campaign Porsche's five seasons' veteran – including Richard Lloyd Racing, the Alméras brothers, Jochen Dauer, Antoine Salamin, Vern Schuppan, Obermaier and Walter Lechner – their 962s manifest in a variety of new, used, clone or mixed configurations, although none of them apart from Jöst and Brun had much to show for their efforts in terms of results.

Two 962Cs vie with each other along Brands Hatch's Bottom Straight during the 1989 480km (300 miles): Uwe Schäfer and Walter Lechner in the yellow Brun Motorsport car finished 9th, while the Richard Lloyd Racing/Porsche GB-entered car of David Hunt and James Weaver dropped out after fifteen laps.

The long-tail Jöst 962C LH #C145 of Bob Wollek and Hans Stuck started 5th on the grid and came 3rd in the 1989 Le Mans 24-Hours.

The Brands Hatch 480km was the fourth round of the 1989 WEC, and the Repsol Brun Motorsport 962C of Oscar Larrauri and Jesús Pareja finished 6th.

JAGUAR ON THE PROWL

Meanwhile, TWR-Jaguar was reeling somewhat from the unexpectedly tough fight Sauber-Mercedes had put up in 1988, and developed the new XJR-10/11 V6 turbo car in parallel with the existing XJR-9's normally aspirated 7.0-litre V12 design. The V12 was still considered competitive, but the go-ahead for the V6 turbo had been given in 1988, and it was now apparent that if any use were to be made of it before the commencement of the all-atmospheric regulations in 1991, it would have to be introduced sooner rather than later, so the turbo duly made its debut at Brands Hatch. Related, though distinctly different versions of the twin-turbo V6 were being

The TWR-Jaguar JV6 3.5L Turbo V6-powered XJR-11 of Alain Ferté and Andy Wallace leaves the pits during the Donington 480km in September 1989, retiring at 115 laps, five behind the winning Sauber-Mercedes C9.

built for Europe and America for the IMSA series, the most notable distinction being that the Group C engine in the XJR-11 was a 3.5-litre unit, while the XJR-10 IMSA unit was only 3.0-litres.

The new car had been designed around 18-inch radial tyres instead of the previous year's 19-inch cross-plies. But because the V6's debut was not anticipated until mid-season, it was decided to adapt the V12 chassis to take the 18-inch rubber in the interim. Frustratingly, Dunlop had fallen behind in the development of radial tyre technology in racing applications, so the Jaguars lacked grip for most of the races. There was no chance of reverting to the old 1988 set-up, as the suspension geometry on the V12s had been redesigned for the smaller tyres. The shortfall in grip led to greater fuel consumption, and the season turned into something of a disaster for TWR-Jaguar, despite the efforts of Jan Lammers and Patrick Tambay in the lead car and John Nielsen and Andy Wallace in the second car, in the absence of Brundle and Cheever, who were off pursuing their F1 careers.

DEARTH OF WINS

If it seemed unlikely that TWR would end up without a single victory all season, it was Le Mans that dished up the greatest disappointment, where the XJR-9s went quickly in practice as well as in the race, but were struck down by a succession of mechanical problems, including dropped valves, broken exhausts and broken transmission, which the team was convinced were caused by vibrations set up by the tyres turning on their rims. Le Mans was a crushing defeat for TWR-Jaguar, despite their final 4th and 8th placings, and 1990 would see the Silk Cut Jaguars using Goodyear tyres.

CHAPTER 6

JAPANESE EXPANSION 1991–92

One of nine Nissans entered for Le Mans 1990, the Lola-based R90CK of Mark Blundell, Julian Bailey and Gianfranco Brancatelli heads the Brun Motorsport 962C of Walter Brun, Oscar Larrauri and Jesús Pareja; neither car finished.

With its mandatory attendance requirement at all rounds of the WSPC Championship, Nissan, Toyota and Mazda were effectively coerced into taking in the full 1989 race calendar, and all three made a good showing in their own different ways during their first full season. They all insisted on sticking to their chosen engine development strategies and, of the three, Nissan was the most impressive. Previously, Nissan's efforts with its March-based chassis had been problematic, largely due to internecine disputes between the Japanese and European factions within the racing organisation. Ironically, Japanese drivers Suzuki and Hoshino earned themselves 4th place at the Suzuka opener using a 1987/88 car to humble the Jaguars and all but one of the Porsches. Thereafter, Nissan elected to conduct its racing programme through its Milton Keynes-based offshoot, Nissan Motorsports Europe, originally set up for touring cars and run by Howard Marsden. They then commissioned Lola to build a completely new composite car to accept an improved 3.5-litre version of the VEJ/VHR 30 V8 power plant that had first raced in 1988. Marsden hired veteran Keith Greene to manage the team and then surprised everyone by inviting British hot shots Julian Bailey and Mark Blundell to drive, neither of whom so far had any sports car credentials. Andrew Gilbert-Scott, a veteran of one endurance race at

Pit stop for fresh tyres, refuelling and driver change for the Nissan Motorsports International 3.5-litre twin-turbo V8-engined Nissan R89C, driven by Masahiro Hasemi, Kazuyoshi Hoshino and Toshio Suzuki at the 1989 Le Mans. The engine expired after eleven hours.

Silverstone in 1987, was recruited as an occasional substitute for Blundell. If this seemed a radical driver choice for such a major manufacturer to make, Nissan's past performances were unlikely to have had more experienced pilots rushing to sign contracts.

However, the new Nissan R89C looked the part and went well in a straight line, since the VEJ-30 engine was powerful, if difficult to set up. The brakes were ranked as poor until carbon discs were fitted, and the cabin tended to pop its windscreen out due to flexing of the bodywork. NME soon developed it into a potential race winner, and despite Bailey suffering a couple of race-ending shunts whilst on a charge, it was a good year all round for the fledgling team, claiming 5th in the WSPC Team's Championship at season's end.

MAESTRO MECHANICS

Like Nissan, Toyota opted for the V8 turbo path, using a 3.2-litre power unit in a honeycomb and composite chassis built in-house by their racing arm, TOM'S Racing Developments, and TRD in Japan. Again, the company entrusted its fortunes to European expertise, giving the Hingham, Norfolk-based TOM'S GB the task of running the V8 89-CVs and a fallback 2.1-litre turbo-powered 88-C for the first rounds and Le Mans. Two highly experienced ex-Team Lotus Formula 1 mechanics were in charge, Dave Simms and Glenn Waters, who were veterans of the Jim Clark/Graham Hill and Ronnie Peterson/Mario Andretti eras, respectively. Johnny Dumfries was the lead driver, keen to prove himself after losing his Jaguar seat – and, indeed, his Team Lotus F1 seat as John Player Special was dropped in favour of Camel for 1986 in a cigarette sponsor switch – with John Watson and Geoff Lees taking turns in the second seat. The 2.1-litre 88-C was qualified second at Dijon by Dumfries and went on to take 4th place. Le Mans was Toyota's worst showing ever, though, with both the Japanese-tended 89-CVs and the single TOM'S GB-run 88-C retiring before half distance. For Jarama, TOM'S GB was using one of the new chassis. Unfortunately, the car as delivered turned out to be fast in practice but heavy on fuel in a race situation. The team could not quickly fix the problem by working on the engine or reprogramming the electronic management chips because TRD ministered to these in Japan. Despite a basically sound package and a display of controlled aggression throughout the season, particularly by Dumfries, thirsty engines proved to be Toyota's undoing, and there was scant reward for much hard effort.

ROTARY CLUB

Mazda made a welcome return to the WSPC series, deciding, after a brief flirtation with the C2 class at its inception, to run to IMSA GTP regulations when that option became available in the WEC, having been wedded to Wankel rotary technology since the early 1970s. Apart from contesting Fuji and Le Mans, Mazda spent considerable time and effort developing its rotary race engines. Most of the benefits were manifest in the All-Japan Group C Championship and IMSA's GTU and Camel Lights categories, especially by Jim Downing, who used Mazda power to great effect in his Argo Lights chassis.

As it turned out, Mazda's involvement in the 1989 WSPC was a token affair, with just a single 767B chassis run during the season by Silverstone-based Alan Docking Engineering, with the principal focus being on the all-important Le Mans 24-Hours. Here, the two 767Bs and the 767 achieved exactly what they set out to do, being the only Japanese finishers, taking 7th, 9th and 12th positions overall and, not surprisingly, whitewashing the GTP category because there were no other entries. Spectacularly noisy – painfully deafening, not to put too fine a point on it – the Mazda was now challenged in terms of sheer decibels by the Cosworth DF-Zs being run by the works Spices. In terms of pace, the Mazda was not powerful enough to challenge C1 cars and rarely able to do much more than beat the C2s, so drivers David Kennedy and Pierre Dieudonné were condemned to being GTP midfield runners.

PROTEUS PROTEIN

Run under the works Aston Martin banner of Proteus Technology, the new Aston Martin AMR1 was revealed in 1989. 'Protech' was formed by Peter Livanos and Aston Martin Chairman Victor Gauntlet to utilise the talents and facilities of Ray Mallock Engineering and Hugh McCaig's Ecurie Ecosse for the development of the Max Bostrom all-composite chassis design. The AMR1 was powered by a 700bhp 24-valve, 6.0-litre V8 engine developed by V8 forced induction specialists Reeves-Calloway in Connecticut. The AMR1 chassis was compact and sophisticated, and the V8 was tilted up at the rear to allow huge venturi in the underbody. Equally voluminous ducts surrounded the front and sides of the cabin, giving the AMR1 its distinctive Coke Bottle shape and promoting huge downforce in the process. However, from the outset, it suffered from the same ailments that had afflicted all earlier Aston Martin racing cars: overweight and excessive bulk in the engine bay. The fundamental issue was the mass and size of the engine, which made the prototype weigh nearly 1,000 kilogrammes.

The previous EMKA and Nimrod projects – and before them, Robin Hamilton's massive DBS-based RHAM/1 Le Mans coupé – had all used the Aston Martin Lagonda engine but failed to win a race. So, when the new car was unveiled, it was familiar territory, and expectations were not high. The prototype was wrecked in testing at Donington, and the second car was not completed in time for Suzuka, landing Protech with a $250,000 FISA no-show fine. Thereafter, drivers David Leslie, Brian Redman, Michael Roe, Costas Los and Stanley Dickens all struggled all season to earn one 6th place, two 7ths and an 8th, plus an 11th for Redman, Roe and Los out of a two-car entry at Le Mans.

The cars improved throughout the year, though, with suspension and aerodynamic modifications and a weight reduction to 906 kilogrammes, and Calloway also produced a 6.3-litre version of the V8 for Mexico, which went well enough. But then, the Ford Motor Company, which had acquired the Aston Martin Lagonda group, decided they were not interested in supporting the planned 1990 AMR2 evolution. There was still some doubt about the future of Le Mans as a points-scoring round in the WSPC, and having also purchased Jaguar in the meantime, Ford was unenthusiastic about supplying suitable 3.5-litre engines to two works teams conforming to the 1991 regulations. That spelled the end of the latest Aston Martin Sports Car Challenge – till the marque resurfaced on track in 2005 with the Prodrive-built DBR9 LMGT1, followed by the 2008 DBR1-2, a development of the Lola B08/60 – leading to its successor, the open-top Prodrive-built AMR-One.

Running in the GTP category, the Mazdaspeed-entered Mazda 757 of David Kennedy and Takashi Yorino came 19th overall in the 1986 Silverstone 1,000km. Power came from the three-rotor Mazda 13G motor, rated at 2.0-litres.

Mazdaspeed's 767B, powered by the Mazda 13J-M (2.6-litre) quad-rotary engine, was driven to 9th overall and 2nd in IMSA GTP at Le Mans 1989 by Takashi Yorino, Hervé Regout and Elliot Forbes-Robinson.

The Ecurie Ecosse Aston Martin AMR1 was powered by the Aston Martin 6.0-litre RDP 87 V8 engine, and the car of David Leslie and Michael Roe came 6th in the 1989 Donington 480km, followed by the sister car driven by Brian Redman and David Sears in 7th.

The Mazda 737C of David Kennedy, Jean-Michel and Philippe Martin came 18th at Le Mans 1985.

Along with Toyota and Nissan, Mazda was a prominent presence in Group C racing, particularly from 1989, when all contenders were obliged to run every round of the series. The firm had long been active in motorsports, especially in the European and American markets, going back to its participation in European endurance races in the late 1960s and early 1970s with a view to demonstrating the performance, durability and reliability of the Wankel rotary engine. Mazda Auto Tokyo, which had turned the first RX-7 into a Le Mans car, received support from the factory and, in 1983, became independent as Mazdaspeed Corporation, specialising in Mazda motorsports.

Mazda triumphed at Le Mans in 1991 with the four-rotor Mazda R26B-powered Mazda 787B in the hands of Johnny Herbert, Volker Weidler and Bertrand Gachot.

In 1984, Mazda abandoned the idea of turbocharging the rotary engine (RE), and pursued multi-rotor engines to gain more power. In 1987, Mazda became the first Japanese car to finish as high as 7th overall at Le Mans. But then, in 1989, the FIA announced a new regulation that no rotary-engined cars would be allowed to compete in the World Sports Prototype Endurance Championship (WSPC).

The Mazda Le Mans cars that had evolved step by step up to that point were based on the unique rotary engine technology, and the fact that the RE could no longer run at the WSPC was a huge blow to the Mazda team. Mazda's management issued a decree to 'build a car that can win Le Mans' and invited six-time Le Mans winner Jacky Ickx to serve as an advisor. In 1989, despite a significant improvement in performance, at Le Mans, the best their three cars could achieve was seventh, ninth and twelfth places.

Fortunately, other manufacturers were not able to develop vehicles in time, and the new regulations would not be implemented until 1991. The Mazda 787B was based on the 1986 Mazda 757, which British designer Nigel Stroud was in charge of. The cockpit was a bathtub-type twin-tube monocoque moulded using the prepreg method, in which lightweight and strong carbon composite fibre materials are laminated together and heat-treated in a special kiln. The steering mechanism and pedal box were housed in the front and connected to the crushable structure. At the rear, the power unit and transmission assembly were arranged vertically. Since Mazdaspeed did not have a gearbox specifically designed for the RE, the five-speed transmission assembly for the Porsche 962C was used as the transmission mechanism from the 757 series onwards. The gearbox for the horizontally opposed engine was placed upside down to accommodate the RE's high output shaft position. The power unit went from a 3-rotor RE to a 4-rotor RE, while further improvements included carbon brakes, honed during a 24-hour test at Paul Ricard Circuit. It had been a close-run thing, but in the final year of the RE, the Mazda 787B became the first Japanese car ever to win Le Mans.

In 1991, the Mazda 787B #002, driven by Johnny Herbert, Volker Weidler and Bertrand Gachot, won Le Mans by two laps, averaging 205.333km/h, the only victory for a car using a rotary engine and the first win by a Japanese manufacturer. The four-rotor R26B engine featured three spark plugs per rotor, with variable length trumpets, rated at 2,616cc, delivering a maximum power output of 900bhp mated to a Porsche five-speed gearbox.

HARDY SPICER

The upcoming 3.5-litre class was a godsend for Spice Engineering since Jeff Hazell and Gordon Spice were now presented with an opportunity to equip then-current C2 chassis technology with a slightly larger Cosworth V8. The SE89Cs tipped the scales close to the mandatory 750kg limit and ran with John Nicholson-prepared Cosworth DFZ V8s, set up for endurance racing and the free-fuel formula. The regular drivers were Ray Bellm, Eliseo Salazar, Thorkyld Thyrring and Wayne Taylor, with tin-top specialist Tim Harvey standing in. When running flat out, the Spices proved capable of keeping up with the slower normal C1 cars all season and, on the twistier circuits, had a real chance of outright victory, even though their Cosworth V8s were down-tuned, and they were markedly agile through the turns. With minor mechanical problems and only a couple of top ten finishes, Spice still regarded the season as a success. However, having failed to obtain sufficient budget to run a full schedule as a team driver, principal Gordon Spice called it a day after a one-off outing at Le Mans to concentrate on the business aspect of his company.

Two other teams joined Spice Engineering in embracing the 3.5-litre 'atmo' concept – one promisingly, one not so promisingly. The France Proto team consisted of the remnants of 1988's MT Sport Racing set up by Spice shareholder Jean-Louis Ricci, who contracted Henri Pescarolo and Alain Ferté to drive a modified SE88 C2 chassis running a Heini Mader DFZ V8. An excellent 8th in Dijon scored the first points by a C1 atmospheric car, but for most of the season, the team concentrated on its C2 car, dodging the $250,000 fines by swapping between the two categories.

Meanwhile, in late season, with C2 already won, Chamberlain Engineering set up their SE89C's 3.3 DFL to free-fuel specification for the last race in Mexico. The driver partnership of Fermín Vélez and Nick Adams was immediately competitive, and a top ten finish was on the cards until the car was tipped off by Jochen Mass, dropping it to 14th overall.

Brian Ireland and Roger Rimmer ran the works Tiga team, whose GC289#372 was quick but prone to mechanical problems. At Donington, the Tiga proved sufficiently fuel-efficient to enable Jari Nurminen and Tony Trevor to win. The Porto Kaleo team, previously known as Kelmar, fielded Tiga GC288s converted to front radiator GC289 spec, placing 3rd in C2 in the final round in Mexico. Louis Descartes's new all-composite ALD C289 Cosworth, which appeared at Dijon-Prenois, was a quantum leap on the old

In the pits access road during the 1989 Donington 480km (300 miles), the sixth round of the Championship, is the 3.3-litre Cosworth V8-engined Chamberlain Racing Spice SE89C of Fermín Vélez and Nick Adams, which came 15th.

Privateer Didier Bonnet entered a pair of 3.5-litre BMW-engined ALDs for the 1989 Le Mans race, but neither managed to qualify.

sheet-aluminium BMW-powered cars. Meanwhile, Descartes built a pair of old-style cars for Didier Bonnet, chassis 05 and 06, which proved as slow as the earlier versions. Failing to qualify for the all-important Le Mans 24-Hours, and mostly failing to finish or even qualify elsewhere, he opted out of the championship.

TAKE COURAGE

Yves Courage's Cougars were now in C22S trim and powered by Porsche 962C customer-specification engines, driven by Pascal Fabre and a number of up-and-coming French and Belgian hopefuls. With Fabre at the wheel, the Cougar was able to outpace the majority of the Porsches, excluding the Joest Racing and Brun Motorsport lead cars, especially on tighter circuits in KH short-tail trim, logging a series of top ten finishes. Predictably, Courage's season revolved around Le Mans, where he adopted the best of both worlds by entering three Porsche-powered cars – two 3.0-litre C1s, and a C2 with a 2.8-litre engine. None of the C1s finished, but the C2 cruised to a five-lap class win after the leaders had retired. The first Lancia privateer, Gianni Mussato, commissioned a new Dallara-built honeycomb and composite chassis clad in Ferrari-red LC2 bodywork, and it was campaigned in 1989 by Andrea de Cesaris, Bruno Giacomelli and Franco Scapini, though the engine electronics proved too complex for a private team to sort.

Predictably, WM-Peugeot made its final visit to Le Mans, though both P489 cars broke down and repeatedly caught fire.

The C2 category finally concluded after seven successful seasons. This had not been FISA's original plan,

The Courage-entered 3.0-litre Porsche-powered Cougar C22 S #03 driven by Pascal Fabre and Hervé Regout came 9th in the 1989 Donington 1,000km.

Brun Motorsport's 962C was driven into 10th place at the 1989 Le Mans 24-Hours by Harald Huysman, Uwe Schäfer and Dominique Lacaud.

Entered by Mussato Action Car, the 3.0-litre Ferrari 308C turbo-powered Lancia LC2 of Bruno Giacomelli and Franco Scapini retired after 28 laps of the 1989 Donington 480km, classified 30th.

Created to be the quickest car along the Mulsanne Straight, the WM P489 was powered by the Peugeot PRV ZNS4 3.0-litre twin-turbo V6 – which caught fire in the 21st hour at Le Mans 1989. Drivers were Jean-Daniel Raulet, Philippe Gache and Pascal Pessiot.

which envisaged the class running until the end of 1990. However, as the year progressed, it became increasingly clear that most of the existing C2 outfits wanted to convert to the 750-kilogramme 3.5-litre free-fuel formula as soon as possible, so the FIA saw little point in continuing it. Contrarily, its passing was genuinely mourned by many enthusiasts, who relished its varied and variable fields and close racing.

RACE DISTANCES SHORTENED FROM 1990

There was a major sea change in 1990, as the FIA reduced race lengths from the time-honoured 1,000km or six hours to 480km to lure the TV channels and elicit more in the way of coverage. They also abandoned fuel limitation rules, which had maintained the balance between the teams for so long.

Sauber-Mercedes repeated its dominance, except at Silverstone, where the unfancied XJR-11 scored a notable 1–2 success. Le Mans was not on the WSC calendar in 1990, so Sauber-Mercedes chose to sit it out, while Jaguar returned with its XJR-12s and won convincingly against a returning Porsche works team, which had been sitting out the WSC for a couple of seasons.

Donington Park's 480km was the seventh round of the 1990 WSC, with the Mercedes-Benz C11s taking 1st and 2nd. Here, the Jochen Mass/Heinz-Harald Frentzen runner-up leads the 4th-placed Nissan R90CK of Kenny Acheson/Gianfranco Brancatelli.

Nissan R90CKs on air-jacks in the Silverstone pitlane during qualifying for the 1990 480km. Number 24 of Mark Blundell/Gianfranco Brancatelli was not classified, having taken too long to complete the final lap, while Julian Bailey/Kenny Acheson's broke its suspension.

Running at Le Mans in 1991, the Mazda 787B was 150kg lighter than the lightest rival 962C. Aware that this was their final chance of victory at Le Mans before the regs shut down the rotary engine, Mazdaspeed retained Jacky Ickx as a consultant. One of three 787Bs entered, this came 8th, driven by Yojiro Terada, Pierre Dieudonné and Takashi Yorino.

The other in-form team was Nissan, which scored numerous podiums throughout the year, taking over the role of chief challenger to Sauber-Mercedes in the last couple of rounds when TWR's resources were diverted into the design of its 1991 car.

Peugeot arrived on the Group C scene for the final couple of races in 1990, and its 3.5-litre V10-engined 905 contrived to appear a generation ahead of its rivals. The 905 cockpit was accessed via removable plexiglass roof panels doubling as doors. It was fast but fragile: indeed, 1991 began with a Peugeot victory at Suzuka. After teething troubles, it dominated the next few races to the extent that Peugeot went away and completely redesigned the 905 to reappear as the 905B, outwardly similar but radically different under the skin. Sauber-Mercedes, by contrast, soldiered on with the old C291, having misjudged the level of competition from Peugeot and Jaguar.

Le Mans 1991 went the way of Mazda's rotary-engined car, ahead of a trio of V12 Jaguars. But the real revelation was the Jaguar XJR-14. The purple car featured a full-on F1 Cosworth V8, and an aerodynamically re-thought body not much bigger than an F1 car. This is probably one of the all-time great sportscars, as it appeared in 1992 in the guise of a Mazda, and again in 1996 with a Porsche engine in their WSC chassis and went on to win Le Mans in 1996 and 1997.

INTERNAL WRANGLE

Months of uncertainty regarding the future of Le Mans dominated the WSPC's closed season as 1989 morphed into 1990. The seeds of the dispute between the FIA and FISA in Paris and the *Automobile Club de l'Ouest* had been sown a year earlier with the FIA's new plan for the WSPC and the virtual annexation of all the commercial interests involved. Late in the day, the great race was allowed to go on, but it again remained outside the championship, which did not greatly affect entries or materially change its status as one of the world's premier benchmark motor races. Of course, not many people seriously doubted that it would be run. Too much was at stake for it to be cancelled as the result of an internal wrangle within the sport. The fact is that the Sarthe regional economy, and indeed, to some extent, the French national economy, relied too much on the annual influx of cash that the 24-hour race brought in to allow it to be summarily destroyed. Therefore, it was inevitable that a bitter battle would ensue, but that a classic compromise would be reached to save the face of the parties involved.

Ahead of the 1990 season, most of the face-saving had been at the Paris end of the dispute. Later, the ACO almost completely caved in to FISA's demands. Paris had set itself to gain almost total financial control of the race: television rights, timing and paddock catering. And they were sure that ultimately, the lure of being allowed back into the World Sports Prototype Championship would be a sufficient lever to force the ACO around to their way of thinking, a strategy that proved correct in the end.

However, while the 1990 edition was being negotiated, it slowly dawned on the FIA that despite what one of their officials had optimistically said as fact the previous year, FIA, FISA and the championship needed Le Mans much more than Le Mans needed them. Things started to get a little nasty with claims and counterclaims being thrown around, while the FIA said it would ban any driver that took part in any future renegade 24 hours, after they had arranged for the withdrawal of the circuit's licence on the grounds that a quickly introduced and previously unheard of regulation required that no circuit should have a straight longer than two kilometres, because of the Mulsanne Straight being longer than that.

MULSANNE MAYHEM

At this point, safety became part of the dispute. The ACO continued to sneer and call for help from the French government's higher echelons. The Minister of Sport summoned FIA chief Jean-Marie Balestre to be interviewed. In the meantime, the major manufacturers started to make it known that they were not amused by the continued assault on the future of this jewel in sportscar racing's crown, and a few made it known that Le Mans was actually the reason they put up with the rest of the rather lacklustre and under-publicised championship. In the end, the ACO lost its hallowed *Ligne des Hunaudiéres* in the interest of safety with the insertion of two chicanes, necessitating a reappraisal of previous top speed goals. It was fascinating to

One of Joest Racing's 962Cs heading for the pits during the 1990 Le Mans 24-Hours, the white livery with ID flashes reprising the works Porsche sports prototypes of the late 1960s. Driven by Hans Stuck, Derek Bell and Frank Jelinski, it came 4th overall.

Leaving the pitlane at Le Mans' newly reconfigured pits garage and hospitality complex, the Mazda 787B of Johnny Hebert, Volker Weidler and Bertrand Gachot took an unassailable lead with three hours left to go in the 1991 race.

hear the drivers' views, several of whom claimed a dislike of the straight but, because of its length, were happy to use it to relax physically for a short while on every lap, despite the fact that the cars were going flat out. They were now confronted with two more tricky complexes to negotiate, and there were also the effects on the cars to take into account, since most mechanical failures occur when a car is under cornering and braking loads. Despite appearances to the contrary, the arguments were never really over the question of safety, although the Le Mans circuit had been justifiably criticised in the past for its flaws, particularly its antiquated pits complex and the lack of three-tier Armco around most of the circuit, which normally constituted public roads for much of its circumference.

NEW PITS GARAGES

After the 1990 race, the ACO set out to rebuild the old circuit and amenities to state-of-the-art standards, and, in the modern era, there is no question that they did an amazing job. The improvements included completely new pits garages, a broader pitlane with a safer approach leading away from the Ford Chicane, a more substantial pit wall, first-floor hospitality suites, a media centre and race control, with covered spectating area on top of most of the building. The paddock area was much revised, with garages and catering establishments, plus extra camera posts around the circuit and a long-awaited enlarged motor museum by the main entrance.

One year into the WSPC's new look, many of the anticipated teams failed to show up for the new C1 Atmospheric Class, some because their sponsors were unwilling to stump up for a programme of events with no Le Mans 24-Hour race in it. Crowds were conspicuously thin, except at Le Mans, and the mass media almost totally ignored the category. The hope for worldwide television coverage had failed to materialise. At Spa-Francorchamps, press and team personnel almost outnumbered paying spectators during qualifying. Silverstone, a traditionally popular venue with British sportscar race fans, attracted possibly its smallest paying crowd for a world championship event ever.

An infield usually thronging with corporate hospitality tents was strangely bereft. FISA's control had simply priced the pitches beyond the level that most companies were prepared to pay.

There was also a growing suspicion that the 3.5-litre rules had merely been created by the governing body to encourage manufacturers to make suitable engines that would eventually enter Formula 1. Finally, the Jarama race was cancelled at a week's notice for reasons that were never satisfactorily explained to the unimpressed teams.

One manufacturer looking beyond the immediate future was Mercedes-Benz, who had now dropped Sauber from its team title and was actively working towards the 1991 Formula.

The Brun Motorsport Hydro Aluminium-sponsored Thompson-chassis 962C #003 of Oscar Larrauri and Harald Huysman gets a wheel change during practice for the 1990 Silverstone 480km – the former 1,000km and Six Hours having been superseded by the shorter distance – in which it came 6th.

Former Arrows and Alfa Romeo F1 pilot Mauro Baldi, who also drove for Jöst and Lancia in Group C, shared the winning Mercedes-Benz C11 with Jean-Louis Schlesser here at the 1990 Nürburgring 480km.

Meanwhile, they absolutely steamrollered the WSPC in 1990, taking eight out of the nine constituent races, gathering another world title for Jean-Louis Schlesser and a joint first for his season-long partner, Mauro Baldi. It was an awesomely impressive performance, rivalling Porsche's triumphs in the early years of Group C and those of Jaguar mid-period.

Any hopes that TWR-Jaguar might have harboured for some leeway while Peter Sauber's technicians sorted the new C11 chassis were summarily dashed because it was dominant straight out of the box. The silver cars took every championship race with the single exception of Silverstone, where ignorance of the rules eliminated one car in practice, and the other suffered a rare engine breakage whilst leading the race. Mercedes-Benz decided not to run at Le Mans, notionally as a protest about the scrappy dealings between Paris and the *AC de l'Ouest*, but actually because they preferred to concentrate on the WSPC's actual qualifying rounds.

Mazda took the opposite view to Sauber-Mercedes. Their aspirations were focused on success in the French Enduro, so, despite the race being excluded from the championship, Mazda ditched the WSPC and appeared only in France with two new GTP 787s and a single 1989 767B, all with four-rotor engines. Ironically, they had their worst race for years, managing only to get the 767B to the finish line.

Meanwhile, the Sauber-Mercedes C11, which superseded the ageing but still effective C9, which, as you will recall, had its origins in the C7s and C8s of the mid-1980s, was once again penned by Leo Ress and was Sauber's first composite design. The monocoque, built by Dave Price's Woking-based DPS Components, sported an improved version of the M119 engine with the 1990 generation of Bosch's engine management system, which gave more power and economy. Also new was a stronger gearbox, while a switch from Michelin to Goodyear tyres completed the package, which was extensively tested over the winter of 1989 and 1990, proving easier for the drivers to steer and handle over an endurance race distance.

The opening round of the 1990 WEC was the Suzuka 480km, where the Mercedes-Benz pair of 5.0-litre turbo V8 C11s triumphed in 1st and 2nd places. Here, the winning car is refuelled on lap 23, while Mauro Baldi helps Jean-Louis Schlesser belt up. In the background to the right of the yellow airline is team manager Jochen Neerpasch.

During the Group C era, versatile Irishman Kenny Acheson drove Porsche 956B and 962C for John Fitzpatrick, Richard Lloyd and Advan Alpha-Nova, Toyota 4T-GT and TS010 for TOM'S Toyota, Sauber C9 for Sauber-Mercedes (best season: 1989), Nissan 89C for NISMO, and XJR-12 for Silk Cut-TWR.

Driver change for the victorious 5.0-litre turbo V8 Mercedes-Benz C11 at Spa-Francorchamps during the 1990 480km race: Jochen Mass steps out as Karl Wendlinger prepares to climb aboard during a refuelling and tyre-change stop.

YOUNG GUNS GO FOR IT

As the factory increased its influence within the team, it became apparent that the dropping of Sauber's name from the title indicated much more than it first suggested. The Mercedes C11s were now very much works cars, Jochen Neerpasch calling all the shots and Peter Sauber taking instructions from Stuttgart. Schlesser, Baldi and Mass remained on the driver roster, whilst Kenny Acheson, who had impressed in 1989, was let go and replaced by three junior team recruits, namely Michael Schumacher, Heinz-Harald Frentzen and Karl Wendlinger, the reigning German F3 champion, who took it in turns to drive with Jochen Mass.

This caused some upset within the Sauber-Mercedes operation and was seen by some people as an attempt by Untertürkheim to attract much-needed publicity to their racing campaign by bringing on the next generation of Austro-German Formula 1 hopefuls. The move was a success, nevertheless. None of the three had yet reached their 22nd birthday, but all displayed maturity and speed, evidenced by Schumacher's fastest lap in Mexico and the win by Wendlinger (and Mass) under pressure at Spa.

Dave Price and fellow British engineer Bob Bell left around this time and joined Acheson at Nissan.

At Silverstone, Schumacher's crew allegedly worked on the German's C11 outside the pitlane zone, which was expressly forbidden. As a result, he and the car were eliminated from the race. Spa saw both cars stay out on wet tyres on a drying track while the rest pitted for slicks, a ploy that would have cost them the race if Brundle had not suffered a fuel leak in the leading Jaguar.

Mexico was another near disaster for Mercedes. Schlesser and Baldi won, despite delaying a change to slicks too long, but both were then disqualified for taking on a fraction too much fuel. Fortunately, Mass and Schumacher were lying 2nd at the time and so rescued the win. Some of these were driver errors and some were down to pit mismanagement, but they were bungles that it was hard to envisage Dave Price having allowed to happen. Nevertheless, these rare mechanical gremlins and pit procedures were the only chinks in Mercedes-Benz's armour.

WATSONIAN ASIDES

One of the stars on the Porsche driver roster early in the Group C era was John Watson, picking up drives for Jaguar and Toyota later on as well. Historically, his climb through the racing hierarchy took him from club racer and Formula 2 privateer to F1 team leader and Grand Prix winner (shaving his beard after winning in Austria following a bet with team owner Roger Penske), with a final decade piloting Group C sports prototypes. Today, John is an F1 pundit, high on the media hit list as a 'man to go to' for a pithy comment on anything from safety issues to regulation changes. For the last 50 years, he has owned the same 911, a 2.7 Carrera RS, bought in 1974 from his race team owners, Hexagon-of-Highgate, whose F1 Brabham he drove.

Watson's final F1 season was 1983, marked by a win in the US GP West at Long Beach. He started the race 22nd on the grid, passing car after car to take the victory. Some achievement. But John believes overtaking ability is inherent:

In my day, overtaking was a skill you learned and developed, made easier because the cars didn't have the same level of aerodynamics they have today, and consequently the braking efficiency was nowhere near where it is nowadays. So you could do things in my era which would be virtually impossible these days. I could judge speed and distance pretty well, particularly coming into a braking zone, and when you're overtaking somebody you brake later than you would do on your own, and you then compromise the car you're overtaking by gathering your car up in a way that makes sure he isn't able to come back. Be assertive, and don't fall into the trap of getting caught behind a car for three or four laps, because you'll lose your momentum. It's not a matter of, 'I might overtake,' it's, 'I am overtaking you!' And quite often, the driver in that position will yield; your first strike is the one that really sets the ground rules: get out of my way, I am coming through, and once you develop that sort of reputation, people think, 'Oh shit, here he comes,' so you create your own legend.

John's F1 career drew to a close in 1983, having lost out in negotiations with McLaren over his retainer to upcoming Alain Prost. There was a single comeback GP at Brands in 1985, placing 7th for McLaren, which is not bad after a two-year lay-off, but in the meantime, he had stepped into the works Rothmans Porsche squad, driving 962s alongside hot shoe Stefan Bellof, most notably taking the win at Fuji in 1984.

Because the F1 McLaren's TAG turbo engine was built by Porsche, I got to speak to people in the Rothmans Porsche Group C team, and Sean Roberts fixed it for me to drive when they were running a third car or, for example, when Derek (Bell) was doing an IMSA round which clashed with a Group C WSC race. And in '84 the development of the PDK gearbox was taking place, and a car was entered at Imola and then at Nürburgring a couple of weeks later, but the PDK gearbox was not perfect at that stage so they withdrew the car, but I did the Spa 1,000km with Vern Schuppan, and then the penultimate round at Fuji with Stefan Bellof. That was an interesting insight into a young guy who was just unbelievable in a 956 or a 962, and the team loved him, especially Klaus Bischof (now Porsche Rolling Museum manager) who ran that particular car. They were friends as well as team members, and when you get a kid who is extending the potential of a car to the limits like Stefan did, and on some occasions exceeded the limits, that's what teams love. They love to see the equipment being driven to a new threshold, and that's what Stefan did. Derek couldn't do it, Ickx and Mass couldn't do it, but Bellof did.

Tragically, though, Bellof, then the reigning WSC champion, died at Spa the following September.

Co-driving this budding star in his championship-winning year provided Wattie with a niche in the Porsche works team.

In '85 I drove the third 962 with Vern and Al Holbert at Le Mans, but that was more like a Mobil Economy Run, and the race was won by Ludwig, Barilla and Winter in Reinhold Jöst's Porsche, and they must have been inventing the bloody fuel, because that car did things economy-wise that the factory Porsches certainly weren't doing!

Wattie also drove WSC events for Jaguar, handling the Group 44 XJR-5 at Le Mans in 1984, the Silk-Cut XJR-8 in 1987, placing 2nd in the WSC rankings with Jan Lammers, and the XJR-9LM in 1988, switching to TOM'S Toyota with the 89C-V in 1989. Swansong enduro in 1990 was helming the Richard Lloyd Racing Porsche 962C, finishing 11th at Le Mans. He has mixed views about the 24-Hours. 'I would like to see Le Mans become what it was in its infancy, which in the 1930s was a race for road-going production cars.' So, which was his favourite: Porsche, Jaguar or Toyota? 'Well, TWR was just down the road…!' comes the pragmatic reply.

For the 1985 Le Mans 24-Hours, John Watson joined 1983 winners Vern Schuppan and Al Holbert, dropping out in the 21st hour with engine failure.

JAGUAR REVAMPS

The 1990 season promised much but yielded little for Jaguar. After their miserable season on Dunlop radials, they switched to Goodyear tyres. The XJR-11 Turbo V6 was used for the entire calendar, although the V12s were resurrected in XJR-12 form for the Le Mans race. Since 1989, Tom Walkinshaw had restructured his Group C team to regain the championship's initiative. The biggest transformation was the establishment of a specialist technical centre, though rejected by long-time designer Tony Southgate who opted out, to be replaced by ex-Arrows man Ross Brawn – and future F1 team owner – to handle chassis design and development, while ex-BMW employee Gerhard Schumann was recruited to oversee the engines. Brawn did not make any radical changes to the Southgate chassis, instead laying out plans for the 1991 XJR14 atmospheric car, while Schumann refined the V6 turbo engine by replacing Zytek engine management with Bosch 1.7 Motronics. There were also changes on the driver roster: Patrick Tambay left, and John Nielsen concentrated exclusively on IMSA. Andy Wallace and Jan Lammers remained in the WSPC and were teamed together, while Alain Ferté, who had been brought in late in 1989 to relieve the jet-lagged Nielsen, secured a full-time seat, joining Martin Brundle in the lead car.

Although a decade on he would become the nation's favourite F1 television presenter, Martin Brundle's own F1 career had faded again with the demise of the Brabham F1 team, but he was welcomed back to TWR like a prodigal son. He was arguably the quickest driver that TWR had, and he won Le Mans for them and was a crowd-pleaser without a doubt. Chilean driver Eliseo Salazar, who had been slated to drive the number three car at Le Mans that eventually won, found Brundle had been popped into his seat after the Norfolk boy's own car had retired on Sunday morning. Salazar had qualified in car number three and was held in reserve all through the first half of the race and then placed in the failing car, number four, which immediately cooked its engine. The Walkinshaw team's only other win had come at the quaintly named British Empire Trophy in May, where after Sauber-Mercedes unexpectedly went awry, the Jaguars kept up the run of Silverstone luck to take a one-two in front of a small crowd.

The new Jaguar XJR-11s were certainly the best of the rest, but very soon after the start of the year, it became clear that the only way that TWR could hope to score a win over Sauber-Mercedes was by default, and the Swiss-German squad did not make enough serious mistakes for that to be a viable strategy. If that were not bad enough, TWR made mistakes of its own, notably, the incident at Donington that saw the 3rd and 7th-placed cars removed from the results for using a few litres too much fuel.

The start of the 1990 Silverstone 480km, with the Mercedes-Benz C11 of Baldi/Schlesser leading the two TWR Jaguars XJR-11s of Brundle/Ferté – the eventual winner – and Lammers/Wallace (2nd place) plus the Nissans and Toyota. The Mass/Schumacher Mercedes is absent, having been disqualified for receiving outside assistance during qualifying.

NISMO HEADWAY

Nissan made progress during the season, although that did not actually include any wins, and the British-based Nissan Motorsports Europe was broken up at the end of the season. As things got going, Nissan Motorsports Europe was able to run two cars using the same V8 power plant as before in an updated version of last year's Lola chassis, the R90C. So, there was room for a couple of extra drivers. Kenny Acheson took over the second car and was joined by Gianfranco Brancatelli after some musical chairs involving Martin Donnelly and Raoul Boesel. Mark Blundell and Julian Bailey stayed in the lead car. Out went veteran race manager Keith Greene, and in came Dave Price and Bob Bell from Sauber. To save cash, which was always in short supply, Nissan Motorsports Europe entries at the first round in Suzuka were taken up by the Japanese arm, NISMO. Driving an R89C, Anders Olofsson and Masahiro Hasemi finished 3rd. Thereafter, Nissan Motorsports Europe took over and, for the rest of the year, suffered the same malaise as Jaguar, having to pick up what Mercedes had left for them.

Apart from niggling problems like wheel nuts falling off at Monza and Silverstone, the Nissans' basic drawback was their thirst for fuel. The V8s were exceptionally reliable and powerful but rarely had enough petrol to reach the finish at racing speeds. For Le Mans, Nissan made their usual big effort, entering five works R90C cars: two from Nissan Motorsports Europe, chassis numbers #03 and #04; another two prepared by the US-based NPTI, #02 and #05; and one from Japan, #01. There were also two semi-works R89Cs, one from Team Le Mans, which was #03 and the other in the care of Yves Courage, #01. Amazingly, twenty-one drivers were employed for the event, and Nissan also pumped vast amounts of money into the race itself, so its logo was everywhere during the lead-up to the race weekend. All the works cars qualified well, with Blundell taking pole by a substantial margin, using what was known in the turbo era as a grenade engine. Things looked good, but by Sunday afternoon, it had gone sour. Bailey, Blundell and Brancatelli were leading on Saturday evening when the latter smashed into Suzuki's Toyota at the end of the pit straight and retired during the night. Brabham, Robinson and Daly in the first NPTI car were challenging for the lead when they developed a fuel leak, and that was effectively the end of that. The other American car trailed home in 17th, and the Courage car crossed the line in 22nd place.

Midway through the year, rumours circulated about Nissan's long-term future in sportscar racing. Chassis builder Lola was told that its services would no longer be required for 1991; the plan was to temporarily park the Group C assault and concentrate resources on IMSA. At season's end, Nissan Motorsports Europe had garnered enough points to finish 3rd, just behind Jaguar in the teams' table. This was a respectable enough performance, but it did not save them from dismissal. Nissan had no further use for its Nissan Motorsports Europe Group C project, and all the team personnel found themselves unemployed.

The Silk Cut TWR Jaguar XJR-11 of Martin Brundle – pictured – was disqualified from the 1990 Donington 480km, along with the second XJR-11 of Wallace/ Lammers, for using excess fuel.

TOM'S TIP-OFF

Toyota's 90CV was an updated version of the previous season's car. TOM'S GB, based at Hingham, Norfolk – almost literally a stone's throw from Group Lotus at Hethel – used the same fuel-thirsty V8 power unit as before. But to keep it competitive, the displacement was increased during the year from 3.2 to 3.6 litres, which simply made it even thirstier. Faced with a car that there was little chance of getting to the finish, let alone winning, regular drivers Johnny Dumfries and Geoff Lees, aided and abetted by Roberto Ravaglia, plus John Watson, Aguri Suzuki and Hitoshi Ogawa, had a challenging season. The only points were scored by TOM'S Japan, who substituted at Suzuka, Lees and Ogawa, taking 4th place with a 3.6-litre car. Things had not been helped by a spate of early-season crashes that destroyed or seriously damaged at least five chassis. Lees and Dumfries took out three cars at Monza alone, and Suzuki shunted at Spa and then again at Le Mans, where he collected Brancatelli's Nissan, vaulted the barriers, and caught fire. The Japanese had had enough

Joest Racing's 962C, driven by Bob Wollek and Hans Stuck, comes in for a pit stop on its way to 3rd place in the 1989 Le Mans 24-Hours, seven laps behind the winning Sauber-C9.

Nifty pit work as Hans Stuck swaps with Bob Wollek for a stint in the Joest Racing Porsche 962C during the 1989 Le Mans 24-Hours, where they finished 3rd.

and decided to concentrate on F1. Paradoxically, it was at Le Mans that Toyota had probably had its best race, with Lees, Ogawa and Sekiya seeing off all the Nissans and Mazdas to take 6th place in the other TOM'S car, a joint effort by the GB and Japan teams. There was also the Sigma Auto Racing Developments – SARD – entered 90CV, but that did not finish.

Powered by the Type 935 3.2-litre flat-six turbo, the Joest Racing Porsche 962C of Bob Wollek and Frank Jelinski came 7th in the 1990 Donington 480km.

Reinhold Jöst's two works-assisted Blaupunkt Porsche 962Cs represented the fifth factory effort. After a relatively successful 1989 season, which saw the Abtsteinach outfit take second in the teams' table with a run of point-scoring performances, Porsche sensed a new lease of life for the 962. Like Mercedes-Benz, they swung fully behind their chosen representatives, although like his Swiss-German rivals, Jöst clearly remained in full control of his organisation and kept it a distinctly separate entity from the Weissach factory. Porsche's Norbert Singer was now assisting with team management but based at Joest Racing and not so much at Weissach.

The 962Cs were new works specification tubs fitted with the latest 3.0-litre and 3.2-litre flat-six engines, and there was little doubt that the team would have been a potent force if only the decision had not been made to swap from Goodyear to Michelin rubber. This decision was made because Porsche was not keen to be the third-string customer for Goodyear's products behind Mercedes and Jaguar. And, of course, the championship had been won on Michelin in 1989, despite some dark muttering from the Sauber-Mercedes team about the quality of the tyres. Regular pilots Bob Wollek, Frank Jelinski and Jonathan Palmer struggled all through 1990 on the Michelin rubber, and they simply were not able to make the cars handle optimally. The best Jöst's cars could usually do was run behind the Sauber-Mercedes, TWR-Jaguars and Nissans to lead the private Porsche teams home. This earned them 5th place in the Teams' championship, behind C2's Spice Engineering.

To boost his budget, Reinhold Jöst ran two other private 962Cs for Stanley Dickens, John Winter, Henri Pescarolo and Jean-Louis Ricci, sporting combinations of Mizuno and Primagaz sponsorship – and Goodyear tyres. Neither car did any better than the factory versions, though. The 962 was by now a car out of time, and it showed. But Walter Brun very nearly embarrassed everyone at Le Mans. Instead of the accustomed long-tail bodywork commonly fitted at Le Mans and high-speed circuits, Brun took a gamble and sent Oscar Larrauri out in short-tail, low-downforce trim on sticky Yokohamas in qualifying. The idea worked so well, thanks in part to the retarding effect of the new Mulsanne chicanes, that he was the only driver able to get into the Nissan's quick qualifying times.

The Porsche 962C of Joest Racing was driven into 8th place by Henri Pescarolo and Jean-Louis Ricci at the Donington 480km in 1989.

Argentinean Oscar Larrauri spent nine seasons in Group C, driving a Lancia LC1 for Scuderia Sivama, Porsche 956 and 962C over eight seasons with Brun Motorsport, and 962CK6 for Kremer Racing.

The Hydro Aluminium-sponsored Brun Motorsport 962C of Harald Huysman and Oscar Larrauri in the Donington Park pitlane during the 1989 480km race, where they finished 5th.

The set-up was retained for the race, in which Brun and Jesús Pareja drove like mad for most of the 24 hours, after Larrauri fell sick on the Saturday evening, and nearly claimed 2nd place, only to experience a blown engine with fifteen minutes to go. Elsewhere, during the year, a second 962C run for Larrauri and Harald Huysman, paid for by the Norwegian's Hydro-Aluminium sponsors, did not feature on the podium but notched up enough points finishes to bring the Swiss slot-machine millionaire's team 6th place in the final table.

MANHOLE COVER

Brun Motorsport had a large amount of its hardware wiped out in a ridiculous incident at Montreal's notorious island-park Circuit Gilles Villeneuve that saw both Huysman and Pareja hitting a loose manhole cover, the latter crashing and stopping the race. The manhole ripped the bottom out of Pareja's car, rupturing the fuel tank, which then spilt into the engine compartment, turning the 962 into an inferno. The Montreal organisers eventually admitted liability and paid Brun a reported $700,000 compensation for his cars. However, the Spaniard was lucky to escape with nothing worse than superficial burns.

Kremer Racing, also using Yokohama tyres, passed another season, mostly trailing around in the middle of the pack. They had prepared a new carbon chassis 962CK6/05-2, which was a slight improvement on the 1989 model, but was only raced at Suzuka and Spa. Otherwise, it was kept as a spare – a scrutineering dummy, while the team campaigned the Thompson-built honeycomb chassis cars CK6/06-2 and CK6/07-2. As their regular lead driver, ex-Zakspeed F1 pilot Bernd Schneider managed 4th at Montreal and 5th at Silverstone. He was joined by South African renter driver Sarel van der Merwe. A second entry for Nova Engineering came 5th at Suzuka and all but one of the European races by the new Strandell Convector team, who first leased Kremer's earlier composite monocoque and then acquired a new factory chassis 962.162.

Touring car specialist Scotsman Anthony Reed was Convector's lead driver, swapping over to the Japanese Alpha Team and sharing third place with Tiff Needell and David Sears in the first Porsche home. The wealthy German Jürgen Oppermann bought his way into Obermaier Racing, bringing with him the means to purchase new cars. Oddly, considering it was the last proper year of the fuel regulations formula, the team decided to buy three brand-new Porsche 962s, and then tried to sell them again before the calendar reached halfway. Harald Gröhs briefly led at Montreal, staying out for a couple of extra laps as the leaders went in for fuel. But Oppermann and Otto Altenbach were in over their heads, with Oppermann spending a lot of time on repairs.

Richard Lloyd persevered with his honeycomb 956 GTI clone #201, sponsored by Italya Sport, with Manuel Reuter, Stefan Andskar, James Weaver and Perry McCarthy sharing driving duties. Reuter took 3rd in the chaos of Montreal and 6th at Spa with Andskar, but a two-car entry at Le Mans turned sour when #201 burned out after a puncture, while the other car, a Porsche-built 962C, chassis #161, at least finished 11th in the care of John Watson, Bruno Giacomelli and Canadian Alan Berg.

Further down the running order, Tim Lee-Davey, Franz Conrad, Antoine Salamin, the Alméras Brothers (Jean-Marie and Jacques), and Jochen Dauer all raced their 962Cs. The Montpellier-based Alméras Brothers tended to be somewhat erratic but provided variety with their experimental low-dive bodywork.

Montpellier-based specialist Porsche tuners Alméras Frères was founded in 1971 by brothers Jean-Marie and Jacques Alméras, who ran a 962C in the WSPC in 1989 and developed unique bodywork for their prototype 911 GT1, photographed with the author as the passenger on the Millau viaduct.

The 3.5-litre Cosworth DFRS V8-engined Spice SE90C came 5th in the 1990 Donington 480km, driven by Eric Van de Poele and Bruno Giacomelli, with Eric at the wheel here.

CHAMBERLAIN ENGINEERING

In 1986, former Clubmans' racer Hugh Chamberlain entered C2 with a Tiga-Hart, partnered by Will Hoy, their best result being 7th in class at Spa. Chamberlain bought a new chassis from C2 champions Spice Engineering for 1987, and Nick Adams became lead driver, and he and Graham Duxbury won their class at the non-championship Kyalami 480km. Owner-driver Jean-Louis Ricci added his own Spice to Chamberlain's team later in the year, and the partnership continued into 1988. Their respective Spices were runners-up in the C2 Teams' championship behind Spice Engineering, with Ricci and co-driver Claude Ballot-Léna sixth in the drivers' standings. In 1989 Chamberlain switched from their turbocharged Hart engine to the ubiquitous Ford Cosworth V8, and Nick Adams and Fermín Vélez won the season's first four races, winning the C2 Teams' and Drivers' championships. In 1992, Chamberlain Engineering won the 1992 FIA Cup for Teams, and Ferdinand de Lesseps won the Drivers' title.

BOLD SPICE

The last successful factory entries were from Spice, who had pioneered the free-fuel formula and were hoping to reap long-term benefits. Despite being down on power compared to the turbos, there were some outstanding performances, but they were often stymied by a lack of finance, having to rely almost entirely on cash from a selection of renter drivers, which mitigated against continuity. Two SE90Cs, updated versions of the 1989 car, were equipped with Nicholson Cosworth DFRS engines and ran as a pair when funds permitted, though often only one made it into the picture, Le Mans being a typical example, although amazingly Gordon Spice and his drivers saw off Toyota and all the Porsche teams including Jöst, Kremer and Brun in the final Teams' table, finishing the year 4th behind Sauber-Mercedes, TWR-Jaguar and Nissan Motorsport.

ENGINE SWAPS

If Spice's fiscal difficulties were constraining, their customer, Hugh Chamberlain's, were equally so, and an ambitious two-car operation featuring regular drivers Nick Adams, Cor Euser and Charles Houseman was also hampered by mechanical issues, exchanging Hart 415T engines for Ford Cosworth V8s. Equally, Louis Descartes inserted a Nicholson-built DFZ engine in his C289 composite C2 chassis, but with no success. The Italian CSAI Federation commissioned a new Alba from Giorgio Stirano, designated the AR20 and powered by the Motori Moderni Subaru flat-12. The Alba consistently failed to qualify until a late change to a 4.5-litre Buick engine enabled it to get onto the grid at Montreal, and finish 16th and last at Mexico City.

Anyway, Peugeot was also present at the Nürburgring and later rounds at Magny-Cours, Suzuka and Autopolis. FISA had allowed them a special dispensation to race their new 3.5-litre 905 prototype without penalties for the rest of the season. At this point, Jean Todt was best known as a successful rally navigator, and his years as Ferrari team boss and FIA president were in the future. As principal of Peugeot-Talbot Racing, his team's debut appearance was eagerly awaited, and when Keke Rosberg and Jean-Pierre Jabouille were persuaded out of F1 World Championship retirement to drive, it was seen as one of the most positive developments in the Group C WSCC championship for some time. However, of all the recent arrivals in sports car racing, Peugeot was seen as the most likely to move into F1 as a result. Two new V10-powered chassis, EV11 and EV12, were built with the assistance of aeronautics manufacturer Dassault, with development and testing work carried out on the former chassis. EV12 qualified 12th in Canada but retired after 22 laps with low fuel pressure. EV12 was used again in

Jochen Mass and Jean-Louis Schlesser's Mercedes-Benz C291 flat-12 leads the Peugeot 905 V10 of Mauro Baldi and Philippe Alliot during the 1991 Nürburgring 430km – the race distance shortened yet again – the fifth round of the EC. Neither car finished.

Mexico with EV11 as a spare. It took 11th spot on the grid and finished 13th, hampered by problems with tyre grip and a faulty starter motor.

Meanwhile, Mussato's Lancia, now called the SP90, crashed and burned to destruction in the middle of the night with Fabio Magnani at the wheel. There were the Japanese-based Schuppan and Alpha 962C squads, Moretti's Momo IMSA version, the GTP Mazdas and, perhaps most interestingly, an attempt to make the ageing Lola T700 chassis a viable proposition.

And that was the end of Group C in its last proper restricted fuel season, with the exception of the C1s and C2s that took advantage of Le Mans' non-championship status to have a fling in world-class endurance racing.

CHAPTER 7

PEUGEOT MOPS UP 1992–93

Dramatic aerodynamic facade of the low-slung Peugeot 905 photographed by Alex Denham in the pits during Peter Auto's Group C Revival race at the 2022 Spa Classic meeting.

The existence of the World Sportscar Championship, the modern incarnation of long-distance endurance racing, was called into question at the end of the 1991 season, and it only just survived – and then effectively only for another season. The first year of the new formula – renamed the Sportscar World Championship – was bound to be filled with difficulties, and the birth of the 3.5-litre sportscar championship was particularly fraught. It was supported by just three manufacturers: Jaguar, who won the title; Peugeot, who finished runner-up; and Mercedes-Benz, who finished third. But at the beginning of the season, there were no more than seven new-generation cars on the grid. The numbers clawed their way up to double figures by the end of the season, but even as Toyota joined in, Mercedes-Benz announced their withdrawal. Most of the manufacturers were wrong-footed by confusing statements from FISA. Le Mans, always the prime event of the series, was run outside the World Championship in 1989 and 1990. The Japanese teams, Nissan, Mazda and Toyota, were more interested in doing the prestigious 24-Hour race with its exalted publicity status than doing the full season and delayed the development of their 3.5-litre cars.

MAD MAX

The seeds were sown for this debacle a couple of years earlier. Max Mosley, then chairman of the FISA Manufacturers Commission, conceded at Suzuka in April 1990 that the existing unlimited cars would be allowed one year's grace. That meant that the Porsche 962, Jaguar XJR, Mercedes-Benz stock blocks and Mazda rotary engines would be allowed to compete in 1991, but only to make up the grids, and with handicaps imposed to make sure they could not win. Their handicaps, it turned out, were so severe that they deterred Nissan and Toyota from competing, and several Porsche teams thought better of it, too, causing a catastrophic financial drought in the sportscar racing scene.

TIMES PAST

Three years earlier, in 1988, the World Sports Prototype Championship was flourishing. Even though Porsche was in decline, Jaguar and Sauber-Mercedes were battling hard for victories, with Toyota, Nissan and Mazda appearing at the key races. A successful C2 Class was running, too, in which Spice Engineering was the dominant manufacturer, and some races were very well supported. When FISA took full control in 1989 to pave the way for the 3.5-litre formula, it was mandated that all the participating teams would be obliged to contest all the races and not cherry-pick events like Le Mans. That ensured 36 cars at every race. Each team was paid $3,000 per car, per start, no matter whether it was Monza or Mexico, Silverstone or Suzuka. There were no expenses for travel nor any prize money. Bernie Ecclestone demanded $600,000 from race organisers, circuit owners and promoters for the privilege of staging each race. So, FISA became very rich, and the teams became relatively poor and, unsurprisingly, when the glorious new era was heralded in April 1991, there were just sixteen entries registered for the Sportscar World Championship. Spectators were now obliged to pay Formula 1 ticket prices to see half a grid of disparate cars, so they stayed away. The championship's nadir was at Magny-Cours, the circuit in central France that had turned away 20,000 people in July because they could not access the F1 Grand Prix, and there were fewer than 10,000 spectators at the Nevers track in mid-September to watch the World Sportscar Championship race, many of whom had received free tickets from Peugeot. The 962Cs of Kremer Racing finished 6th and 8th, with Courage Competition 9th and Obermaier Racing 10th in a race monstered by Peugeot.

FRENCHMAN'S CREAK

Despite the ups and downs of administrative management, Le Mans has always been the nucleus of the World Sportscar Championship – or World Endurance Championship, whatever name the series went by – and it was Le Mans that kept the championship in being in 1992. Amusingly, Le Mans has, more or less, always been Great Britain's second-largest motor race after the British Grand Prix, in the sense that, in mid-June every year, around 50,000 people pour across the Channel to attend it. We used to think that was about the headcount for the non-championship Race of Champions and Daily Express International F1 races at Brands Hatch and Silverstone in the 1970s, with 70,000 turning out for the F1 Grands Prix. But Le Mans? In 1992, more people journeyed from the UK to attend Le Mans than the combined attendance at the Group C races at Silverstone, Donington and Brands Hatch.

ONE-SIDED AFFAIR

The Sportscar World Championship season was something of a one-sided contest in 1991, because the TWR Silk Cut Jaguar team performed with distinction throughout. Ross Brawn's XJR-14 was immediately the class of the field, even though the first trials were carried out only three weeks before the opening round at Suzuka. There was a setback in Japan, which benefited Peugeot, but the Jaguars were consistently four seconds a lap quicker there. After Monza, where they finished 1st and 2nd, and at Silverstone, where they were 1st and 3rd, the Kidlington team's speed advantage had virtually disappeared when challenged at the Nürburgring in August, but that was another 1–2 result, securing the Teams' championship title. Over the greater part of the season, the Silk Cut Jaguars ran rings around Peugeot and Mercedes-Benz, both in terms of speed and reliability, and a couple of late-season defeats could not deny that.

As previously mentioned, the newish French GP venue at Magny-Cours near Nevers in central France was an unlikely venue as a game-changer. The result of the sixth round of the series at Magny-Cours on 15 September should have put Silk Cut Jaguar well in shape for the main title. But what no one had foreseen was that the Peugeot-Talbot Sport team would turn the tables and dominate the race with a 1–2 result.

The winning duo of the 430km race were Keke Rosberg and Yannick Dalmas, and in 2nd place, 43 seconds behind, were Suzuka winners Philippe Alliot and Mauro Baldi. Faster than Jaguar in testing and quickest in all four practice and qualifying sessions, setting the fastest lap and displaying total reliability, the margin might have been a lot larger, but for a messy pit stop that was beyond the team's control. Although the purple Jaguars were comprehensively outpaced at Magny-Cours by a margin of two seconds per lap on average, the result was not a complete disaster. David Brabham helped Teo Fabi to a podium 3rd place, and Derek Warwick finished 5th after an eventful run, which included a flash fuel fire and an impromptu diversion into a gravel trap. The important feature of the French race from Jaguar's point of view was that Sauber-Mercedes could not earn any points at Magny-Cours and, therefore, were not realistic challengers any more. Ongoing technical problems with porous engine blocks – all 30 units – blighted the effort of the Swiss-German team that had been almost invincible in the previous two years.

Meanwhile, the Jaguar XJR-14s performed particularly well on faster circuits like Suzuka, where the Group C

The 3.5-litre flat-12 Mercedes-Benz C291 of Karl Wendlinger and Michael Schumacher came 2nd in the 1991 Silverstone 430km, ahead of the 3.5-litre Cosworth HB-powered Jaguar XJR-14 of Martin Brundle/Derek Warwick.

Running in C1, the Peugeot 905 used the 3.5-litre Peugeot SA35 V10 engine, though Keke Rosberg/ Yannick Dalmas recorded a DNF at Silverstone's 430km in 1991.

Derek Warwick readies himself in the cabin of the XJR-14 for the 1991 Silverstone 430km, where he finished 1st.

record stood at 120.08 mph to Derek Warwick, and at Monza, where Martin Brundle set the Group C record at 145.48mph, and at Silverstone, where the 130.8mph outright record was also held by Brundle, and the Nürburgring's 124.58mph outright record went to Teo Fabi.

Peugeot, on the other hand, made real progress at the Nürburgring with the 905 Evolution and showed it to be superior at Magny-Cours, where the fastest lap was set by Philippe Alliot at 111.32mph, while the Jaguar drivers complained of a lack of grip and hence no traction. The XJR-14s continued to be the pace setters in the faster corners but were handicapped on the slow turns. However, Michael Schumacher claimed a place on the front row of the Magny-Cours grid in the Mercedes-Benz C291, while Jean-Louis Schlesser topped the Sunday morning warm-up times. Their Goodyears were working well when the suspension had been set up properly, and that, conversely, was the crux of Jaguar's difficulties: the XJR-14 lacked mechanical grip. Accordingly, the Jaguars were laden with aerodynamic appendages to increase the downforce. The Peugeot 905s were in difficulties, too, with tendencies to jump and porpoise at speed, although subtle changes to settings cured the problems. This was not a new problem: the phenomenon had affected the Lotus Type 80 'wingless' ground-effect F1 car back in 1979, and that was quickly given wings and spoilers to help counteract the problem.

Pit stop during the final race in the 1991 World Sportscar Championship at Japan's Autopolis 430km for the winning Mercedes-Benz C291 of Michael Schumacher and Karl Wendlinger, powered by the 3.5-litre M291 flat-12 engine.

The Jaguar team might have considered Magny-Cours as an aberration, a venue that suited the Peugeots and their Michelin tyres and where the XJR-14s proved difficult to set up properly. No such consolation could be justified at the next round in Mexico, where the Peugeots were again at least a second a lap quicker, even though the Jaguars were well set up, and where even their reliability factor was superior on race day. It demonstrated that more development work would be needed on the XJR-14 in preparation for the 1992 World Championship, and ahead of that, a new major sponsor would have to be found to replace Silk Cut cigarettes. By late season, there were already signs that the Jaguar budget had been cut back in terms of manpower and development.

LATE IN THE DAY

On 27 October, at Autopolis, the 2.9-mile circuit in Japan, Mercedes-Benz came right back into the reckoning. The infuriating manufacturing problem that had dogged their M291 3.5-litre flat-12 engine casings had been sorted, and Michael Schumacher made a supreme effort to snatch a place on the front row in the C291, and he and Karl Wendlinger beat the two Jaguars by two minutes to take the victory. By now, it was clear that Schumacher was a future champion, having set the pace in Peter Sauber's team, and was looking set to enter Formula 1 with Benetton in 1992.

In the second Mercedes-Benz C291, Jean-Louis Schlesser and Jochen Mass were consistently circulating two seconds a lap slower than their 22-year-old teammates in the lead car. Nonetheless, it was interesting to reflect that Jochen Mass was one of team manager Jochen Neerpasch's drivers back in the early '70s when he drove a works Köln Capri. By the same token, Schumacher, Wendlinger, Frentzen and possibly Wendlinger's co-driver Fritz Kreutzpointner could all be said to be Neerpasch protégés. There is a certain gratification in knowing, with hindsight, that one of the greatest-ever Formula 1 drivers came to the fore in Group C endurance racing.

Back at Autopolis '91, and the reliability of the two Mercedes race engines was discovered to be down to a recognised manufacturing fault, and even though the two best engines in the batch were kept for the race, one of them broke during the warm-up. Porsche, winners of 42 World or European Championship events since Group C was conceived in 1982, had by now faded rather quietly from World Championship racing, and would re-emerge with the 911 GT1 in the BPR Global GT series.

Michael Schumacher contemplates the controls of his Mercedes-Benz C291 in the pitlane at Autopolis, where he and Karl Wendlinger took the victory in 1991.

The TWR Jaguar XJR-14 of Martin Brundle heads the Mercedes-Benz C291 of eventual winners Karl Wendlinger and Michael Schumacher at the Autopolis 430km, Japan, the eighth and final round of the 1991 World Sportscar Championship.

JOEST RACING

Reinhold Joest set up Joest Racing in 1978, winning several WEC rounds. Rivalling the works Rothmans Porsche team, Joest Racing went on to win Le Mans in 1984 and 1985.

Reinhold Jöst is the most successful private entrant of Porsches in Group C. A key figure in world motorsport, he raced Porsches for twenty years, and his team won Le Mans four times for Porsche and, subsequently, a further eight times for Audi Sport.

For two decades, Reinhold Jöst drove a succession of Porsches in the crucial period when the marque was making its breakthrough into the big time. Retiring in 1982 to focus on running his team, Jöst was selected in 1999 to run the ultra-successful works Audis that dominated the World Sportscar Championship for thirteen years. When I spoke to him in the Jöst (Jöst) Motorsport motorhome at Silverstone during the 1,000km, he was commendably modest about his achievements.

Reinhold's competition career began in hill climbs in 1962 in a Porsche 356 Carrera Speedster.

Reinhold Jöst and Willi Kauhsen came 4th in the 1971 Spa-Francorchamps 1,000km in the Auto Usdau Porsche 917.

Waiting in the Silverstone pitlane to go out for qualifying for the 1983 1,000km, the Klaus Ludwig/ Henri Pescarolo New Man Joest Racing 956#104 eventually came 2nd overall. Behind is the Lyncar MS83 of Costas Los/Richard Down/Les Blackburn which did not finish.

> *It was light and nice to drive, but a year later, I built a new 356 Carrera coupé, which was really the top car at the time. This was the European Hillclimb Championship, with rounds at Eberbach in the Odenwald near Heidelberg, Rossfeld-Berchtesgaden and Schauinsland-Freiburg. They were big events with factory Porsches and Alfa Romeos running.*

Jumping ahead two decades, he goes on:

> *When the Group C regulations came in, we built a 936C for the '82 season, which was a coupé built on nearly the same chassis, but the wheelbase was longer with the same engine and gearbox. We were up against the factory Porsche 956s, but that car wasn't available to customers in its first year. My driving career stopped in '82, and after twenty years, it was very hard, but it was the right decision at the time. My last big race was the Kyalami 9-Hours in November '81 with Jochen Mass, and we won that. That's not a bad way to finish a racing career!*

In 1983, Reinhold bought two 956s. 'Dr Porsche met us at the traditional end-of-year party, and then the next day, he invited us to his private residence, which was very nice and very family-oriented.' Although Reinhold was racing against the works Rothmans 956s, Porsche nonetheless took care to supply him with the best equipment.

> *Absolutely; it was always very good working with Porsche. In '83, we were running 2nd when Klaus Ludwig had an accident and*

The start of the DRM round 3 on 1 May 1983, at Berlin's unique AVUS racetrack, won by Bob Wollek in Joest Racing's 956 #104 (right), with pole sitter Volkert Merl 4.6sec behind him in the second Joest Racing 956 #004. Leopold von Bayern (left) finished 5th in the Joest Racing 936/80 #004. Opened in 1921, AVUS consisted of an 8km lap along a dead-straight stretch of Autobahn, bookended by a couple of vast hairpins at either end – one, formerly steeply banked with a rough brick surface and now a vast truck park, the other absorbed by overgrown woodland, of which photographer Antony Fraser and the author discovered the shrouded spectator banking during a photoshoot on a Porsche 997.

needed a new rear tail, and this cost a lot of time, but in '84, I knew exactly what we had to do to win this race. Porsche refused to send works cars to Le Mans because of the fuel restrictions, and so we won with Klaus Ludwig and Henri Pescarolo driving. We beat the works cars in '85 with drivers Paolo Barilla, John Winter and Klaus Ludwig, and in '86, we were leading, but after Joe Gartner's fatal accident in the Kremer 956, the pace car was out for two hours, and the engine cooled down too much in the night air, and eventually the oil pump failed. We were going for a triple, basically '84, '85, '86.

After that, Joest Racing contested the North American IMSA GTP series. 'In 1990, we won the 1991 Daytona 24-Hours with Bob Wollek, Henri Pescarolo, Frank Jelinski and Hurley Haywood in the 962. Our last year with the IMSA 962 was 1993 with the double-decker rear wing.'

After that, Jöst's association with Porsche went on hold until the WSC95, which won Le Mans in 1996 and '97. 'The last race we did with Porsche was Road Atlanta at the end of the '98 season, and then I signed the contract with Audi at the start of '99.'

The trio of 962C LHs entered for the 1989 Le Mans by Joest Racing; from left, the #C125 of Bob Wollek and Hans Stuck, which came 3rd, #007 of Frank Jelinski, Pierre-Henri Raphanel and 'John Winter', which succumbed to a water leak, and #004/#104C of Henri Pescarolo, Jean-Louis Ricci and Claude Ballot-Léna which came 6th.

Suitably battle-scarred after 24 hours' racing, Derek Bell, Hans Stuck and Frank Jelinski placed 7th at Le Mans 1991 in the 3.2-litre twin-turbo Konrad Motorsport/Joest Racing 962 C#149> #012.

Reinhold Jöst masterminded four Le Mans wins for Porsche in 1984, 1985, 1996, and 1997. This made Joest Racing the most successful private Porsche team, winning the prestigious Porsche Cup eight times. Since 2000, Joest Racing and Audi Sport have won the Le Mans 24-Hours eight times.

SPRINT RACING

By the end of 1991, the writing was on the wall for Group C. The shortened races – which did not appeal either to television or 'sprint' race fans, and actually irked endurance race fans – and the cost of 3.5-litre cars spiralling upwards due to F1 and aerospace technology inroads were driving spectators, sponsors and competitors away in droves. Jaguar and Mercedes-Benz – who clinched a late-season win with their C291 as consolation for a terrible season – both announced their withdrawal from Group C, largely because they were not keen to spend money only to lose out to less prestigious marques such as Toyota and Peugeot.

The long climb back towards a respectable level of entertainment began in 1992 when races were restored to 500 kilometres at least. Private teams were allowed to compete more fairly and less expensively against the manufacturers. The goal was to return to 1,000-kilometre race distances, as a car that cannot make it over 1,000 kilometres has no chance of lasting a 24-hour marathon. By 1992, however, the Group C nomenclature was barely mentioned in the media, apparently having been superseded by the World Sportscar Championship. So far as the FISA World Council was concerned, the twenty cars needed to register for the ten-round World Championship would not include those registered for the FIA Cup Series, which was reserved for the seven rounds in Europe. It was quite clear that the existing teams would not be able to produce twenty cars, even if they wanted to, and the World Council stipulated that major manufacturers would be held financially responsible for the non-appearance of any cars. Understandably, Peugeot, Toyota and Mazda would not enter into such a commitment on behalf of private owners, bearing in mind that each no-show penalty would cost $250,000, which the organisers would claim. There was much politicking behind the scenes. Peugeot team manager Jean Todt declared that if the turbocharged cars like the 962 ran at Le Mans, then Peugeot would not turn up, and not surprisingly, FISA was under pressure from Porsche, which had given an enormous commitment to the World Sportscar Championship Series over the years, as well as Toyota and Mazda.

Pretty in pink: the Pleasure Racing Mazda 787B of Tetsuji Shiratori and Masatomo Shimizu came 8th in the Suzuka 500km, round 1 of the 1992 All-Japan Sports Prototype Championship and a round of the Fuji Long Distance Series.

THE END GAME

The series did run in 1992, but with a heavily curtailed schedule of races and only Peugeot and Toyota as the major players participating. Very few privateers had either the funds or the inclination to enter, and after a few races, the World Sportscar Championship ceased to exist. Former regulars like Kremer Racing and Courage opted out. Mercedes-Benz was reeling from the engine debacle that had afflicted the C291 and dropped plans to enter an updated C292.

Having invested heavily in the 905, Peugeot won all but the opening Monza race, which was taken by the Toyota TS010 of Geoff Lees and Hitoshi Ogawa. Typically, 1992's pitiful grids numbered under a dozen cars, of which only four were competitive. The Euro Racing Lolas often scored good placings but were well behind the works cars, and the Mazda MXR-01, now running not rotary engines but instead, 1992's Jaguar XJR-14 Judd-built customer engines, were rarely on the pace, although they did run strongly at Le Mans.

The series was done, although Group C Toyotas and Peugeots took up the cudgels at Le Mans again in 1993, with Peugeot once more victorious. The final race featuring Group C cars was at Le Mans in 1994 when Toyota were narrowly beaten by the Dauer-Porsche 962C.

With the 1993 SWC season cancelled by the FIA, elsewhere, the All-Japan series also collapsed, while IMSA staggered on with small grids, GTP morphing into ALMS, the American Le Mans series, in 1999. ALMS spawned the European Le Mans Series in 2004.

Third place in the 1994 Le Mans 24-Hours went to Hans Stuck/Thierry Boutsen/Danny Sullivan in the 3.0-litre 935 turbo-powered Dauer 962. Winners were Yannick Dalmas, Hurley Haywood and Mauro Baldi in the other Dauer 962.

So, the FIA's decision to revoke fuel economy rules, shorten races for television coverage, and introduce F1-based 3.5-litre rules finally killed off Group C. Cynics suggest that F1 supremo Bernie Ecclestone was keen to lure Mercedes and Peugeot into F1, and the demise of Group C did achieve that. And, sure, there is a book to be written about the next phase in the endurance racing saga, involving Le Mans Prototypes (LMPs) that succeeded Group C, a formula that continues to power the top echelon of long-distance racing.

MOVING SWIFTLY ON

Summing up the demise of Group C, the category floundered because certain egotistical individuals, including the Parisian rule-makers, had overreaching ambitions and too much power within the sport, while the manufacturers, by now, had too little at stake in Group C as a whole to make it worthwhile making a stand. Porsche, Mercedes-Benz, Toyota and Audi went on to capitalise magnificently on the

On the starting grid ahead of the 2022 Le Mans 24-Hours, the Oreca 07 Gibson GK428 4.2-litre V8 of the Franco-Swiss Cool Racing Team ran in LMP2 and came 11th overall, driven by Yifei Ye, Ricky Taylor and Niklas Krütten.

GERMAN GIANT

Teammates in 1971 when racing in the European Touring Car Championship for Ford Köln, Jochen Mass and John Fitzpatrick hang out again in the paddock at the 2014 Goodwood Revival in the 1982 John Paul JLP-4 IMSA 935.

As we approach the end of the Group C saga, we round it off by chatting to a driver who was in it from the off. Spanning over five decades, Jochen Mass's racing career included winning the European Touring Car Championship with Ford Capris in 1972, Formula 1 with March, Surtees and McLaren, and World Champion Sportscar driver in 1976 with the 936. While outright Le Mans success eluded him until 1989 with the Sauber-Mercedes C9, he did win the German sportscar championship with Porsche in 1985. By rights, he should have won Le Mans a few times.

> *We had small, silly things to go wrong. With Jacky, I had no misgivings about the 24-Hours, but I did have misgivings about the safety at Le Mans because the arrogance of the Automobile Club de l'Ouest was just mind-blowing. The pits were atrocious, and the sheer danger caused by negligence was what I disliked about Le Mans. When we drove there, there were still no chicanes, which was, in fact, a lot better, because now it is inviting a lot more accidents than before. But I liked it while I was doing it. I was always of the disposition that, if you don't like it and if you think it's wrong, don't do it.*

Porsche or Sauber-Mercedes? 'Generally speaking? The Porsche was more of a workhorse than the C9 and C11, which felt more refined.'

The 1989 Nürburgring 480km gets under way, with the Sauber-Mercedes pair of Jean-Louis Schlesser/Jochen Mass's winning car just ahead of Baldi/Acheson, who finished 2nd, just 2 seconds in arrears. Baldi started from pole, and Schlesser set fastest lap. In pursuit are George Fouché/Giovanni Lavaggi (3rd) in the Kremer 962C, Andrew Gilbert-Scott/Julian Bailey's Nissan (DNF), Oscar Larrauri/Franz Konrad (6th) in the Brun 962C and Johnny Dumfries/Geoff Lees' Toyota (7th).

Coming up the pitlane during Le Mans 2015 is the 3.7-litre V8 works LMP1 Toyota TS040 Hybrid, driven to 8th overall by Anthony Davidson, Sébastien Buemi and Kazuki Nakajima.

The 4.5-litre Gibson GK458 V8-powered Oreca 07 of DKR Engineering ran in the LMP2 Pro-Am class at the 2022 Le Mans, driven to 22nd place by Laurents Hörr, Jean Glorieux and Alexandre Cougnaud.

LMP2 (Pro-Am) Ligier JS P217 Gibson 4.2-litre V8 refuels during the 2022 Le Mans 24-Hours.

new LMP regulations, and the longevity of the present LMP categories – twenty seasons and counting – suggests that, actually, there was little amiss with the original tenets of Group C; it was just badly handled at the end, and the vested interests of the power brokers got the better of it. Come to think of it, there were similar loggerhead moments in Formula 1, such as the FISA-FOCA war of 1978 – a confrontation between Mr Ecclestone and J-M Balestre over the control of F1 – and the Drivers' Strike at Kyalami in 1982, led by Niki Lauda, in protest at the FIA seeking to impose a Super Licence on them.

Whatever, the die was cast. LMP cars made their debut in the 2004 Le Mans 24-Hours, split into LMP1 and LMP2 classes, with LMP1s using larger custom-built engines and LMP2s using smaller production-based engines. Soon enough, manufacturers and privateers including Ferrari, Porsche and Mazda embraced the LMP classes. Cars fell into three main categories, each with different performance levels and regulations. Hypercar (LMH/LMDh) remained the top-tier class in 2024, featuring the most advanced technology, with cars producing around 670–700bhp. Brands including Toyota, Ferrari and Porsche have competed in this class, their cars built for cutting-edge performance with complex hybrid systems. Next up is LMP2, positioned just below Hypercars and enabling a balance of performance and cost-efficiency. Powered by a 560bhp Gibson V8 engine, these cars are lighter and less expensive than Hypercars and are a mainstay of the European Le Mans Series (ELMS) and FIA World Endurance Championship (WEC). The current regulations will remain valid until 2028. LMP3 cars are designed for teams on a budget and as a stepping stone for up-and-coming drivers. Although less powerful than LMP2s, they are powered by 455bhp 5.6-litre Nissan VK56 V8 engines, delivering a maximum speed of 290km/h. Subdivisions include the LMP2 Pro-Am, LMP GTE Pro and LMP GTE Am classes.

In 2025 the LMP3 class is scheduled to undergo significant changes to remain competitive until 2029. The major update is the introduction of a new 3.5-litre twin-turbo V6 engine developed by Oreca, replacing the ageing Nissan VK56 V8. This new engine promises improvements in fuel efficiency performance and noise reduction, all while keeping costs manageable for teams. Key models such as the Ligier JS P325, Duqueine D09, ADESS AD25 and Ginetta G51-LT-P3 Evo are to the fore, and in 2024, the Ligier JS P320 and Duqueine D08 have been prominent in the championships, while Porsche won the 2024 FIA world endurance drivers' title with the 963.

EPILOGUE

So, what are we to make of the Group C episode in terms of manufacturer benefits and rewards? Obviously, Porsche sustained its record for racing excellence and doughty resistance to challengers, while Jaguar flowered brightly if intermittently; TWR was always under pressure from Jaguar's corporate subjection to Ford. And Ford totally missed an opportunity despite Cosworth engines being almost ubiquitous in C2. Mercedes-Benz achieved glorious stardom, thanks to Sauber having first gained a foothold in the ring, and the Japanese makers got what they wanted in terms of a prominent presence in the top echelons of the sport. Lancia flew the flag for Ferrari half-heartedly but capitalised instead in the theatre of world-class rallying. Peugeot, late to the party, dropped a lot of money into the ring and picked up the pieces. Did the whole scenario dance to FISA's tune? In any game, there has to be a rule-maker and a set of rules to conform to, otherwise it's *Formule Libre*.

In summary, then, the administration and direction of The Sport are more professional and efficient nowadays than they were 35 years ago; cars are more reliable, drivers in general more professional, team crews have multiplied in number, circuits are safer though sanitised, and trackside facilities have incomparably improved. Media coverage of endurance events is still sparse, in spite of social media, and its fanbase still consists of ardent devotees rather than the general public. And that, at least, gives endurance racing an exclusive cachet. Best of all, diehard Group C aficionados and a new audience can get a fix of the real thing – as it was – in Peter Auto's Spa Classic and Classic Le Mans series and, from 2025, the Masters Historic series.

Four decades on, Porsche celebrates its mid-'80s Group C heyday at its Leipzig test facility, featuring Joest Racing's 3.0-litre 700bhp Porsche 962C #015 that came 4th at Le Mans in 1990, driven by Hans Stuck, Frank Jelinski and Derek Bell.

Appendix I

SPECIFICATION TABLES

MODEL: PORSCHE 956

Designer: Norbert Singer
Valentin Schäffer: engine; Eugen Kolb: body; Horst Reitter: chassis
Years: 1982–84

Layout and Chassis

Chassis: aluminium monocoque

Engine

Engine capacity: 2.65-litres Type-935 flat-6
Turbochargers: twin KKK K26 turbos
Bore and stroke: 92.3 × 66.0mm = 2,649cc
Compression ratio: 7:1
Maximum power: 620bhp@8,000rpm
Maximum torque: 442lb ft @ 5,400rpm with 1.2 bar of boost
Transmission: 5-speed rear-wheel drive
Fuel capacity: 99 litres

Suspension and Steering

Front: independent by double wishbones, Bilstein gas dampers, progressive titanium springs, adjustable anti-roll bar
Rear: independent pushrod, lower wishbones, rocker arms, Bilstein gas dampers, progressive titanium springs, adjustable anti-roll bar

Wheels and Tyres

Front: 16in Speedline/BBS, Dunlop 280/650 x 16
Rear: 16in Speedline/BBS, Dunlop 350/650 x 16

Brakes

330mm ATE, 2 x 4-pot Brembo calipers each

Dimensions

Length: 4,800mm
Width: 199.898mm
Height: 1.1m
Weight: 820kg

Performance

0-62mph: 2.8sec
Top Speed: 217mph

MODEL: JAGUAR XJR-9

Designer: Tony Southgate
Assembled by Tom Walkinshaw's TWR base
Years: 1988–89

Layout and Chassis

Body: carbon composite monocoque
Chassis: carbon fibre and Kevlar monocoque

Engine

Engine capacity: 7.0-litre Jaguar 60° sohc V12
Fuel injection: Zytek, naturally aspirated
Bore and stroke: 99mm x 84.0mm = 6,995cc
Compression ratio: 12:1
Maximum power: 750bhp@7,200rpm
Maximum torque: 611lb ft @ 5,500rpm
Fuel capacity: 107 litres

Transmission

March/TWR 5-speed, rear-wheel drive

Suspension and Steering

Front: double wishbones, pushrod activated coil springs over dampers
Rear: Magnesium uprights, titanium coil springs over dampers

Wheels and Tyres

Front: 16in TWR, Dunlop Denloc 225/50ZR16 radials
Rear: 16in TWR, Dunlop Denloc 245/55ZR16

Brakes

TWR ventilated discs

Dimensions

Length: 4,780mm
Width: 2,000mm
Height: 1.1m
Weight: 880kg

Performance

0–62mph: 2.5sec
Top Speed: 245mph

MODEL: SAUBER-MERCEDES C11

Designer: Leo Ress: chassis; Willi Muller & Gerd Witthalm: engine
Years: 1990–91

Layout and Chassis

Chassis: carbon-Kevlar monocoque

Engine

Engine capacity: 5.0-litre twin-turbo 90° Mercedes-Benz M119 V8
Injection: Bosch Motronic MP 1.8
Turbochargers: twin KKK K26 turbos
Bore and stroke: 96.5 x 89.5mm = 4,973cc
Compression ratio: 8.5:1
Maximum power: 750bhp@8,000rpm
Maximum torque: 295lb ft @ 3,900rpm with 2.0 bar of boost
Transmission: 5-speed, rear-wheel drive
Fuel capacity: 100 litres

Suspension and Steering

Front: double wishbones, pushrod-operated coil springs over shock absorbers, torsion bar stabiliser
Rear: inboard transverse coil spring/damper units actuated by pushrods, torsion bar stabiliser

Wheels and Tyres

Front: 13in x 17in
Rear: 14.5in x 18in; Goodyear.

Brakes

13in ventilated steel discs
Brakes: Brembo, AP Racing calipers

Dimensions

Length: 4,800mm
Width: 2,000mm
Height: 1.03m
Weight: 905kg

Performance

0–62mph: 2.5sec
Top Speed: 252mph

MODEL: MAZDA 787B

Designer: Nigel Stroud
Year: 1990–91

Layout and Chassis

Chassis: carbon/Kevlar composite monocoque

Engine

Engine capacity: 2,616cc naturally aspirated 4-rotor Mazda R26B 'Wankel' RE
Bore and stroke: four rotors, each with a 654cc chamber
Compression ratio: 11.9:1
Maximum power: 690bhp@9,000rpm
Maximum torque: 448lb ft @ 6,500rpm
Transmission: Mazda/Porsche 956 5-speed, rear-wheel drive
Fuel capacity: 100 litres; Idemitsu brand

Suspension and Steering

Front: double wishbone, pull rod-operated inboard Bilstein springs and dampers. Rear: double wishbones, top rocker-operated inboard Bilstein springs and dampers.

Wheels and Tyres

Front: RAYS wheels, Dunlop 300-640 x 18
Rear: 355-710 x 18

Brakes

Brembo carbon-fibre

Dimensions

Length: 4,782mm
Width: 1,994mm
Height: 1.003m
Weight: 830kg

Performance

0–62mph: 2.5sec
Top Speed: 258mph

MODEL: PEUGEOT 905/B

Designers: André de Cortanze, Enrique Scalabroni
Years: 1990–93

Layout and Chassis

Chassis: Dassault Aerospace carbon-fibre monocoque

Engine

Engine capacity: 3.5-litre naturally aspirated SA35-A1 80° V10
Injection: Bosch Motronic MP 1.8
Bore and stroke: 91.0mm x 53.8mm = 3,499cc
Maximum power: 641bhp@12,500rpm
Maximum torque: 332lb ft
Transmission: 6-speed Peugeot sequential, rear-wheel drive
Fuel capacity: 90 litres, Esso brand

Suspension and Steering

Front: double wishbones, push-rod-actuated coil springs and dampers, anti-roll bar
Rear: double wishbones, rocker-actuated coil springs over dampers, anti-roll bar

Wheels and Tyres

Front: 32 x 63/17
Rear: 34 x 70/18; Michelin.

Brakes

Carbon-fibre ventilated discs

Dimensions

Length: 4,800mm
Width: 1,960mm
Height: 1.04m
Weight: 780kg

Performance

0–62mph: 2.6sec
Top Speed: 220mph

Appendix II

PARTICIPATING MAKES

ADA
01, 1984, C2, rebadged 1982 De Cadenet-Lola LM
03, 1988, C2, March chassis
02B, 1989, C2, Gebhardt chassis
Alba
AR2, 1983, C Jnr-C2
AR3, 1984, C2
AR4, 1985, C2 (AR3 chassis rebuilt for IMSA GTP Lights)
AR5, 1985, C2
AR6, 1986, C2
AR20, 1990, C
ALD
01, 1985, C2
02, 1986, C2
03, 1987, C2
04, 1988, C2
C289, 1989, C2
C91, 1991, C2
Alfa Romeo
SE048SP, 1990, C1, never raced
Allard
J2X-C, 1992, C2
Argo
JM19, 1986, C2
JM19B, 1987, C2
JM19C, 1988, C1
Arundel
C200, 1984, C2, rebuilt in 1986 as Bardon DB1
Aston Martin
AMR1, 1989, C1
Bardon
DB1, 1986, C2
BRM
P351, 1992, C1
Brun Motorsport
C91, 1991, C1
Cheetah
G603, 1983, C1
G604, 1984, C1
Chevron
B36, 1986, C, modified Group 6 car
B62, 1986, C2
Cougar
C01, 1982, C
C01B, 1983, C
C02, 1984, C1
C12, 1985, C1/C2
C20, 1987, C1
C20B, 1988, C1/C2
C22, 1988, C1
C22LM, 1989, C1
C20S, 1990, C2
C24S, 1990, C1
C26S, 1991, C2
C28LM, 1992, C3
C30LM, 1993, C2
Dahmen
DC884, 1984, C1
De Cadenet
LM, 1982, C/C Jnr, Lola T390 chassis
Dome
RC82, 1982, C/C1, March Engineering chassis
RC83, 1983, C1, Dome chassis
Ecosse
C284, 1984, C2, based on De Cadenet-Lola Group 6 chassis
C285, 1985, C2
C286, 1986, C2
EMKA
C83/1, 1983, C
C84/1, 1985, C1
Ford
C100, 1982, C, TC Prototype chassis

GKW
862 SP,1986, C2, unraced
Gebhardt
JC843, 1985, C2
JC853, 1985, C2
C88, 1988, C2
C91, 1992, C2
Grid
S1, 1982, C
S2, 1984, C1
Harrier
RX-83C, 1983, C Jnr
Jaguar
XJR-5, 1982, IMSA GTP, built by Group44 Racing
XJR-6, 1986, C1, henceforward built by TWR
XJR-8, 1987, C1
XJR-9, 1988, C1
XJR-11, 1990, C1
XJR-12, 1990, C1
XJR-14, 1991, C1
XJR-17, 1992, C1
Konrad
KM-011, 1991, C1
Kremer Racing
CK5, 1982, C/C1, based on modified Porsche 936
Lamborghini
Countach QVX, 1985, C, built by Spice Engineering on Tiga GC84 chassis
Lancia
LC1, 1982, Group 6/B
LC2, 1983, C/C1
Lola
T610, 1982, C C1
T616, 1984, C2
T92/10, 1992, C1
Lotec
M1C, 1982, C
C302, 1985, C2
C190, 1990, C2
March
82G, 1982, C
83G, 1983, C1, competed as Nissan Silvia Turbo C
85G, 1985, C1, competed as Nissan Skyline Turbo C
86G, 1986, C1
87G, 1987, C1
88G, 1987, C1
88S, 1988, C1
Mazda
717C, 1983, C Jnr
727C, 1984, C2
737C, 1985, C2
757, 1987, C2
767, 1988, C2
767B, 1989, C2
787, 1990, C1
787B, 1991, C1
MXR-01, 1992, C1, powered by Judd V10
McLaren
C8, 1982, C, built on Trojan/McLaren M8F chassis
Mercedes-Benz
C11, 1991, C2, chassis built by Sauber
C291, 1991, C1
C292, 1991, C1
Mirage
M12, 1982, C1
Mooncraft
MCS Guppy, 1983, C2
Mussato
MXJ-92, 1992, C2, unraced
Nimrod
NRA/C2, 1982, C
NRA/C2B, 1983, C/C1
Nissan
Skyline Turbo C, 1983, C1, Group 5 Skyline RS
Fairlady Z, 1985, C1, aka Lola T810
R85V, 1985, C1, chassis by March Engineering
R86V, 1986, C1, March chassis
R87E, 1987, C1, March chassis
R88C, 1988, C1, March chassis
R89C/10, 1989, C1, Lola chassis
R90CP, 1990, C1, aka Lola T90/10
R90CK, 1990, C1
R91CP, 1991, C1, aka Lola T91/10
R91CK, 1991, C1, updated R90CK
R92CP, 1992, C1, updated R91CP
P35, 1992, C1, never raced
Norma
M6, 1990, C1
Olmas
GLT-200, 1988, C2
Peugeot
905, 1991, C1
905B Evo, 1992, C1
Porsche AG
936C, 1982, C, modified by Joest Racing
956, 1982, C/C1
956B, 1984, C1
962C, 1985, C1
962 GTi, 1985, C1, Richard Lloyd Racing
962 CK6, 1985, C1, Kremer Racing
ROC
002, 1991, C1
Rieger
CJ 84, 1984, C2
Rondeau
M379C, 1982, C/C2
M382, 1982, C/C1
M482, 1983, C/C1
Royale
RP40, 1987, C2
SARD
MC86X, 1986, C1
Sauber
SHS C6, 1982, C/C2
C7, 1983, C
C8, 1985, C1
C9, 1987, C1

Sehcar
C6, 1983, C, based on Sauber SHS C6
C830, 1983, C/C1, based on Ford C100
Spice
SE86C, 1986, C2
SE87C, 1988, C2
SE88C, 1988, C2
SE89C, 1989, C1/C2
SE90C, 1990, C1
Sthemo
SM01, 1983, C-Jnr
SMC2, 1984, C2
Strandell
85, 1985, C2
Tiga
GC284, 1984, C2
GC285, 1985, C2
GC286, 1986, C2
GC287, 1987, C2
GC288, 1988, C1
GC289, 1989, C2
TOJ
C390, 1982, C/C1
Toyota
Celica C, 1982, C
82C, 1983, C
83C, 1983, C
84C, 1984, C1, Dome chassis built by TOM'S
85C, 1985, C1, Dome chassis built by TOM'S
86C, 1986, C1, Dome chassis built by TOM'S
87C, 1987, C1, Dome chassis built by TOM'S
88C, 1988, C1, Dome chassis built by TRD
88C-V 1988, C1, Dome chassis built by TRD
89C-V 1989, C1, Dome chassis built by TRD
90C-V 1990, C1, TRD chassis
91C-V, 1991, C1
92C-V, 1992, C2
TS010, 1992, C1
93C-V, 1993, C2
URD
C81, 1982, C/C2
C83, 1983, C
Veskanda
1985, C1, built by K&A Engineering for Australian CAMS series
WM
P82, 1982, C
P83, 1983, C
P83B, 1984, C1
P86, 1986, C1
P87, 1987, C1
P88, 1988, C1
P489, 1989, C1
Zakspeed
C1/4, 1983, C, Ford C100
C1/8, 1983, C/C1, Ford C100

Corvette Racing's C8-R 5.5-litre Chevrolet V8 of Nick Tandy/Tommy Milner/Alexander Sims completes a pit stop during the 2022 Le Mans 24-Hours.

Appendix III

ANNUAL RESULTS

1982 WORLD SPORTSCAR CHAMPIONSHIP

Races & overall winners

1. Trofeo Filippo Caracciolo 1,000km, Autodromo Nazionale Monza. 1st Henri Pescarolo/Giorgio Francia, Rondeau M382
2. Pace Petroleum 6 Hours, Silverstone. 1st Michele Alboreto/Riccardo Patrese, Lancia LC1
3. Rudolf Caracciola Wanderpreis 1,000 Kilometres, Nürburgring. 1st Michele Alboreto/Riccardo Patrese/Teo Fabi, Lancia LC1
4. 24-Hours of Le Mans. 1st Jacky Ickx/Derek Bell, Porsche 956
5. Trophee Diners Club 1,000km, Spa-Francorchamps. 1st Jacky Ickx/Jochen Mass, Porsche 956
6. Trofeo Banca Toscana 1,000 Kilometres, Mugello. 1st Piercarlo Ghinzani/Michele Alboreto, Lancia LC1
7. WEC Japan 6 Hours, Fuji Speedway. 1st Jacky Ickx/Jochen Mass, Porsche 956
8. Shell Oils 1,000km, Brands Hatch. 1st, Jacky Ickx/Derek Bell, Porsche 956

Drivers' championship

1. Jacky Ickx
2. Riccardo Patrese
3. Derek Bell
4. Teo Fabi
5. Michele Alboreto
6. Henri Pescarolo
7. Jochen Mass
8. Giorgio Francia
9. Rolf Stommelen
10. Vern Schuppan

Manufacturers' championship

1. Porsche
2. Rondeau
3. Aston Martin-Nimrod
4. WM-Peugeot - WM
5. Ford
6. Sauber
7. Lola
8. Cougar

1983 WORLD ENDURANCE CHAMPIONSHIP

Races & overall winners

1. Trofeo Filippo Caracciolo, Monza. 1st Bob Wollek/Thierry Boutsen, Lancia LC2
2. Grand Prix International 1,000km, Silverstone. 1st Derek Bell/Stefan Bellof, Porsche 956
3. Bitburger ADAC-1,000-km-Rennen, Nürburgring. 1st Jacky Ickx/Jochen Mass, Porsche 956
4. 24-Hours of Le Mans. 1st Vern Schuppan/Hurley Haywood/Al Holbert, Porsche 956
5. Trophee Diners Club 1,000km, Spa-Francorchamps. 1st Jacky Ickx/Jochen Mass, Porsche 956
6. World Endurance Championship, Fuji Speedway. 1st Derek Bell/Stefan Bellof, Porsche 956
7. Castrol 1,000km, Kyalami. 1st Derek Bell/Stefan Bellof, Porsche 956

Drivers' championship

1. Jacky Ickx
2. Derek Bell

3. Jochen Mass
4. Stefan Bellof
5. Bob Wollek
6. Thierry Boutsen
7. Jan Lammers
8. Jürgen Lässig
9. Axel Plankenhorn
10. Vern Schuppan

Manufacturers' championship

C1

1. Porsche
2. Lancia
3. Aston Martin-Nimrod
4. Nissan-March
5. Sauber
6. Toyota-Dome
7. URD

C2

1. Alba-Giannini
2. Mazda
3. Harrier
4. March-Toyota

1984 WORLD SPORTSCAR CHAMPIONSHIP

Races & overall winners

1. Trofeo Filippo Caracciolo 1,000km, Monza. 1st Derek Bell/Stefan Bellof, Porsche 956
2. Grand Prix International 1,000km, Silverstone. 1st Jacky Ickx/Jochen Mass, Porsche 956
3. 24-Hours of Le Mans. 1st Klaus Ludwig/Henri Pescarolo, Porsche 956
4. ADAC 1,000km, Nürburgring. 1st Derek Bell/Stefan Bellof, Porsche 956
5. British Aerospace 1,000km, Brands Hatch, 1st Jan Lammers/Jonathan Palmer, Porsche 956
6. Budweiser GT 1,000km, Mosport Park. 1st Jacky Ickx/Jochen Mass, Porsche 956
7. Rothmans Spa 1,000km, Spa-Francorchamps. 1st Derek Bell/Stefan Bellof, Porsche 956
8. 1,000 Kilometres di Imola, Autodromo Dino Ferrari, Imola. 1st Hans Stuck/Stefan Bellof, car
9. Mount Fuji 1,000km, Fuji Speedway. 1st John Watson/Stefan Bellof, car
10. Kyalami 1,000km, Kyalami. 1st Sandro Nannini/Riccardo Patrese, Lancia LC2
11. Sandown 1,000km, Sandown Park. 1st Derek Bell/Stefan Bellof, Porsche 956

Drivers' championship

1. Stefan Bellof
2. Jochen Mass
3. Jacky Ickx
4. Derek Bell
5. Henri Pescarolo
6. Jonathan Palmer
7. Jan Lammers
8. Hans-Joachim Stuck
9. David Hobbs
10. Walter Brun

Manufacturers' championship

C1

1. Porsche
2. Lancia
3. Alba-Giannini
4. Alba-Ford
5. Tiga
6. Lotec
7. Rondeau
8. Lola
9. Mazda
10. Toyota

C2

1. Alba-Giannini
2. Lola J
3. Tiga
4. Gebhardt
5. Rondeau
6. Lotec
7. Ecosse-Cosworth
8. Mazda
9. ADA
10. Gebhardt

1985

Races & overall winners

1. 1,000km Mugello, Mugello. 1st Jacky Ickx/Jochen Mass, Porsche 956B
2. Trofeo Filippo Caracciolo 1,000km, Monza. 1st Manfred Winkelhock/Marc Surer, Porsche 956
3. Silverstone 1,000km, Silverstone. 1st Jacky Ickx/Jochen Mass, Porsche 956B
4. 24-Hours of Le Mans. 1st Klaus Ludwig/Paolo Barilla/John Winter, car
5. Duschfrish ADAC 1,000km, Hockenheimring. 1st Derek Bell/Hans Stuck, Porsche 956B
6. Budweiser GT 1,000km, Mosport Park. 1st Derek Bell/Hans Stuck, Porsche 956B
7. 1,000km of Spa, Spa-Francorchamps. 1st, Bob Wollek/Mauro Baldi, Lancia LC2
8. 1,000km of Brands Hatch. 1st Derek Bell/Hans Stuck, Porsche 956B
9. Fuji 1,000km, Fuji Speedway. 1st Kazuyoshi Hoshino/Akira Hagiwara/Kenji Matsumoto, March-Nissan 85G
10. Malaysia 800 Selangor, Shah Alam. 1st Jacky Ickx/Jochen Mass, Porsche 956B

Drivers' championship

1. Hans-Joachim Stuck & Derek Bell
3. Jacky Ickx & Jochen Mass
5. Klaus Ludwig & Bob Wollek
7. Paolo Barilla
8. Alessandro Nannini
9. Manfred Winkelhock & Marc Surer

Teams' championship

C1

1. Rothmans Porsche
2. Martini Lancia
3. New Man Joest Racing
4. Kremer Porsche Racing
5. Richard Lloyd Racing
6. Brun Motorsport
7. Jaguar
8. Obermaier Racing Team
9. Spice Engineering
10. John Fitzpatrick Racing

C2

1. Spice Engineering
2. Ecurie Ecosse
3. Ark Racing
4. Jens Winther
5. Carma F.F.
6. Labatts
7. Roy Baker Promotions
8. Mazdaspeed
9. ADA Engineering
10. Strandell Motors

1986 WORLD SPORTS PROTOTYPE CHAMPIONSHIP

Races & overall winners

1. Monza 360km, Hans-Joachim Stuck/Derek Bell, Rothmans Porsche 962C
2. Silverstone 1,000km Derek Warwick/Eddie Cheever, Silk Cut Jaguar XJR-6
3. Le Mans 24-Hours, Hans Stuck/Derek Bell/Al Holbert, Rothmans Porsche 962C
4. Norisring 200 miles Klaus Ludwig, Joest Racing Porsche 956B
5. Brands Hatch 1,000km, Bob Wollek/Mauro Baldi, Richard Lloyd Racing Porsche 956 GTi
6. Jerez 360km, Oscar Larrauri/Jesús Pareja, Brun Motorsport Porsche 962C
7. Nürburgring 1,000km, Mike Thackwell/Henri Pescarolo, Kouros Racing Sauber-Mercedes C8
8. Spa 1,000km, Spa-Francorchamps, Thierry Boutsen/Frank Jelinski, Brun Motorsport Porsche 962C
9. Fuji 1,000km, Fuji, Paolo Barilla/Piercarlo Ghinzani, Joest Racing Porsche 956

Drivers' championship

1. Derek Bell
2. Hans-Joachim Stuck
3. Derek Warwick
4. Frank Jelinski
5. Eddie Cheever
6. Oscar Larrauri & Jesús Pareja
8. Paolo Barilla
9. Thierry Boutsen
10. Mauro Baldi

Teams' championship

C1

1. Brun Motorsport
2. Joest Racing
3. TWR Silk Cut Jaguar
4. Rothmans Porsche
5. John Fitzpatrick Racing
6. Kouros (Sauber-Mercedes) Racing Team
7. Richard Lloyd Racing
8. Porsche Kremer Racing
9. Obermaier Racing
10. Ecurie Ecosse

C2

1. Ecurie Ecosse
2. Spice Engineering
3. ADA Engineering
4. Jens Winther
5. Kelmar Racing
6. Gebhardt Motorsport
7. Lucien Rossiaud
8. Automobiles Louis Descartes
9. Roy Baker Racing
10. WM Secateva
11. Martin Schanche Racing

1987 WORLD SPORTS PROTOTYPE CHAMPIONSHIP

Races & overall winners

1. Grand Premio Fortuna (360km), Jarama. 1st Jan Lammers/John Watson, Jaguar XJR-8
2. 1,000km Jerez, Circuito Permanente de Jerez. 1st Eddie Cheever/Raul Boesel, Jaguar XJR-8
3. 1,000km Monza, Autodromo Nazionale, Monza. 1st Jan Lammers/John Watson, Jaguar XJR-8
4. Autoglass 1,000km, Silverstone. 1st Eddie Cheever/Raul Boesel, Jaguar XJR-8
5. 24-Hours of Le Mans. 1st Derek Bell/Hans Stuck/Al Holbert, Porsche 962C
6. 200-Meilen von Nürnberg, Norisring. 1st Mauro Baldi/Jonathan Palmer, Porsche 962C
7. Shell Gemini 1,000km, Brands Hatch. 1st Raul Boesel/John Nielsen, Jaguar XJR-8
8. International ADAC 1,000km-Rennen, Nürburgring. 1st Eddie Cheever/Raul Boesel, Jaguar XJR-8
9. Kouros 1,000km Spa, Circuit de Spa-Francorchamps. 1st Martin Brundle/Johnny Dumfries/Raul Boesel, Jaguar XJR-8
10. Mount Fuji 1,000km, Fuji Speedway. 1st Jan Lammers/John Watson, Jaguar XJR-8

Drivers' championship

C1

1. Raul Boesel
2. Jan Lammers
3. John Watson
4. Eddie Cheever
5. Derek Bell
6. Hans-Joachim Stuck
7. Oscar Larrauri
8. Mauro Baldi
9. Jochen Mass
10. Johnny Dumfries

C2

1. Gordon Spice
2. Fermín Vélez
3. Ray Mallock
4. David Leslie
5. Mike Wilds
6. Marc Duez
7. Thorkild Thyrring
8. Costas Los
9. Ranieri Randaccio
10. Martin Schanche
11. Will Hoy

Teams' championship

C1

1. Silk Cut Jaguar
2. Brun Motorsport
3. Porsche AG
4. Joest Racing
5. Liqui Moly Equipe
6. Kremer Racing
7. Spice Engineering
8. Primagaz Courage Competition
9. Swiftair Ecurie Ecosse
10. Japan Mazdaspeed

C2

1. Spice Engineering
2. Swiftair Ecurie Ecosse
3. Kelmar Racing
4. Tiga Ford DK
5. Team Lucky Strike Schanche
6. Chamberlain Engineering
7. URD Junior Team
8. GP Motorsport
9. Cosmik RBR
10. Automobiles Louis Descartes

1988 WORLD SPORTSCAR CHAMPIONSHIP

Races & overall winners

1. 800km Jerez, Circuito Permanente de Jerez. 1st, Jean-Louis Schlesser/Mauro Baldi/ Jochen Mass, Sauber-Mercedes C9
2. 360km Jarama, Circuito Permanente Del Jarama. 1st, Eddie Cheever/Martin Brundle, Jaguar XJR-9
3. 1,000km Monza, Autodromo Nazionale Monza. 1st, Eddie Cheever/Martin Brundle, Jaguar XJR-9
4. Autosport 1,000km, Silverstone. 1st, Eddie Cheever/ Martin Brundle, Jaguar XJR-9
5. 24-Hours of Le Mans. 1st, Jan Lammers/Johnny Dumfries/Andy Wallace, Jaguar XJR-9
6. Grand Prix ČSSR, Autodrom Brno. 1st, Jean-Louis Schlesser/Jochen Mass, Sauber-Mercedes C9
7. 1,000km Brands Hatch, Brands Hatch. 1st, Martin Brundle/Andy Wallace/John Nielsen, Jaguar XJR-9
8. ADAC 1,000km Nürburgring, Nürburgring. 1st Jean-Louis Schlesser/Jochen Mass, Sauber-Mercedes C9
9. 1,000km Spa, Circuit de Spa-Francorchamps. 1st Stefan Johannson/Mauro Baldi, Sauber-Mercedes C9
10. Fuji 1,000km, Fuji Speedway. 1st Eddie Cheever/ Martin Brundle, Jaguar XJR-9
11. Lucas Supersprint, Sandown Park. 1st Jean-Louis Schlesser/Jochen Mass, Sauber-Mercedes C9

Drivers' championship

1. Martin Brundle
2. Jean-Louis Schlesser
3. Mauro Baldi
4. Eddie Cheever
5. Jochen Mass
6. Klaus Ludwig
7. John Winter
8. Frank Jelinski
9. Bob Wollek
10. Jan Lammers

Teams' championship

C1

1. Silk Cut TWR-Jaguar
2. Team Sauber Mercedes
3. Blaupunkt Joest Racing
4. Brun Motorsport
5. Spice Engineering
6. Porsche AG
7. Swiss Team Salamin
8. Porsche Kremer Racing
9. Richard Lloyd Racing
10. From A Racing

C2

1. Spice Engineering
2. Chamberlain Engineering
3. Kelmar Racing
4. GP Motorsport
5. Charles Ivey Racing
6. ADA Engineering
7. Team Lucky Strike Schanche
8. PC Automotive
9. Roy Baker Racing
10. MT Sport & Automobiles Louis Decartes

1989 WORLD SPORTSCAR CHAMPIONSHIP

Races & overall winners

1. Japan WSPC Suzuka (480 km), Suzuka Circuit. 1st Jean-Louis Schlesser/Mauro Baldi, Sauber-Mercedes C9
2. Coupe de Dijon (480 km), Dijon-Prenois. 1st Bob Wollek/Frank Jelinski, Porsche 962C
3. Trofeo Repsol (480 km), Circuito Permanente Del Jarama. 1st Jean-Louis Schlesser/Jochen Mass, Sauber-Mercedes C9
4. Brands Hatch Trophy (480 km), Brands Hatch. 1st Kenny Acheson/Mauro Baldi, Sauber-Mercedes C9
5. ADAC Trophy (480km), Nürburgring. 1st Jean-Louis Schlesser/Jochen Mass, Sauber-Mercedes C9

6. Wheatcroft Gold Cup (480 km), Donington Park. 1st Jean-Louis Schlesser/Jochen Mass, Sauber-Mercedes C9
7. Coupes de Spa (480km), Circuit de Spa-Francorchamps. 1st Kenny Acheson/Mauro Baldi, Sauber-Mercedes C9
8. Trofeo Hermanos Rodriguez (480 km), Autodromo Hermanos Rodriguez, Mexico City. 1st Jean-Louis Schlesser/Jochen Mass, Sauber-Mercedes C9

Drivers' championship

1. Jean-Louis Schlesser
2. Jochen Mass
3. Mauro Baldi
4. Kenny Acheson
5. Frank Jelinski
6. Bob Wollek
7. Oscar Larrauri
8. Jan Lammers & Patrick Tambay
10. Andy Wallace

Teams' championship

C1

1. Team Sauber-Mercedes
2. Joest Racing
3. Repsol Brun Motorsport
4. Silk Cut TWR-Jaguar
5. Nissan Motorsports International
6. Aston Martin
7. TOM'S Toyota
8. Porsche Kremer Racing
9. Spice Engineering
10. Richard Lloyd Racing

C2

1. Chamberlain Engineering
2. Team Mako
3. PC Automotive
4. France Prototeam
5. Tiga Race Team
6. Porto Kaleo
7. Roy Baker Racing
8. Pierre-Alain Lombardi
9. Automobiles Louis Descartes
10. Didier Bonnet

1990 WORLD SPORTSCAR CHAMPIONSHIP

Races & overall winners

1. Fuji Film Cup (480 km), Suzuka Circuit. 1st Jean-Louis Schlesser/Mauro Baldi, Sauber-Mercedes C11
2. Trofeo F. Caracciolo (480km), Autodromo Nazionale Monza. 1st Jean-Louis Schlesser/Mauro Baldi, Sauber-Mercedes C11
3. Shell BRDC Empire Trophy (480 km), Silverstone Circuit. 1st Martin Brundle/Alain Ferté, Jaguar XJR-11
4. Coupes de Spa (480km), Circuit de Spa-Francorchamps. 1st Jochen Mass/Karl Wendlinger, Sauber-Mercedes C11
5. Coupe de Dijon (480km), Dijon-Prenois. 1st Jean-Louis Schlesser/Mauro Baldi, Sauber-Mercedes C11
6. ADAC Sportwagen Weltmeisterschaft (480km), Nürburgring. 1st Jean-Louis Schlesser/Mauro Baldi, Sauber-Mercedes C11
7. Shell Donington Trophy (480 km), Donington Park. 1st Jean-Louis Schlesser/Mauro Baldi, Sauber-Mercedes C11
8. Players Ltée Mondial (480 km), Circuit Gilles Villeneuve. 1st Jean-Louis Schlesser/Mauro Baldi, Sauber-Mercedes C11
9. Trofeo Hermanos Rodriguez (480 km), Autodromo Hermanos Rodriguez. 1st Jochen Mass/Michael Schumacher, Sauber-Mercedes C11

Drivers' championship (Simply Group C, as no C2 any more)

1. Jean-Louis Schlesser & Mauro Baldi
3. Jochen Mass
4. Andy Wallace
5. Karl Wendlinger
6. Michael Schumacher
7. Jan Lammers
8. Martin Brundle
9. Julian Bailey
10. Mark Blundell & Kenny Acheson

Teams' championship

1. Team Sauber-Mercedes
2. Silk Cut TWR-Jaguar
3. Nissan Motorsports International
4. Spice Engineering
5. Joest Racing

6. Porsche Kremer Racing
7. Brun Motorsport
8. Richard Lloyd Racing
9. TOM'S Team Toyota

1991 SPORTSCAR WORLD CHAMPIONSHIP

Races & overall winners

1. Fuji Film Cup (430 km), Suzuka Circuit, 1st Mauro Baldi/Philippe Alliot, Peugeot 905
2. Trofeo F. Caracciolo (430km), Autodromo Nazionale Monza. 1st Derek Warwick/Martin Brundle, Jaguar XJR-12
3. Castrol BRDC Empire Trophy (430 km), Silverstone Circuit. 1st Derek Warwick/Teo Fabi, Jaguar XJR-12
4. 24-Hours of Le Mans, Circuit de la Sarthe, 1st Volker Weidler/Johnny Herbert/Bertrand Gachot, Mazda 787
5. ADAC Sportwagen-Weltmeisterschaft (430km), Nürburgring, 1st Derek Warwick/David Brabham, Jaguar XJR-12
6. Championnat du Monde de Voitures de Sport (430 km), Circuit de Nevers Magny-Cours, 1st Keke Rosberg/Yannik Dalmas, Peugeot 905
7. Trofeo Hermanos Rodriguez (430 km), Autodromo Hermanos Rodriguez, 1st Keke Rosberg/Yannik Dalmas, Peugeot 905
8. SWC in Autopolis (430 km), Autopolis, Japan, 1st Michael Schumacher/Karl Wendlinger, Sauber-Mercedes C11

Drivers' championship

1. Teo Fabi
2. Derek Warwick
3. Philippe Alliot & Mauro Baldi
5. Cor Euser
6. Charles Zwolzman
7. Jochen Mass & Jean-Louis Schlesser
9. Michael Schumacher & Karl Wendlinger

Teams' championship

1. Silk Cut Jaguar
2. Peugeot Talbot Sport
3. Team Sauber-Mercedes
4. Euro Racing
5. Mazdaspeed
6. Porsche Kremer Racing
7. Courage Competition
8. Team Salamin Primagaz
9. Repsol Brun Motorsport
10. Konrad Motorsport

1992 SPORTSCAR WORLD CHAMPIONSHIP; CURTAILED SCHEDULE

Races & overall winners

1. 1,000km of Monza, Autodromo Nazionale Monza, 1st Geoff Lees/Hitoshi Ogawa, Toyota TS010
2. 500km of Silverstone, Silverstone Circuit, 1st Derek Warwick/Yannik Dalmas, Peugeot 905
3. 24-Hours of Le Mans, Circuit de la Sarthe, 1st Derek Warwick/Yannik Dalmas/Mark Blundell, Peugeot 905
4. Triton Showers Trophy 500 km of Donington, Donington Park, 1st Mauro Baldi/Philippe Alliot, Peugeot 905
5. 1,000km of Suzuka, Suzuka Circuit, 1st Derek Warwick/Yannik Dalmas, Peugeot 905
6. Championnat du Monde de Voitures de Sport (500 km), Circuit de Nevers Magny-Cours, 1st Mauro Baldi/Philippe Alliot, Peugeot 905

Drivers' championship

1. Yannik Dalmas & Derek Warwick
3. Mauro Baldi & Philippe Alliot
5. Geoff Lees
6. Jan Lammers
7. Ferdinand de Lesseps
8. Maurizio Sandro Sala
9. Johnny Herbert
10. David Brabham

Teams' championship

1. Peugeot Talbot Sport
2. TOM'S Toyota
3. Mazdaspeed
4. Chamberlain Engineering
5. Euro Racing
6. Team SCI

ACKNOWLEDGEMENTS

I grew up reading *Motor Sport* and *Autosport* magazines, and got my first break as a kid journalist writing autocross reports when Simon Taylor, Richard Feast and Robert Fearnall held the reins at *Autosport* in the late 1960s. In the early '70s I had a weekend job helping press officer Graham Macbeth in the Brands Hatch press box – what we'd call the Media Centre nowadays – from which I was plucked by Noel Stanbury, who was busy enabling and establishing the commercial link between tobacco firm John Player & Sons and Team Lotus, and went on to become Team Lotus's Commercial Manager through the 1980s. My stint running the John Player Motorsport Press Office out of Noel's racing promotions agency Stanbury-Foley in Stratford, London E15, lasted from 1972 to 1975, the era when Emerson Fittipaldi, Ronnie Peterson and Jacky Ickx surfed the F1 waves in the JPS-Lotus Type 72s. I mention all this as a preamble, partly to establish I have a modicum of inside knowledge, but also because, subsequently, I bought a complete set of *Motor Sport* magazines stretching from 1950 to 1995, amongst which were reviews of the halcyon 1980s decade of Group C racing, which gave me a head start researching this book.

The amazing website Racing Sports Cars (RSC) has been another fantastic resource. It's facilitated the process of identifying specific years, races, and cars and drivers, and I wholeheartedly endorse RSC for the breadth of information provided. As for the images presented here, I'd like to acknowledge the manufacturers Mercedes-Benz, Mazda, Nissan, Toyota, and Porsche for generously providing access to their hallowed photo archives so that I could obtain pics of their Group C racing cars, drivers and team personnel. I'd also like to credit my old friend and colleague from the *On Four Wheels* days in Covent Garden, Laurie Caddell, who helped me identify drivers and cars in a few of the more obscure photos, too.

Over the years, I've interviewed many of the drivers, entrants and contestants who competed in Group C, including the illustrious Foreword writer Mike Wilds, and Jürgen Barth, who supplied the Preface. You'll have read fascinating comments and observations from some of them in the text, focusing on car control and specification evolutions, circuit and co-driver preferences, and reactions to regulation changes.

Individual photographers who attended many Group C rounds and have generously provided images for the book are Nigel Barrett (an erstwhile Porsche 911RS racing driver himself), who, by dint of the number of images selected, emerges as my chief collaborator. Then there's Gareth Rees, who had a lifelong career at Nissan and also gave me privileged access to his photos taken at numerous Group C events. Antony Fraser, my colleague and confidant for two decades and with whom I've attended several iterations of Le Mans Classic and Nürburgring 24-Hours came up with race and driver portrait shots. Andreas Beyer and Rebecca Olausson, who I worked with in Mexico; Jason Parnell with whom I travelled extensively when composing material for the Lotus Cars in-house mag in the 2000s; Sarah Hall, who came to Le Mans with me in 2018, and Alex Denham, who's been my snapping companion covering several events, including Le Mans 2022, when we drove a Corvette Stingray C8 from the UK to La Sarthe and back as guests of Oliver Gavin and Cadillac-Chevrolet's Corvette Racing Team.

IMAGE CREDITS

Alex Denham, p.14, p.50 (top), p.163; **Antony Fraser**, p.6, p.19 (bottom), p.20 (right), p.22 (top left and bottom), p.37 (right), p.40 (bottom left), p.68, p.84, p.101 (top), p.124; **Gareth Rees**, p.13, p.16 (top), p.31 (top and bottom), p.40 (top left), p.62 (top), p.70, p.73, p.74 (bottom), p.75, p.79, p.85 (top), p.91 (top and bottom), p.92 (top), p.144, p.149 (bottom), p.170; **Jason Parnell**, p.24, p.43 (top); **Johnny Tipler**, p.15 (top), p.16, p.32, p.38 (bottom left), p.45, p.69, p.82, p.110

(top), p.114 (left), p.129 (right), p.171 (right), p.172 (top), p.173 (all); **Laurie Caddell**, p.86 (right); **Mazda Heritage Gallery**, p.39 (bottom), p.41 (top and bottom), p.42 (right), p.77, p.80, p.131, p.145 (middle), p.146 (bottom left and bottom right), p.150 (top right), p.151 (bottom); **Mercedes-Benz Classic**, p.12, p.15 (bottom), p.26, p.51 (top), p.53 (bottom), p.54 (top and bottom), p.55 (top and bottom), p.56 (top and bottom), p.57 (top and bottom), p.58 (left and right), p.59 (top and bottom), p.60 (all), p.127, p.128, p.129 (left), p.130, p.132, p.134, p.138 (left and right), p.140 (right), p.150 (top left), p.152 (right), p.153, p.154 (right), p.156, p.165 (top), p.166, p.167 (top and bottom), p.172 (bottom); **Mercedes-Benz Photo Archive**, p.162; **Mike Wilds**, p.2 (frontispiece); **Nigel Barrett**, cover image, p.17, p.18 (top), p.19 (top), p.20 (left), p.25 (top and bottom); p.28, p.29 (top and bottom), p.30, p.33 (top and bottom), p.34 (top and bottom), p.35, p.36, p.37 (left), p.38 (top left, top right and bottom right), p.40 (bottom right), p.42 (left), p.43 (bottom), p.44, p.49, p.51 (bottom), p.52, p.53 (top), p.61, p.62 (middle and bottom), p.63, p.67 (bottom), p.74 (top), p.86 (left), p.87 (top and bottom), p.89 (top and bottom), p.90, p.92 (bottom left and bottom right), p.93 (top and bottom), p.94, p.95, p.96, p.97 (top and bottom), p.98 (top and bottom), p.99 (top and bottom), p.100, p.101 (bottom), p.102 (top and bottom), p.103, p.104 (top and bottom), p.105 (top and bottom), p.106, p.107, p.108, p.109, p.112 (top and bottom), p.113, p.114 (right), p.115 (top), p.117, p.118 (left and right), p.119 (left and right), p.120 (left and right), p.121, p.123, p.126 (left and right), p.133, p.135 (top and bottom), p.139, p.140 (left), p.141 (all), p.142, p.145 (top and bottom), p.146 (top left), p.147 (top and bottom), p.148 (top and bottom), p.149 (top), p.150 (bottom left), p.151 (top), p.152 (left), p.154 (left), p.155, p.157, p.158 (all), p.159 (all), p.161, p.165 (middle and bottom), p.168 (top left and top right), p.169 (top right and bottom right), p.171 (left); **Nissan Photo Archive**, p.143; **Peter Robain**, p.160; **Porsche Photo Library**, p.11, p.18 (bottom), p.21, p.46, p.48, p.64, p.67 (top), p.78, p.85 (bottom), p.110 (bottom), p.111 (left and right), p.115 (bottom), p.116, p.125, p.137, p.174, p.189; **Reinhold Jöst**, p.9, p.168 (bottom left), p.169 (top left); **Sarah Hall**, p.39 (top), p.50 (bottom), p.136; **Ultima Sports**, p.22 (bottom).

In a relatively small 17-car field, Jacky Ickx and Jochen Mass won the 1985 Mugello 1,000km in the works 962C, here leading the Marc Surer/Manfred Winkelhock 962C #110 (left), which finished 2nd, the Brun Motorsport 956 #111 of Oscar Larrauri/Massimo Sigala which spun off, and the Kremer Racing 956B #115 driven by Klaus Ludwig/George Fouché/Gianni Mussato into 5th place.

INDEX